THE
ASSASSINATION
CHAIN

THE ASSASSINATION CHAIN

by
SYBIL LEEK
and
BERT R. SUGAR

Foreword by
JACK ANDERSON

Corwin Books
New York

Photo Credits

The photographs in the eight-page insert are published with permission as indicated here, on a page by page basis, from top to bottom, left to right, according to layout. Page One: courtesy of UPI, Assassination Information Bureau; Page Two: all courtesy of Assassination Information Bureau; Page Three: all courtesy of Assassination Information Bureau; Page Four: courtesy of Wide World, UPI; Page Five: courtesy of Assassination Information Bureau, UPI, UPI; Page Six: courtesy of UPI, Wide World, Joseph Louw; Page Seven: courtesy of the F.B.I. via UPI, WTOP-TV Eyewitness News Photo via UPI; Page Eight: courtesy of CBS via UPI.

Designed by Soho Studio.

THE ASSASSINATION CHAIN

Copyright © 1976 by Sybil Leek

Library of Congress Card No. 76-3951
ISBN 0-498-01982-9

Manufactured in the United States of America

Published by
CORWIN BOOKS
275 Madison Avenue
New York, N.Y. 10016

CONTENTS

FOREWORD

Court testimony, fantastic conjecture, forensic testimony, guilty-by-association theories, ballistic evidence, unexplained coincidences, eyewitness reports, conspiracy schemes—after a dozen years, they're all still there.

The only thing certain about the assassination attempts that riddled America's political trust for ten years is that nothing is certain—and that nothing seems beyond questioning.

The various and conflicting theories offered by Mark Lane, Jim Garrison, Earl Warren, Allard K. Lowenstein, Donald Freed, Theodore Charach, and others may be partly right. Or totally wrong.

One thing is certain. They reflect the stubborn national neurosis that grips the country; the nagging sense that all is not known. And the harder the Government tries to shut the door on the questions that plague the official explanation of the assassinations, the stronger the feeling of uneasiness grows.

So, it is hardly surprising that a recent Gallup Poll showed that more than eighty percent of the American people question the Government theories and continue to believe one of the several conjectures on the assassinations of John F. Kennedy, Robert F. Kennedy, Martin Luther King, and the attempted assassination of George Wallace.

Whether you believe them totally or only in part, *The Assassination Chain* serves the purpose of furnishing you with all of the theories of what might have happened on those tragic days in American history.

—JACK ANDERSON

INTRODUCTION

It is never easy to live with ghosts, especially those who seemed to have been well and truly exorcized only to rise up again as year succeeds year. It becomes disconcerting when, even after a decade, there are some ghosts who will not rest. Grim sentinels of our destiny, as well as their own, they are determined to join us on the two hundredth anniversary of the United States. These ghosts are not gaunt, defleshed skeletons who lived in the distant past and, as such, now should be honored. They are the ghosts of our contemporaries. In life they touched on our lives and, when they became ghosts, each year increased their luminosity as if they could never be content with anything less than the limelight.

They are still with us, these ghosts who once spoke with silver tongues, who now rise up with a clamor that we can no longer ignore because tangible worldly things bolster up the ghosts to give them a new type of life.

You do not have to be an historian to remember three of the most momentous dates of the last thirteen years:

November 22, 1963 ... A President died and a ghost
was born.

April 4, 1968   ... A Nobel Prize winner died and
another ghost was born.

June 5, 1968   ... A Presidential candidate died
and the third ghost was born.

And yes, we have to remember May 15, 1972, when a
strong Southern man, the governor of his state, was im-
mobilized as the bullet of a would-be assassin shattered
his spine.

In remembering these dates, you probably feel a sense
of shock that these years represent a decade when assassination attempts thinned the ranks of American leadership. Then a second shock wave floods the system with
the realization that nothing seems certain except the
acts of assassination and after all these years nothing
seems beyond questioning. To the enigma of ghosts who
cannot rest comes another mystery of the stubborn nagging neurosis that grips this country today—a neurosis
that takes all the various and conflicting theories offered
by many serious students, public figures, and assassination critics and increases the disturbing sense that all is
not known. The harder the Government tries to slam
the door on the questions that plague the official explanation of the assassinations, the stronger the feeling of
uneasiness grows.

When we first read "The Warren Report," we, like so
many others, were inclined to believe every word of
seven tried-and-true public servants who, like Caesar's
wife, were beyond reproach. But after Watergate and
some of the CIA and anti-Castro Cuban operatives in
the White House crawled out from under the official
rocks, we began to have doubts—horrible nightmarish
doubts much worse than those that followed the
knowledge of the assassinations and put black dates on
every calendar each year following. We need to know
what really happened on November 22, 1963, because
recently we have been forced to face the revelations of

hired assassins who are every bit as terrifying and weird as the Lee Harvey Oswalds and the Sirhan Sirhans of the world.

With the latest revelations, there is the shock of knowing that the climate of assassinations has spread to those who work within the Government itself, while enjoying the aura of respectability that comes from participating in projects of supposed national security or from a misguided sense of "patriotism." The distinctions we once made in our minds are fast blurring to a point of disappearing, especially when we are informed that the CIA is in league with the Mafia and a would-be assassin of President Ford turns out to be associated with the FBI. The Government, by its now-acknowledged undertaking to carry out assassinations in other countries—whether it be by gun, poison on light bulbs, poisoned cigars or darts, or by drugs—has placed itself on the same level with the chain of assassinations. And since they may be the same people, there is a further fueling to our need to know exactly what happened that day in Dallas in 1963.

Once there was a clean line of demarcation in our minds—the Government on one side, standing for law and order, and those on the other side, indulging in murder and mayhem. Now, like many other people in this country, we totter feebly on a thin, frail tightrope, afraid that if we fall on either side, we shall find ourselves face to face with the same people, assassins who sometimes wear the cloak of governmental respectability. It is a new macabre twist to the old cloak-and-dagger types beloved of classical crime writers.

It is possible that the trail from Dallas to Memphis to Los Angeles to Laurel, Maryland, is already too cold—stark-shrouded by death, missing witnesses, and pages in history books already written, as well as the contrivances of men anxious to protect their professional reputations and their complicity in the crime of the ages. But always there is this terrible urgent need to know and the fact that "The Warren Report" as well as other official documents raise more questions than they answer.

In common with eighty-two percent of all Americans who do not accept "The Warren Report," we find every page a stimulant to find the real answers. For, in each of the four assassination attempts, the official version of what is reported to have happened is at variance with too many known facts. In attempting to find the discoverable roots, we can neither believe nor reject these known facts, but can merely investigate them first. Even in investigating them, there are pitfalls and traps, many blind alleys, meaningless clues, and far-fetched ideas scattered around, outnumbering and sometimes hiding the real clues. More than a decade after the assassination of President John Kennedy, some of the real clues have not been allowed to surface. Some coincidences have become clues and some clues have disintegrated into coincidences.

The real success of any investigation of this sort starts with rumors and their combination with known facts then supplying what we think may be our own unique blend of assessment and perspective. When an act is explainable in terms other than those accepted, we intend to pursue it. When evidence is gratifying but not helpful, we intend to discard it. We think one has to start at the tip of the iceberg and then go into the dark waters that cover five-sixths of this iceberg. In this case, the assassination of President John F. Kennedy is surely only the tip of the iceberg. We have concentrated on this because it is the most prominent, the most known, and the most lurid in its melodramatic aspects. It is melodramatic because it is like a Grande Guignol opera in which the victim is slain early in the play, and the audience believes it knows the villain, who must of course display all the known evils that appeal to public hatred.

The assassination of President Kennedy was the "Murder of the Century," if not the ages; and it is the first link forged in the assassination chain that meshed the Eastern Seaboard with the West in a frightening death rattle, and unleashed ghosts to walk forever until an acceptable truth gives them the peace they and the living are entitled to. For if, and remember at this point we said "if," the implications of the John F. Kennedy assassination are that existing Government institutions are involved in either the act of assassination or the cover-up of the act, then the consequences for all of us are terrifying. We have to ask what it does say about our famous democracy, our republicanism, our love of freedom and our independence. These are the issues at stake and the main reasons why we must come to grips with the assassinations and not merely accept the platitudes and the summarizations issued under the guise of authentic documents by Government agencies.

Some of the evidence we present in this book is based in part on speculation and rumor. It is speculation born of coincidences that cannot be explained away and the rumors matured into hard evidence, as more and more of the Warren Commission documents are reluctantly released by the National Archives. We intend to link the chains in these assassinations, to take you through them, step by step, acknowledging and even describing those scenarios that are plausible, and then to develop our own scenario, the only one consistent with the facts as now known. For to do less would be to merely rehash every available theory in one volume and arrive at no conclusion. No one has ever comprehensively looked at all the facts. Not having a probable theory is like eating raw meat. . . . It fills the stomach, but it is hard to digest. You will find that we have digested and analyzed every known fact, every known theory, and several of those that have not hitherto been known.

There is a precedent of history that has been preserved for the selfish use of men, causes, and countries. America fought the Spanish-American War ostensibly to both revenge the sinking of the *Maine* and to free Cuba from the despotic rule of Spain. But newspaper tycoon William Randolph Hearst had promised his readers a war, and a war they were going to get, even if his correspondents at the front had difficulty in finding it. Hearst sent telegrams to his correspondents, admonishing them: "You provide the coverage; I'll provide the war."

The sinking of the *Lusitania* by a German U-2 boat on May 7, 1915, with the loss of 1,198 lives, including 120 American "neutrals," has traditionally been cited by historians as the turning point of World War I and entirely the fault of a bloodthirsty German admiralty. But, recently, a substantial body of opinion has surfaced, indicating that the English, if not wishing the sinking of one of their own passenger liners to occur, certainly had done nothing to prevent it. They provided no aid to a ship in the danger zone where a U-boat had already sunk three other ships. Moreover, the "passenger" ship carried not only 1,388 passengers but also 173 tons of ammunition, using the passengers as a shield for the more precious cargo to break the German blockade of England, not unlike England's blockade of Germany. The blockade secure, anti-German feeling in the United States rose to a point where Americans inevitably came in on the side of the British in 1917, and Winston Churchill said: "It was an event most important and favorable to the Allies."

We always thought that the twisting of history was a thing of the past. Cover-ups, which were safe to reveal long after the historic facts, had been recorded and passed down for a few generations. Watergate brought the twisting of history right into our own times. And now the assassinations, with the facts of "The Warren [Commission] Report" collapsing, as Senator Schweiker of Pennsylvania says, "like a deck of cards," might be added to the list of perversions of history worthy of a second look.

If there were twists and perversions that were unseen by the public, taking for granted the acts of officials, then the press was twice as blind. For while several theories have surfaced in books and magazines, newspapers—

particularly *The New York Times*—have not seen fit to print them and were eager to defend "The Warren Report" against all reason. Some even profited by "The Warren Report" by putting out the text in a book that *had* to have been set in print before the official release of the information. *The New York Times*, the most visible and prestigious newspaper in America, is a prime example of the American press that has neither printed nor investigated new evidence that has turned up about the assassinations.

It almost seems as if many newspapers have been deliberately used to buoy up the shaky grounds on which "The Warren Report" was structured. For instance, *The New York Times* ran a page-one interview of the exact findings of "The Warren [Commission] Report" four full months before its release, with the headline: PANEL TO REJECT THEORIES OF PLOT IN KENNEDY'S DEATH. In company with other opinion-shaping papers, *The Times* has continually supported and apologized for the findings in the report. On September 27, 1964, the date of the release of the final report, *The Times* said: "The Commission analyzed every issue in exhaustive archaeological detail." That fact is not borne out by the recent release of Commission memoranda from the National Archives. Moreover, such a fact could not have been ascertained, even if true, without a thorough reading of the twenty-six volumes of the report, something that could not have been done in one week, let alone one day.

The opinions of critics were either relegated to back pages or ignored altogether. So, the major newspapers, and especially *The Times*, participated in the cover-up—if we can call "The Warren Report" a cover-up—by their own "conspiracy of silence," clearing their stories with the very governmental agencies that were involved. *The Times* and the many other newspapers that greeted "The Warren Report" findings that "no conspiracy existed" apparently did so as a wish-fulfillment that some of the deeper fears of Americans were groundless. It was the ultimate example of Pollyanna journalism.

But were those fears groundless? Just because the newspapers and broadcast media abdicated their public responsibility to investigate a matter of such national importance, should that stop others? If it should, then the fact is that it certainly did not. Those who did study "The Warren Report" found some incongruous, unsubstantiated conclusions based less on creditable evidence than on incredible assumptions and implausible assessments. It was their duty to come forward with more concrete facts, better reasoning, and even hypotheses built on a better foundation. This was left as the contribution of those who have been denigrated by newspapers as "assassination buffs" and "cranks." However, the Mark Lanes, the Edward Epsteins, and the Assassination Information Bureaus did not plant the seeds of doubt in the minds of people. The doubt was always there—but these people were able to nurture it through rational and painstaking research. It was they who continued to come up with theories that would make the findings of the Warren Commission more and more untenable . . . until the whole thing did indeed fall apart like a pack of fluttering cards. It was the private citizens who provided the impetus and the momentum for both our research and resolve and for several of the theories that we shall pursue. Because, like the mountain challenging the climber, the facts were there to provide the steps for the research, and we could not ignore the challenge any longer.

As we pursue several of the known facts and many of the theories, as well as some of the circumstantial evidence that cannot be explained away, we run into several incisive instances of investigative reporting that were never repeated by newspapers. In this vein, we unearthed the "Two Oswalds" theory, the undermining of the "Magic Bullet," and the continued presence of a man named Eugene Hale Brading at all the crucial places where history was, and is, being made.

It is these theories, among others, that we shall follow and develop with you, rather than the data that is merely coincidental and not meaningful. For, in giving credence to all but the most outlandish theories and circumstances, we still encounter some things that must be acknowledged and, having been so acknowledged, can be discarded, for they will serve no further useful purpose other than making our final conclusion more Byzantine and convoluted.

One of these proven facts that can only muddy the waters of the assassination theories is that on the night before his death Robert Kennedy did indeed have dinner with Sharon Tate and Abigail Folger. It is also a fact that these two women were themselves victims of murder, killed by Charles Manson and his family of followers. Add to this disquieting fact the recent attempted assassination of President Gerald R. Ford by Squeaky Fromme, one of Manson's family, and what do you have? Simply two disturbing facts without a thread that, in our estimation, can serve no other purpose than to divert our attention from the real matter at hand . . . to find the true links in the Assassination Chain.

Another one of those hard-to-explain but what-the-hell-are-we-going-to-do-with-it facts is the strange death of actress Marilyn Monroe and its relationship to the Kennedy family. It was no secret that Miss Monroe had been involved with both Jack and Robert Kennedy. She was seen with Jack Kennedy many times and even left a busy production schedule on the West Coast to show up at Madison Square Garden for his forty-fifth birthday party. It is even known that she was wearing a sheer, sequin-studded, form-fitting dress that protected but part of her abundant feminine charms. Later there were indications that Marilyn and Bobby Kennedy were more than an "item" and that the last phone call she received was from Peter Lawford, who was hosting a party that night to be attended by both Marilyn and Bobby. Regardless of whether the rumors that circulated among those in the know were true or not, how could this further our investigation of the Assassination Chain?

Other writers have ventured the strong opinion, buttressed by facts, that the deposition of Bobby on Marilyn's death was suppressed, that her suicide was a myth because the coroner found that, although she died from a massive lethal dose of barbiturates, no traces were found in her digestive or urinary tracts. Nor was there any residue of the supposed forty-seven Nembutals she had taken to be found in her stomach. Some have read a sinister inference into the fact that the coroner who performed the autopsy on Marilyn was Dr. Thomas Noguchi, the Los Angeles coroner who coincidentally performed the final autopsies on Sharon Tate and Bobby Kennedy. According to one source, the body of Miss Monroe was rearranged before it was found, thus proving that she could not have gone to sleep in that condition without attempting to regurgitate the drugs.

The unanswered questions left by her death on August 4, 1962, led some to conclude that Marilyn Monroe was killed by a right-wing enclave in the CIA, bitter at the Bay of Pigs incident and attempting to set up the Kennedys in a murder made to look like a suicide with the underground effect of a Chappaquiddick. Or a right-wing enclave of the CIA, again angry about the Bay of Pigs, and eager to take revenge on the Kennedys. Or even that Marilyn was accidentally killed by men trying to use her as a decoy to ensnare Bobby Kennedy into her house or, perhaps most outlandish of all, that she was killed by the Kennedys themselves to avert any possible scandal. Even if we examine all of these ideas, it would still be difficult to do more than dignify her death and not amplify it. All that the Monroe death does is to detract from the matter at hand . . . the Assassination Chain.

For now, during America's Bicentennial Anniversary, as never before, more theories and more evidence are surfacing, and a ground swell of suspicion fanned by Watergate and newfound evidence is coming to a head. As these opinions, suppositions, and facts arise, they form another crack in the Assassination Chain. In the early days, the kindest thing to be said about "The Warren Report" was that it was a fairy tale designed to make Americans sleep more peacefully in their beds, but now there are more and more sinister implications, and the fairy-story idea is no longer feasible. More than twenty-five Congressmen have sponsored a bill calling for the reopening of "The Warren [Commission] Report," believing, as do many observers, that in a normal court of law, there would have been inadequate forensic evidence to convict Lee Harvey Oswald. We can extend this lack of forensic evidence to stretch out further into the Assassination Chain and include James Earl Ray and Sirhan Sirhan.

In the first 187 years of our country, there were only seven attempts on the lives of our political leaders. In the succeeding thirteen years, no less than six attempts have been made on contemporary leaders. It is this recent turn to "Bullets not Ballots" that has to be arrested and those who have been able to perpetrate it must be discovered now.

We will develop a number of plausible scenarios that can explain the John F. Kennedy assassination, for the murder of the President is the link-pin that holds together the rest of the chain. If we can build our working hypothesis of what really happened on November 22, 1963, on the basis of research, insight, hindsight, factual data, and personal intuition, we will have gone a long way toward ferreting out and breaking up the Assassination Chain.

Then it is up to you, the American public, who must serve as the final jury in this case, which affects all of us and our republic. If you are convinced, as we are, then it is time to call for a new investigation of the Assassination Chain.

—Sybil Leek
—Bert Randolph Sugar
Melbourne, Florida
February 20, 1976

1 | DALLAS, NOVEMBER 22, 1963

Although John F. Kennedy was elected President of the United States in 1960, the fact that he had Texas-born Lyndon B. Johnson on his ticket as Vice President did little to help him win popularity in the Lone Star State. True, the Kennedy-Johnson ticket carried Texas, but only by a hair's breadth. By 1963, the hair's breadth of the former victory seemed to be receding to a broad, open space of nothingness, and there was the anticipation of a big swing to the Republicans.

If governors of states ever had thrones to sit on, then John Connally, Governor of Texas, would surely have been the first to have one. He is a powerful political figure with relentless ambition and dedication to achieve political fortune, ready to trample anyone standing in his way. One of the people who refused to be trampled was liberal Texas Senator Ralph Yarborough, equally passionate and devoted to his particular branch of politics. Lyndon Johnson provided little help in bridging the gap between his fellow Texans. A family divided breeds its own type of troubles; a division in a political party among three powerful men like Connally, Yarborough, and Johnson could only portend disaster to John F. Kennedy's hopes of carrying Texas in the next Presidential election.

Also, Texas was important as a state that could generate new money for the Democratic party. Traditionally, the party got more financial help from Eastern money sources, while the Republicans relied mainly on Western sources. Not only could it be a new source of money inasmuch as it might be possible to siphon its resources away from the Western strategists, but Texas was a state, more than any other, associated with power on all levels.

By 1963, three people had an obvious personal interest in Kennedy visiting Texas. For Ralph Yarborough, it was yet another chance to show his dedication to the President and prove that he had been right to stand fast by Kennedy in Los Angeles when the rest of the party was rallying to Lyndon Johnson. Governor Connally saw it as an opportunity to show the world once and for all who ran Texas. Lyndon Johnson, hearing rumors that he was in grave danger of being dropped from the Kennedy ticket in the next election, would have been less than human if he had not jumped at the chance to stand at the side of the President in his own state. Probably the least enthusiastic person to want to have a Texan summit meeting was Kennedy himself, but he was shrewd enough to understand the political connotations. With the popularity of Lyndon Johnson wilting in the wings, Governor Connally stood a good chance of being the next Vice President. It was a step up from being Governor and, while the office of Vice President can never completely satisfy the hungry ambitions of any full-blooded politician, at least it is a move in the right direction toward the White House.

The Governor would have to play host to the President visiting his state, and Kennedy was always capable of generating the ultimate in press coverage wherever he went. Presidential aides Kenneth O'Donnell and Lawrence O'Brien set the events in motion. Governor

Connally contacted some of Dallas's most powerful men: J. Erik Johnson, chairman of the Citizens Council; Robert Cullum, president of the Chamber of Commerce; R. L. Thornton, chairman of the Mercantile National Bank; Albert Jackson of *The Dallas Times Herald;* and Joe Dealey, son of the publisher of *The Dallas Morning News*. Kennedy was not likely to appeal to any of them in terms of political popularity. In fact, Connally's choice of allies was a strange collection, and some Texans on the Hill in Washington were quick to notice this. Connally counteracted by saying that the President was above politics—which is probably the most asinine statement ever attributed to a shrewd if not totally intelligent man. Needless to say, in all Connally's meetings with Texans on the Hill, Yarborough was never even invited. If Kennedy's visit to Texas was really designed to help put forth a show of unity among Johnson, Connally, and Yarborough, it should have been obvious in the early planning stages that this was not the way to go about it. At this time, it seems as if Connally first thought to put his old enemy Yarborough not only in his rightful place but definitely out into the wilderness.

As Governor Connally spun his fine subtle web of double intrigue, it was common knowledge that Dallas was a hub of hatred for Kennedy and all he represented. "Big D" was busy looking after its own interests, and Kennedy's interest was too liberal and diffused with a concern for Negroes and other deprived minority groups. The attitude was "Let him come to Dallas and see how much money he can raise from the people he favors." The city was ready to give its best to Governor Connally and, if its best meant money, then it would be there for him from people who were more Republican-minded than Democratic, from a city that had voted Republican in the last Presidential election.

No one can say that the warning lights were not flashing about the proposed visit. The ugly mood in Dallas was no secret, and Senator Fulbright begged Kennedy to reconsider his decision about the visit. There were other warnings, all equally ignored. If the outer world, as well as the White House, knew of the climate of hate in Dallas, it is a safe assumption that a group of watchful men, already irritated by Kennedy's brand of politics, also knew of it. There could be no better place than Dallas for getting rid of Kennedy once and for all. Murder was high on the list of Texas priorities, and Dallas was no exception, having one of the highest homicide rates in the United States. Nearly all homicides were by gunshot wound, there being no requirement in Dallas to register firearms.

But Dallas was merely the choice of venue, just as Kennedy was the choice as a prime target for the one hundred and eleventh murder in the city in the month of November 1963.

Given a place and time for a murder, there is still one other ingredient needed and that is the motive. At the time of President Kennedy's visit to Dallas, the real motives were obscured by a rash of seemingly obvious ones that ultimately served to mislead inquiries and obscure clues. On November 22nd it was enough for Dallas to know that the enemy of all it stood for was actually within its own camp, ready to exert the devastating Kennedy charisma; the same charm that had tempted people to vote for him and to ignore the fact that he was the product of that fabric of society which his political assertions were against. The wealthy son of a wealthy family calling for equality and tolerance seemed incongruous to many Texans. In Texas, money earns respect and paves the way to power. Kennedy entered Dallas as an alien and hated force that not even his position as President of the United States could mitigate.

Very early on the morning of November 22nd, before the President awoke to face the day in his Fort Worth bedroom, five thousand handbills were distributed in the streets. They carried portraits of the President's front and profile as a "wanted by the police" poster would do. The headline read WANTED FOR TREASON, and the rest of the page set out seven points indicating that President

Kennedy was a traitor to his country. Not exactly a pleasing omen of a royal, warm welcome. At the W.E. Greiner Junior High School, a young teacher told her students that they could only view the Presidential motorcade if their parents personally came to the school to get them. "If I saw the President" she said, "I'd just spit in his face."

For days before the Presidential tour, national newspapers were having a field day speculating about who would snub whom. The exclusion of Yarborough from the Texas meetings in Washington had been noted. Yarborough had indicated that he would be very happy not to be included in the visit at all, but this had almost brought down the wrath of Kennedy on him. However, Yarborough's presence was as necessary as that of the Governor and the Vice President. Didn't he realize that they must at least put up the appearance of a united front? Yarborough swallowed his pride and annoyance, knowing that he would still be the target for the animosity of Governor Connally In San Antonio, Yarborough preferred to ride with Congressman Henry Gonzalez rather than the Vice President. In Houston, he chose to ride with his wife in Congressman Thomas's car, and then it was on to Fort Worth where just about everything went wrong with the arrangements.

It was the night of November 21st. First it was the hotel arrangements, with Johnson and his wife having a suite far superior to those reserved for the President and his wife. Nine White House agents went off on a drinking binge that lasted all night. Four of these men were virtually necessary to the security of the President when he went into Dallas the next day. There were aching heads and a lack of alertness when dawn came, and the temper of the President was not improved when he saw *The Dallas Morning News.*

Delighted with the idea of the split within the Democratic party, the paper came out with front-page headlines STORM OF POLITICAL CONTROVERSY SWIRLS AROUND KENNEDY ON VISIT and YARBOROUGH SNUBS L.B.J. While not exactly the favorite son of the state, Vice President Johnson was a regular home product, a Texas "boy." Not content with blazoning political quarrels on the front page, the Dallas paper also carried an inside story, with the headline PRESIDENT'S VISIT SEEN WIDENING STATE DEMOCRATIC SPLIT. Texas, always noted for its blunt approach to most matters, was certainly fulfilling its image during this critical period. If the people advising President Kennedy really thought that his visit would breach the gap between Connally, Yarborough, and the Vice President, the news reporters had no illusions that it would be effective.

The hatred of Dallas's past crept right into the present. An organization styling itself "The American Fact-Finding Committee," a local branch of the John Birch Society aided by Nelson Bunker Hunt, son of Texas millionaire H. L. Hunt, added more tons of fuel to the already well-burning fires. *The Dallas Morning News*, that fateful morning, ran a full-page advertisement sarcastically headed WELCOME MR. KENNEDY TO DALLAS and bordered by a black mourning band. The advertisement accused the President of being responsible for the imprisonment, starvation, and persecution of thousands of Cubans, and of selling food to Communist soldiers who would then be strong enough to kill good American boys in Vietnam. Finally, the advertisement bluntly stated that the President had a secret agreement with the Communist party of the United States. An ominous beginning to the day that ended as one of the darkest in American history. Yet few Americans at that time saw it as prophetic writing on the wall, with every word spelling out doom and desolation to the Kennedy family and the Democratic party.

Even the Dallas weather was nasty. Jackie Kennedy looked out of the window gloomily, hoping that the weather would be bad enough to justify using the bubble top on the Presidential limousine. Still weak after a recent miscarriage, she wanted to look her best. Even on a sunny day, Dallas had a reputation for wind, which could spoil her coiffeur. She felt that many people in the hopefully large crowds in Dallas might like to have a good look at the First Lady. A wealthy woman with an identity of her own, Jacqueline Kennedy's public appearances with her husband had been relatively few. Knowing the strain her husband was under, it was important that she look her best, and she hated the idea of spending hours getting ready and then having the totally feminine effect ruined by exposure to inclement weather.

While Jackie was concerned with her own image, the President exorcised his anger sufficiently to make decisions. He was a man of action and prepared to rise to this emergency. He instructed his appointments secretary, Kenneth O'Donnell, to tell Senator Yarborough that this time he would not be given any choice as to which car he would ride in. He was to be conducted firmly to Johnson's car, even though it was rather like suggesting to a tiger that it should ride on the back of an elephant. Both O'Donnell and Larry O'Brien knew that this would present difficulties, and Yarborough had had to put up with many slighting insults from both Connally and the Vice President. The President was adamant. "Either Yarborough rides with the Vice President and his party, or he can walk."

Even Jackie Kennedy was not immune to Presidential temper. The President was annoyed that Mary Gallagher had not been available the night before to help Jackie decide on her clothes, making her late on this important morning. It was enough to have to cope with the insanity of Texas politics, as well as live down the brutal onslaught of the local newspapers, but he didn't need to be concerned with Jackie's tardiness, too. *Time* Magazine reporter, Hugh Sidey, noted that President Kennedy recovered from his spell of ill-humor, but the Vice President seemed to be moody. No one seemed happy unless it was Governor Connally.

The Secret Service men were busy attending to final details. Noting the improvement in the weather, the decision was made for them to ride in an open limousine, to the annoyance of Jackie. O'Donnell confirmed this on the telephone, while Roy Kellerman gave last-minute instructions to Agents Forrest Sorrels and Winston Lawson, who were standing by in Dallas. But there was still some confusion about the state of the weather. *The Dallas Morning News* confidently predicted rain, but the weather bureau could not be sure, and Sorrels felt that the slight wind had a chance of driving the rain eastward.

The rain in Fort Worth that morning of November 22, 1963, had given way to an unpleasant mistiness outside as the handsome, youthful-looking President emerged from the hotel elevator. Making his way along the path through the lobby to the doorway, cordoned off by the police, he responded to a small flurry of cheers with a gracious wave of his hand. He was bareheaded, wearing a gray-pinstripe suit, impatiently pushing away the offer of a raincoat from one of the security agents. He seemed anxious to get across the street to the parking lot where a small crowd had been waiting since dawn. Although damp and misty, the skies were a bit lighter, and it seemed as if Agent Forrest Sorrels's confidence about the weather was justified. Everyone except Jackie Kennedy was relieved to see the skies lighten, obviating the use of the bubble top. "It's going to be Kennedy weather," said Larry O'Brien, in an effort to bring a slight note of optimism into a day that had started off badly.

Vice President Johnson followed unobtrusively a few paces behind the President. John Kennedy said a few well-chosen words to the waiting crowd, and seemed appreciative that they were warm and responsive. But ahead lay Dallas with its known climate of hate and political hostility toward the Democratic President. The President had been warned that demonstrations were a real possibility. The Secret Service told him it could not protect him from any rifleman on a roof. Kennedy told Kenneth O'Donnell: "If anybody wants to shoot the

President of the United States, it's not a difficult job. All one has to do is get on a huge building someday with a telescopic rifle, and there's nothing anybody can do to defend against such an attempt." Knowing the danger, Kennedy refused to be a captive of fear. As President of the United States, he had to show himself to the people of his country, one of the hazards of the job. His most immediate worry was to be sure that someone got round to the subtle business of getting Ralph Yarborough into Johnson's car. Yarborough was already protesting loudly but indicating to Larry O'Brien that he was prepared to compromise by making a statement to the press. In no way was this suitable to the President. The reluctant Yarborough found himself firmly hustled into the backseat of the Vice President's car, sandwiched between Lyndon Johnson and his wife.

At Love Field in Dallas, it looked as if Kennedy was to get a more enthusiastic reception than anyone had imagined. Security was tight with armed police on every rooftop, while security agents mingled with the crowd. There was a twelve-man official reception committee, handpicked by Connally. Not a single representative of organized labor was among them. There were nine Republicans, two Dixiecrats, and one Liberal called Barefoot Sanders. It was an absurd reception committee for a Democratic President, and everyone knew that Connally had engineered another political maneuver.

Even more absurd was the airport scene of the Vice President and his wife going through the forced motions of greeting the President and his lady as if they had not met previously that morning. Besides, they had already performed the same ceremonial honors at San Antonio, Houston, and Fort Worth—all within the last twenty-four hours. The sullen boredom did not escape the crowd. Agent Kellerman kept close to the President, as he did the expected thing of shaking hands with as many people as possible behind the fence holding back the crowd. Ronnie Dugger of *The Texas Observer* scribbled in his notebook: "The President is showing everyone he is not afraid." There were those who began to feel that the Kennedy charm just might stand a chance of achieving the two things that had initiated the need for this visit to Dallas: to raise funds for the Democratic party and to heal the political strife, at least on the surface, among Connally, the Vice President, and Yarborough.

The sun shone, and Jackie Kennedy complained of the heat and wondered why she had been given red roses when yellow ones were so symbolic of Texas. But things seemed better at this moment than when the day had begun. It might not be so bad, after all.

As the motor caravan prepared to depart Love Field for its parade through the streets of Dallas and to the Trade Mart, the pilot car, manned by officers of the Dallas Police Department, started its ignition. Its function was to alert the police along the route that the motorcade was approaching. Next came the motorcycle police whcse duty it was to keep the crowd back. The lead car was an unmarked Dallas police car, driven by Chief of Police Jesse Curry. Accompanying him were Secret Service Agents Sorrels and Lawson and Dallas County Sheriff J. E. Decker. The usual procedure was for the lead car to keep four or five car lengths ahead of the President's limousine.

The President's car was a 1961 Lincoln convertible with two collapsible jump seats between the front and rear seats. The President rode on the right-hand side of the rear seat, with his wife beside him on the left. Governor Connally was in the right-hand jump seat, with Mrs. Connally beside him. Special Agent William R. Greer of the Secret Service was driving the limousine, and seated beside him was Agent Kellerman, whose responsibilities included maintaining radio communications with the lead and follow-up cars. He also had to scan the route and be ready to jump out and stand by the President when the car stopped. The follow-up car, a 1955 Cadillac eight-passenger convertible with eight Secret Service men, was to follow closely behind the

President's limousine. There were two agents in the
front seat, two in the rear, and two on each of the right
and left running boards. Each agent had a .38-caliber
rifle, and shotguns and automatic rifles were also available. Presidential assistants David F. Powers and Kenneth O'Donnell sat in the right and left jump seats, respectively.

Then came the Vice President's car, a four-door Lincoln convertible. Vice President Johnson sat on the
right-hand side of the rear seat, Mrs. Johnson was in the
center, and Senator Yarborough on the left. Rufus W.
Youngblood, special agent in charge of the Vice
President's detail, sat in the right-hand front seat. The
driver was Hurchel Jacks of the Texas State Highway
Patrol. The Vice President's follow-up car was driven by
an officer of the Dallas Police Department. In this car
were three Secret Service agents and Clifton C. Carter,
assistant to the Vice President.

The remainder of the motorcade consisted of five cars
for other dignitaries such as the Mayor of Dallas and
Texas state congressmen. Behind these were a White
House communications car, three cars for press photographers, a VIP bus for White House staff members, and
two press buses, with a Dallas police car and more motorcycles at the rear to keep the motorcade together and
prevent unauthorized vehicles from joining the cavalcade. Rear Admiral George G. Burkley, the President's
personal physician, was surprised to find himself allocated to the VIP bus when he was used to riding in a
car close to the President.

At eleven-fifty A.M., the motorcade was ready to leave.
In the downtown area, large crowds gave the President a
tremendous reception. *The Dallas Morning News* had
published a map of the motorcade route through Dallas,
and the motorcade proceeded according to plan at 11.67
miles per hour west through downtown Dallas on Main
Street. When it reached the intersection of Houston
Street, the motorcade turned right onto Houston and,
after one block, turned sharply southwest into Elm

Street. On the northwest corner of Elm and Houston stood a seven-story orange-brick building, the Texas School Book Depository. The crowds were thinner now as Elm Street curved gently toward the triple underpass and Stemmons Freeway. It was time for everyone to give a sigh of relief. Downtown Dallas had been traversed without any hostile incidents.

It was now twelve-twenty-nine. The sky had opened up, and the grass on lovely Dealey Plaza was a refreshing oasis of green. At his position on Houston and Elm streets, Agent Sorrels radioed the Trade Mart to expect the President within five minutes. Everything was in good order and on schedule, except for some workers on the overpass where Dealey Plaza sloped down and curved away from the Texas School Book Depository. Agent Lawson wondered why there was a breach in the security arrangements. No one should have been on the top of the overpass. He signaled to a policeman, indicating that the area should be cleared, but the man ignored him. Agent Kellerman, riding in the President's car, had been relieved when the limousine turned into Dealey Plaza. They were on the home stretch now, and everyone was relieved that there had been no unpleasant demonstration against the President. Within five minutes they would be at the Trade Mart. Five more minutes, and everyone could unwind. Mrs. Connally tapped Jackie Kennedy lightly on the shoulder and told her to note how Dallas loved the President and was showing it with their cheers and waving hands.

2|12:30 C.S.T.

It looked like another one of those joyous days of Camelot as the motorcade snaked its way through Dealey Plaza. The good-looking, forever-boyish President was waving and smiling; his pretty wife, pink-suited with an armful of red roses, was opening her eyes wide to take in the vista of heavy-foliaged trees lining Dealey Plaza on the right. It looked as if the Texas trip would pay off in terms of popularity. It had started with the idea of a single visit to San Antonio, with the President making a speech at the opening of the air force medical facility at Brooks Air Force Base. Then someone had come up with the brilliant idea of a visit to Fort Worth. A bitter multibillion-dollar contest over the award of the F-111 airplane had ended with the contract being given to the General Dynamics Corporation facility in that city. The President could make political hay out of the goodwill this engendered in Fort Worth and, since this city was so close to Dallas, it was inevitable that the Texas visit should extend to nearby Dallas.

Someone forgot that when Kennedy had been in Mi-

ami in September, an informer told the Miami police
that there was a plot to kill the President either in Miami or some other southern city. Jerry Bruno, the Kennedy advance man, went to Dallas to set up the visit, and
Kenneth O'Donnell also worked on the trip. In the fan-
tasy world of Camelot, the President and the First Lady
were able to forget that personal danger was always a
constant threat to their happiness. But the sun was shin-
ing in "Big D," and all seemed right with their world.
Like the applause, beloved of actors, President Kennedy
enjoyed the acclaim he received in downtown Dallas,
and there were still some people lightly fringing Dealey
Plaza. Soon they would all be at the Trade Mart where
the President would give his speech, and then his Texas
trip would be over.

Abraham Zapruder, the owner of a dress concern
called Jennifer of Dallas, had been looking forward to
the visit of the President. He had an office on the fourth
floor of the Dal Tex Building, angled across the road
from the Texas School Book Depository. On the morning of November 22, he arrived at his office to be re-
minded by his secretary that he had left his eight-mm.
Bell & Howell camera at home. Wanting a home movie
of the President's visit to show to his friends, Zapruder
went home and collected his camera. Returning to the
office, he began to look around for a vantage site where
he could get a good view of the motorcade. He was a
small man and had complained to his secretary, Marilyn
Sitzman, that it might be difficult for him to get a good
view. He was relieved to see that there were not too
many people on the grassy slopes of Dealey Plaza and,
since the rain had passed over, the light was going to be
good enough to get some creditable footage. He found a
good place where he could stand on a low concrete abut-
ment on the grassy knoll, and his secretary joined
him. As the motorcade slowly turned into Elm Street,
Zapruder raised his camera and was annoyed to find the
view of the Presidential car blocked momentarily by a
street sign.

A small child raised his hand to wave, and the President focused his gaze on him, still smiling. The limousine was moving at a steady eleven miles an hour when a noise like firecrackers exploding startled the people on the grassy slopes. Zapruder got the limousine into his sights as it came from the obscurity of the street sign. At the same time, a sharper sound splintered the air. Agent Greer kept the limousine moving at the same speed, but Kellerman froze as more sharp noises cracked abruptly. Now Kellerman recognized them as gunshots. A dazed Jackie Kennedy seemed transfixed with horror, and Governor Connally sat clasping his ten-gallon hat in his hand. First the President fluttered his hands to his throat and then raised them as if to brush his hair away from his head. Jackie Kennedy threw herself toward her husband as pieces of his skull and brain splattered the back of the car and the motorcyclists at the side of the car. Blood spurted on her pink dress until it turned the color of the red roses now lying crumpled beside her.

The impact of the second bullet threw the President's body well back against the seat of the car as Jackie clambered atop the trunk to reclaim the bits and pieces of what had once been her husband's head, believing that she could put him back together again. Bystanders felt a rush of redness as the warm blood, brains, and splintered skull bones of President Kennedy sprayed out from the car. John Connally was screaming with pain as his wife held him in her arms. She noticed blood flowing from his thigh and wrist. Jackie was screaming in anguish: "My God, what are they doing? My God, they have killed Jack; they have killed my husband. Jack, Jack." Connally screamed, "They're trying to kill all of us." And Agent Kellerman yelled into the intercom to Agent Lawson: "We are hit; get us to a hospital." Then the car accelerated, streaking beneath the underpass. Jackie Kennedy wrenched a cushion from the floor of the car to put under what remained of the head of her husband. Later, she wondered how the cushion happened to be in the car. She crouched over her husband, cradling his torn face and head in her gloved hands, struggling to hold the bits of flesh, bone, and hair together.

Through his viewfinder, Abraham Zapruder saw Kennedy slump and realized he had been wounded. But he kept his camera trained on the limousine and ended up with the most famous home movie in history—a twenty-two-second strip of color film that recorded on seventeen feet "The Crime of the Century."

Dallas police were unable to alert Parkland Hospital to expect its sudden cargo of carnage. The police dispatcher's equipment was not working at this grim moment of history. Governor Connally was the first to be placed on a stretcher, momentarily leaving the moribund Kennedy facedown on the floor. It was not that anyone dared to presume that the President was dead so much as the fact that Connally was more obviously alive. Agent Clint Hill had difficulty in forcing Jackie Kennedy away from her husband so that he could be placed on the second stretcher. He took off his jacket as if in answer to the silent plea in Jackie's eyes, begging him to hide the obscene remains of the torn face and head of her husband. Gently, he placed his coat over the head as the body of the President was wheeled into Trauma Room No. 1, which Mrs. Kennedy was prevented from entering. In Trauma Room No. 2, Mrs. Connally was with her husband.

Among the last people to hear of the injury to the President was his physician, Rear Admiral Burkley. The VIP bus had continued on its way to the Trade Mart, unaware of the tragedy ahead. In the bus were Evelyn Lincoln, Pam Turnure, Mary Gallagher, Liz Carpenter, Marie Fehmer, and Jack Valenti. They evacuated themselves from the bus as it drew up at the back of the Trade Mart and were surprised to find no agents or police there to direct them. Nor was anyone prepared to let them into the Trade Mart because there was no one in authority to recognize them. As far as the few people in the Trade Mart were concerned, the President was still due to arrive. There were arguments and confusion, and only Dr. Burkley sensed that something was wrong, very wrong. As Agent Andy Berger was about to draw away in his police car, Dr. Burkley instinctively realized that he was in the wrong place at the wrong time. He flung himself in the car and finally arrived at Parkland Hospital, where he learned what had happened.

He found the hospital overrun by panic and ill-equipped to deal with such a grave emergency. Had the police dispatcher's equipment not failed when it was needed, Parkland Hospital would have been prepared for its unscheduled appointment with destiny. But such was not the case.

After the initial sense of loss and shock, the Secret Service and security men were the first to realize that they were now divided in their loyalties. Most of them knew that Lyndon Johnson, the moody Vice President, was more in need of their services than those mangled remains of John Kennedy in Trauma Room No. 1. Many were also conscious that the favorites of one President may not be the favorites of the new one. Much of the melee around the hospital was caused by the desertion of too many men running to catch up with the Vice President for whatever reason. There was no one available to give orders, no one with enough authority to tell the press anything meaningful and truthful. Technically, Roy Kellerman, as chief security aide to President Kennedy was still in charge; but his authority was quickly undermined by the actions of Emory Roberts, whose first thought was to get as many men as possible to the side of the Vice President. This split between the Secret Service and security men was significant enough to add to the confusion. Kellerman and Hill remained at the hospital with the body of the President, while Rufus Youngblood and Lem Johns rushed to Johnson. Each agent apparently was free to form his own idea of priorities based as much on personal loyalties that were swayed as by the awareness of the impact a new President would make.

President Kennedy's senior military aide was Major General Ted Clifton. He called the White House, a natural enough gesture. But he called to ask that his wife and Mrs. O'Donnell be told that their husbands were safe. Only after this peculiar attention to duty did he make a second call to the White House to ask if there was "any intelligence on the situation." It seems obvious that his priorities were also somewhat mixed up. Clint Hill, the agent who had risen to the emergency by climbing on the bumper of the ill-fated limousine and then by giving his coat to Jackie to cover the head of her husband, suddenly felt naked in his shirt-sleeves and asked a public-relations man to give him his coat. A Dallas police sergeant was concerned because his automobile was missing. This presented a problem because he had borrowed the car of his deputy chief in order to get to the Trade Mart. In normal circumstances one could understand his concern, but this was not a day resembling normalcy. In the emotional stress, the chief things that came out of it were a phone call to Anne Clifton via the White House, an agent who needed a coat, and a policeman who had lost his car.

Meanwhile a woman who in her heart knew she was no longer a wife and the First Lady of the land was left together with another woman whose fears that she would be a widow were unfounded. It was soon apparent that Governor Connally, although wounded, was not in mortal danger. In the rush and confusion to get the President and Connally into the emergency rooms, many people milled through the corridors of the hospital—press, police, and curious, if not sinister, onlookers.

Liz Carpenter, a hard-working public-relations spokeswoman accompanying the official party, arrived at the hospital and had to be revived by aspirin. Liz realized that someone had to give a talk at the Trade Mart, and it had to be Lyndon Johnson. So she rushed away to see what she could do about it. She could do nothing.

As she left, the hospital staff fell back to doing their routine work such as tagging the body of John F. Kennedy and identifying him as a white male assigned to Trauma Room No. 1, number 2,470. It was noted that he had gunshot wounds needing the immediate attention of more than one doctor. Physician Charles J. Carrico, a young resident doctor, was the first to examine the body of the President. He was still bleeding profusely, but there was no pulse or blood pressure. Yet he was making agonizing attempts to breathe. Carrico frantically pounded and pumped his chest in a vain attempt to restore some semblance of life to the pathetic body. Thirteen other doctors stormed into the small emergency room, including Drs. Burkley and Malcolm Perry who took over from young Carrico and began a tracheotomy.

Jackie Kennedy tried to force her way into the already-crowded room and, for a moment, the activity around her husband gave her a flash of hope that he was still alive and that a miracle would happen.

It was just an hour after President Kennedy had left Love Field. At one in the afternoon, Dr. Kemp Clark reached down and drew a sheet over the once-handsome face of John Fitzgerald Kennedy.

Aboard Air Force One, George Thomas, valet to President Kennedy, was sadly packing away the sports clothes he had laid out to await the return of his employer after a tiring day.

Across the country in New York, a Cuban valet was laying out the clothes for the return of his employer, Richard Milhous Nixon. Only a few reporters noted that he left Dallas just before Air Force One glided onto the runway at Love Field.

It had been a busy day for so many people.

The thirty-fifth President of the United States was officially dead. Soon the wire services spread the news throughout the world. Newsmen had scarcely finished calling in and writing their versions of the assassination, when the news broke that a policeman had been shot in Dallas.

At one-forty-five P.M., the police radio stated: "Have information a suspect just went into the Texas Theater on West Jefferson." Patrol cars carrying fifteen police officers converged on the theater and arrested a man who had walked in without paying. The man resisted arrest and was found to be carrying a revolver. At one-fifty-one P.M., a police car radioed Dallas Police Station that it was on its way with a suspect for the murder of Police Officer J. D. Tippit.

At two-fifteen P.M., Captain Will Fritz, head of the Dallas Police Force, returned from the Texas School Book Depository, where a roll call elicited the fact that one of its employees was missing. His name was Lee Harvey Oswald, and he was the man captured in the Texas Theater. Following interrogation and two lineups for identification, Oswald was charged with the murder of Police Officer Tippit. The time was seven-ten P.M., and more interrogation and another lineup followed. At eleven-twenty-six P.M., Captain Fritz signed the complaint charging Oswald with the murder of President John F. Kennedy. At midnight, detectives took Oswald to the basement assembly room for a brief appearance in front of the press. Half an hour later, Oswald was placed in a maximum-security cell on the fifth floor of the police station to await the arrival of Justice of the Peace David Johnston. At one-thirty on the morning of November 23, 1963, Lee Harvey Oswald was formally arraigned for the murder of President Kennedy.

Reporters were already writing their stories of a lone assassin who had gone berserk and struck down the thirty-fifth President of the United States. As their stories flooded through the media of the world, Lee Harvey Oswald was to be the victim of another assassin. His death would come just as dramatically and suddenly as that of John Kennedy. As he was being transferred from the Dallas Police Station to the more secure sheriff's jail, just two days after the crime he was charged with— which had already shaken the world—Oswald was confronted by Jack Ruby, who fired a single bullet into his stomach from a .38-caliber revolver in full view of the press and over one hundred million television viewers. It was eleven-twenty-one A.M., November 24, 1963. At one-oh-seven P.M., Oswald was declared dead at the same Parkland Hospital that had declared John F. Kennedy officially dead exactly forty-eight hours and seven minutes earlier.

The man suspected of being the lone assassin of President Kennedy was himself the victim of another lone assassin. There would be no long legal battle for Lee Harvey Oswald and the world to face. But there were many questions yet to be answered.

3 | THE LONE ASSASSIN SCENARIO

"The assassination of President Kennedy was the work of one man, Lee Harvey Oswald. There was no conspiracy, foreign or domestic."

That was the general finding of "The Warren [Commission] Report." Chief Justice Earl Warren and six other members of the Commission on the assassination were unanimous on this and all questions.

Lyndon B. Johnson became the thirty-sixth President of the United States at two-thirty-eight P.M., on November 22, 1963. He took the oath of office in the Presidential jet plane as it stood on the runway at Love Field with the body of the late President already on board in its bronze casket. Secret Service men were understandably nervous and could hardly wait to get the oath administered in the shortest possible time. The work of running the country had to go on with a Chief Executive in charge. It was important to get the new President airborne and back to Washington, D.C. Anything that helped to put the climate of hate behind them was a good enough reason for rushing the administration of the oath of office.

If public confidence was to be restored, it was necessary for the President to set up a committee to investigate the assassination of his predecessor. The man who would normally have been brought to trial in a United States court of justice was already dead. Yet the act of assassination had to be thoroughly investigated. And so, by Executive Order No. 11130, dated November 29, 1963, President Johnson created the Warren Commission, which took its name from the appointment of Chief Justice Earl Warren as its chairman. The Commission was charged with the task of satisfying itself "that the truth is known as far as it can be discovered and to report its findings and conclusions to him (the President), to the American people, and to the world." Besides the Chief Justice, there were six other members of the Commission. Four were from the political arena: Richard B. Russell, Democratic Senator from Georgia; John S. Cooper, Republican Senator from Kentucky; Hale Boggs, Democratic Representative from Louisiana; and Gerald R. Ford, Republican Representative from Michigan. From private life, President Johnson nominated two lawyers: Allen W. Dulles, former director of the Central Intelligence Agency, and John J. McCloy, former president of the International Bank for Reconstruction and Development. On December 16, 1963, J. Lee Rankin, a former Solicitor General of the United States, was sworn in as general counsel. Among his fourteen assistants were David Belin and Arlen Specter along with twelve staff members.

On September 24, 1964, the Warren Commission completed its report. In a foreword, the Commission stated that it had operated not as a judge and jury but as a dispassionate fact finder. The report itself ran to 888 pages with 8 chapters and appendices. All the testimony taken by the Commission and its staff from 552 witnesses was published later in 26 massive tomes. The conclusion of the Commission was that Lee Harvey Oswald acted in the capacity of a lone assassin. Through "The Warren [Commission] Report," the lone-assassin theory was established as an historical fact. It was acceptable to the majority of people at the time because of the caliber of the men who worked on the Commission. At no time was there any confession of guilt from Lee Harvey Oswald; but he had supposedly left a trail of clues behind him, a trail that led the Commission to their conclusion that he alone was responsible for the assassination of John F. Kennedy.

The first piece of damning evidence against Lee Harvey Oswald was the Italian Mannlicher-Carcano rifle left behind on the sixth floor of the Texas School Book Depository Building. The FBI traced the rifle to the Klein Sporting Goods Company of Chicago which, in turn, had obtained it from the Crescent Firearms Company, a distributing house in New York. The rifle was ordered on March 13, 1963, with a mail-order coupon clipped from the February edition of the *American Rifleman* Magazine. The order was filled out by hand by an "A. Hidell," P.O. Box 2915, Dallas, Texas. Accompanying it was a money order for $21.45, the price for the rifle and scope, plus $1.50 for postage.

By six-forty-five P.M., on November 23rd, the FBI advised the Dallas police that the handwriting on the order form used to purchase the rifle and scope was identical to the writing on checks and other documents belonging to Lee Harvey Oswald. The post office box to which the rifle and scope had been sent was rented to Lee H. Oswald from October 9, 1962, to May 14, 1963. Further handwriting analysis revealed that the handwriting on the application for the box was identical to that on the order form for the rifle and the documents belonging to Lee Harvey Oswald.

When arrested at the Texas Theatre, Oswald was in possession of a Smith and Wesson .38-caliber revolver. Inquiries revealed that this, too, was purchased by mail order from Seaport Traders, Inc., a division of George Rose and Co., of Los Angeles. The mail order form again listed the purchaser as "A. J. Hidell," age twenty-eight, and the address was the same post office box number in Dallas. Among identification papers in Oswald's wallet at the time of his arrest were a Selective Service classification notice, a certificate of service in the U.S. Marine Corps, and a Selective Service registration certificate—all in the name of Lee Harvey Oswald.

But there was also a Selective Service notice of classification and a marine certificate of service in the name of Alek James Hidell. Experts from the Treasury Department and the FBI testified that the Hidell cards were counterfeit photographic reproductions made by photographing the Oswald cards, retouching the negatives, and producing prints from the retouched negatives. The Hidell signatures on these cards corresponded to the handwriting of Oswald. In his rented room at 1026 North Beckley Avenue, Dallas, there was a certificate of vaccination signed by "Dr. A. J. Hidell," Post Office Box 30016, New Orleans. There was no Dr. A. J. Hidell licensed to practice medicine in Louisiana. Nor was there a post office box 30016 rented in New Orleans to Dr. A. J. Hidell. Oswald *had* rented box 30016 on June 3, 1963, listing Marina Oswald and A. J. Hidell as persons to receive mail in this box. Marina Oswald, Lee's wife, testified that Oswald used the fictitious name of Hidell in connection with his pro-Castro activities in New Orleans. He liked the name and used it as a reference on a job application made when he lived in New Orleans.

Based on this evidence, the Warren Commission concluded that it was Oswald who purchased the Italian rifle found in the Texas School Book Depository. A palm print on the rifle established that Oswald had handled the rifle. The rifle was examined for prints by Lt. J. C. Day of the Identification Bureau of the Dallas police. At eleven-forty-five P.M., on November 22, the rifle was released to the FBI and forwarded to Washington. There, on the morning of November 23, it was examined by Sebastian F. Latona, supervisor of the Latent Fingerprint Division. Latona also testified that the palm print was the right-hand print of Oswald. The Commission requested an independent examination by Arthur Mandella, a fingerprint expert in the New York City Police Department, who confirmed the findings of Latona. Experts testifying before the Commission agreed that palm prints are as unique as fingerprints for the purpose of establishing identification. The palm print, therefore, was proof that the rifle had been in the possession of Oswald and handled by him.

More evidence was supplied by fibers caught in the wooden stock of the rifle. These were dark blue, gray-black, and orange cotton fibers that Paul M. Stombaugh, a special agent assigned to the Hair and Fiber Unit of the FBI, compared with the fibers of the shirt Oswald was wearing when he was taken from the Texas Theatre. The colors, shades, and twists matched. This added to the conviction of the Commission that Oswald owned and handled the weapon used at the time of the assassination.

Further evidence of the ownership of the rifle was provided with the production of two photographs of Oswald. These were taken by Marina Oswald during the period when they lived on Neely Street in Dallas from March 2 until April 24, 1963. One photograph showed Oswald holding a rifle and two newspapers later identified as *The Worker* and *The Militant*. The Commission concluded that the rifle in the photograph was the same rifle found in the Book Depository. Special Agent Lyndal L. Shaneyfelt testified: "I found it to be the same general configuration. All appearances were the same." Together with the second photograph, it was established by expert testimony that both had been taken by an Imperial Reflex camera owned by Oswald. And Marina Oswald testified that this was the camera she had used.

Marina also testified that the rifle taken from the Book Depository was "the fateful rifle of Lee Oswald." It was the only rifle her husband had owned since their arrival in New Orleans from Soviet Russia in June 1962.

oh come on already !

In September 1963, Oswald loaded their possessions into a station wagon owned by Mrs. Ruth Paine, who had invited Marina Oswald and their baby to live in her home in Irving, Texas. Marina Oswald stated that the rifle, wrapped in a green-and-brown blanket, was stored in the garage of the Paines' house among Oswald's other possessions. Three hours after the assassination, a detective and a deputy sheriff saw the blanket roll, tied with string, lying on the floor of the garage. Each man testified that he thought he could detect the outline of a rifle in the blanket even though the blanket was empty.

The conclusion of the Committee was that:

1. Lee Harvey Oswald purchased the rifle used in the assassination.
2. His palm print proved that he had handled it.
3. Fibers found on the rifle probably came from the shirt Oswald wore on the day of the assassination.
4. A photograph showed him holding the same rifle.
5. The rifle was kept among Oswald's possessions from the time it was purchased until the day of the assassination.
6. The rifle used to assassinate President Kennedy and wound Governor Connally was owned and possessed by Lee Harvey Oswald.

From October until November 21, 1963, Oswald lived in a rooming house at 1026 North Beckley Avenue in Dallas. His wife and children stayed with Mrs. Ruth Paine and her husband, Michael, in Irving some fifteen miles from the Texas School Book Depository, where Ruth Paine had helped Oswald to find work as a clerk. Oswald spent the weekends with his family in Irving, being driven there by a neighbor, Buell Wesley Frazier, who also worked at the Depository. Frazier, Marina Oswald, and Ruth Paine testified that Oswald never returned to Irving in mid-week prior to November 21, 1963, except on one previous occasion, October 21st, when he visited Marina in the hospital after the birth of their second child.

On the morning of November 21st, Oswald asked Frazier if he could ride back with him that afternoon as he had to get some curtain rods to put in the apartment. Frazier and Oswald left the Book Depository at four-forty P.M., and drove to Irving. Frazier's sister, Mrs. Linnie Mae Randle, remarked that it was unusual for Oswald to come to Irving in mid-week.

The Commission concluded that Oswald used the excuse of wanting curtain rods as his reason to return home and collect the rifle. Next morning, Oswald was picked up by Frazier to go to work and was carrying a long homemade paper bag. Neither Mrs. Paine nor Marina saw Oswald leave the house but, as Oswald walked across the road to the home of Wesley Frazier, his sister noted that Oswald was gripping a bag in his right hand near the top. She stated that it contained a tapered object and was more bulky at the bottom than the top. She estimated that the parcel was about twenty-eight inches long and eight inches wide; and later, when shown the bag found on the sixth floor of the Depository after the assassination, she thought it seemed like the one she had seen Oswald carrying and placing on the backseat of the car. Frazier stated that Oswald told him the parcel contained curtain rods. He also asked Oswald where his lunch was, but Oswald said he intended to buy his lunch that day. (Frazier thought this was unusual because Oswald always carried his lunch bag with him.)

On arriving in the area of the Book Depository, Frazier parked the car in the company parking lot two blocks from the place where they worked. Oswald got out of the car first, picked up the brown paper bag and ran on ahead to the Book Depository. Frazier noted that he carried the bag with one end under his armpit, holding the lower part of it with his right hand and keeping it close to his body. He thought it was unusual that Oswald did not wait for him and walk with him to the Depository. In fact, he did not see Oswald when he himself entered the building. However, another employee, Jack Dougherty, thought he noticed Oswald, although he could not remember if he had a parcel with him.

The Commission carefully considered the testimony of Linnie Mae Randle and her brother Wesley, who both testified that they thought the length of the parcel was about twenty-eight inches long. The wooden stock of the rifle, its largest component, was 34.8 inches, and the bag found on the sixth floor of the Depository was 38 inches long. They concluded it was not easy for two people to accurately estimate the length of the bag. After the assassination, a homemade bag and tape were found in the southeast corner of the sixth floor near the window where the shots were fired. The bag was more than adequate to accommodate, in a disassembled form, a Mannlicher-Carcano rifle, which was also found on the sixth floor. Three cartons were found to have been placed at the window and could have been used as a gun rest. In addition, there was a fourth carton behind them, which could have been used as a seat. It was concluded that a person could have sat there, assembling the rifle, and still be hidden from view of anyone else on the sixth floor because of the cartons acting as a shield.

Oswald's fingerprints and palm print were found on the bag when the FBI examined it. His palm print on the bottom of the bag indicated that he had handled it. Samples of the wrapping paper and tape used in the Depository were sent to the FBI laboratory in Washington, D.C., and were examined by James C. Cadigan. He found that the wrapping paper and tape used in the Depository were the same type the paper bag was made of. Paul M. Stombaugh of the FBI laboratory also examined the bag and found a single brown delustered viscose fiber and several light-green cotton fibers, which he concluded were from the blanket in which the rifle had been wrapped when it rested in the garage at the Irving House. By this time, the Committee reached the conclusion that Oswald carried the disassembled rifle into the Depository in a homemade paper bag and that he left the bag by the window of the sixth floor after the assassination.

Oswald was hired as a "filler clerk" on October 15, 1963, and normally worked either on the first or sixth floor of the Texas School Book Depository. He had ready access to the southeast corner window on the sixth floor. The cartons on this floor were examined by Sebastian F. Latona in Washington, who found twenty identifiable fingerprints and eight palm prints. All matched up with the fingerprints and palm prints of Oswald, but the carton on the windowsill and the large carton below the windowsill contained no prints that could be matched to those of Oswald. However, a third carton had a palm print and fingerprint that were identified as the left palm print and right index fingerprint of Oswald.

From these it was established that Oswald was at the window from which the shots were fired, but it could not be established at what time he was there. Oswald was seen on the sixth floor thirty-five minutes before the assassination, and testimony to this was given by Charles Givens, the last-known employee to see Oswald inside the building prior to the assassination. Givens was a member of a floor-laying crew working on the sixth floor. At approximately eleven-forty-five A.M., the floor-laying crew left the sixth floor to go to lunch. Givens testified that he saw Oswald standing by the elevator on the fifth floor as the elevator moved down. On discovering he had left his cigarettes behind, Givens took the elevator back to the sixth floor and saw Oswald, with a clipboard in his hand, walking from the southeast corner of the floor toward the elevator. On December 21, 1963, an employee, Frank Kay, found a clipboard hidden behind book cartons in the northeast corner of the sixth floor a few feet from where the police found the Italian rifle after the assassination. Three invoices dated November 22nd were still on the clipboard.

In the six-to-eight-minute period before the motorcade turned onto Elm Street, a construction worker, Howard

L. Brennan, testified that he was sitting on a concrete wall on the southwest corner of Elm and Houston streets. He was looking north at the Depository Building directly in front of him. The sixth-floor window was about one hundred and twenty feet away. Brennan saw a man leave and return to the window a couple of times. He heard a noise that he first thought was a motorcycle backfiring, and glanced up again to the half-open window where he saw the same man he had previously seen. He appeared to be standing up and resting against the left windowsill. Brennan stated that he saw the man fire the last shot and disappear from the window. Within minutes of the assassination, Brennan was able to describe this man to the police. A radio alert to police cars was sent out at approximately twelve-forty-five P.M., describing a slender white male, about one hundred and sixty-five pounds, five feet ten inches tall and in his early thirties.

Brennan also testified that shortly after the assassination he saw two employees leave the building and identified them as having been at windows on the fifth floor. His testimony was confirmed by the two men, Harold Norman and James Jarman, Jr., who also heard Brennan describing to the police the man he had seen at the sixth-floor window. They remembered that he told the police he saw a barrel of a gun sticking out of the window and that the shots came from inside the building. On the evening of November 22nd in a lineup at the police station, Brennan identified Oswald as the man who bore the closest resemblance to the man he had seen at the sixth-floor window of the Depository. The Commission was satisfied that Brennan saw a man at the window who bore a close resemblance to Lee Harvey Oswald.

Ronald Fischer and Robert Edwards also testified that they saw a man in the window about a minute before the assassination, but neither saw any shots fired. A fifteen-year-old boy had an experience he would never forget. Amos L. Euins was on the southwest corner of Elm and Houston streets and observed a man at the sixth-floor window of the Book Depository Building. He saw the man lower his head in order to take aim with a rifle, Amos told a Secret Service agent about twenty minutes after the assassination. At this point, there was enough evidence in the opinion of the Commission to conclude that Oswald's movements as described by these witnesses were consistent with his having been at the window at twelve-thirty P.M.

The first person to see Oswald after the assassination was Patrolman M. L. Baker of the Dallas Police Department. He was riding his motorcycle behind the last press car in the Presidential motorcade. Turning the corner from Main onto Houston, he heard a sound that he recognized as a rifle shot, followed by three more. Baker parked his motorcycle on the northwest corner of Elm and Houston Streets and, since he felt that the shots came from the Book Depository Building, he rushed inside. He met a man who identified himself as Roy Truly, the supervisor of the Book Depository, and together they headed for the freight elevators. Neither came down, so Baker followed Truly up the stairway, west of the elevators. As Baker reached the second floor, intending to go up to the next one, he caught a fleeting glimpse of a man walking in the vestibule toward the lunchroom. Truly continued up to the third floor, and with drawn revolver, Baker ran into the vestibule and at the door of the lunchroom told a man to "come here." The man turned and walked back to Baker. He had been walking toward the side wall of the lunchroom where a soft-drink vending machine stood. As the man turned, Baker noted he had nothing in his hands.

Meanwhile Roy Truly, having missed Baker following him, returned to the second floor and went to the lunchroom to find Officer Baker facing an employee known as Lee Harvey Oswald. Truly identified Oswald to Baker. Despite the fact that Baker was holding a gun directed at Oswald's stomach, the man was calm and not out of breath. And he was silent.

The Commission now had to consider how much time it would have taken Oswald to have gone from the sixth floor to the second floor and to correlate this with the time it took for Baker to park his motorcycle and run up the stairs with Truly. The confrontation in the lunchroom was important. So the Commission ordered Baker and Truly to re-enact their movements, which were timed by a stopwatch. The first test showed that one minute and thirty seconds elapsed between Baker hearing the first shot and arriving on the second-floor landing. The second test reduced this timing to one minute and fifteen seconds. Special Agent John J. Howlett of the Secret Service then played the part of Oswald. Starting from the sixth floor with a rifle, he dropped it at the point where the rifle was ultimately found and, at normal walking pace, went down the stairway to the lunchroom. The time was one minute and eighteen seconds. A second test was conducted with Howlett moving at a fast walk, and the time was cut down to one minute and fourteen seconds. Through these tests, it was established that Oswald and Baker could have arrived on the second floor within seconds of each other. (Three other employees would testify that Oswald *could* have used the stairs to effect his getaway. James Jarman, Jr., Bonnie Ray Williams and Harold Norman had been watching the parade from the fifth floor, directly below the window from which the shots were fired. When they heard shots, they ran to the west windows, where their view of the stairway was obscured. Oswald could have started his descent without being seen.)

Victoria Adams, an employee of the Book Depository, worked on the fourth floor of the building. On hearing shots, she ran down the stairs to the first floor where she said she encountered two fellow employees, William Shelley and Billy Lovelady. Shelley and Lovelady presented testimony that was in conflict with Victoria Adams. They said they were watching the motorcade from the steps of the Depository Building. Then another employee, Gloria Calverly, ran up and said the

President had been shot. The two men moved into the street, turned west into the railroad yard, and re-entered the Depository Building from the rear door several minutes after Baker met Truly. It was at this point that Lovelady said he saw Victoria Adams. If Miss Adams met Shelley and Lovelady, the Commission concluded it was at this point, and so her estimate of the time she descended from the fourth floor was incorrect and she must have come down the staircase some minutes after Oswald.

Officer Baker and Roy Truly left Oswald in the lunchroom and, within a few minutes, Mrs. R. A. Reid, a clerical supervisor, saw him walk through the clerical office of the second floor to the door leading to the front stairway. Mrs. Reid had watched the motorcade from the sidewalk in front of the building. She testified that she heard three shots coming from the building, then ran inside to the large open office reserved for clerical employees. As Oswald passed her, she noticed he had a large full bottle of Coca-Cola in his hand, which he must have gotten from the vending machine after Baker and Truly left. She called to Oswald to tell him that the President was shot, but he kept on walking. The only exit he could have taken from the office was through a door leading to the front stairway. She stated that he was wearing a T-shirt and no jacket. Marina Oswald was later to testify that her husband left home wearing a jacket and then identified a blue jacket found in the Depository Building. Following another stopwatch test, the Commission found that Mrs. Reid encountered Oswald at twelve-thirty-two P.M., some thirty to forty-five seconds after the lunchroom encounter involving Oswald, Baker, and Truly. Oswald could have left the building at twelve-thirty-three P.M., a few minutes before the building was officially sealed off by the police.

According to Officer W. E. Barnett, he positioned himself at the front entrance of the building after first inspecting the fire escape at the side of the Book Depository. In between inspecting the fire escape and taking up a position at the front entrance, Barnett spoke to a police sergeant and witness Howard Brennan. Barnett estimated that about three minutes elapsed between the time he heard the last shots and the time he took on the self-imposed task of guarding the front door, where he noted several people going in and out. Sergeant D. V. Harkness of the Dallas police testified that the building was sealed off by twelve-thirty-six P.M., so there was a three-minute gap in which Oswald could have walked out of the building. No one noticed Oswald's absence for half an hour. Officer Baker and Roy Truly had proceeded to the roof of the building after their encounter in the lunchroom. On descending, they found police questioning warehouse employees. Roy Truly noticed that Lee Harvey Oswald was missing and then furnished Oswald's address, telephone number, and description to Captain Will Fritz of the Dallas Police Force.

Coinciding with this information, the Italian rifle was found at one-twenty-two P.M., in the northwest corner of the sixth floor.

The evidence was rapidly mounting that Oswald *could* have been in position on the sixth floor to fire the shots and could have had time to get away from the scene of the crime.

Leaving the Book Depository at approximately twelve-thirty-three P.M., Oswald went to his rooming house by bus and taxi. He arrived at the rooming house at one P.M., and left a few minutes later. In a reconstruction of the journey to the rooming house, the Commission found that Oswald walked east on Elm Street for seven blocks to the corner of Elm and Murphy, where he boarded a bus that took him back in the direction of the Book Depository to the Oak Cliff section of Dallas. Bus driver Cecil J. McWatters testified that he left his checkpoint on time and took approximately four minutes to drive to Field Street, reaching there at twelve-forty P.M. At this point, a man beat on the door of the bus, boarded, paid his fare, received a ticket, asked for a transfer, and got off at the intersection near

Lamar Street, two blocks from Field Street. The bus driver identified Oswald from among four men presented in a police lineup at six-thirty P.M., on November 22nd. Also on the bus was Mary Bledsoe, a former landlady of Lee Harvey Oswald. She boarded at St. Paul and Elm streets and recognized her former tenant. She noted that his shirt was undone and had a hole in the right elbow. According to her, Oswald sat in the rear half of the bus and got off at Lamar Street. Agents of the Secret Service and FBI reconstructed three times the seven-block walk from the Depository, boarding a bus, and dismounting. They took an average time from the three reconstructions and found that Oswald could have left the Depository at twelve-thirty-three P.M., walked seven blocks in six and a half minutes, made a four-minute run on the bus, and dismounted at twelve-forty-four P.M.

A taxi driver, William Whaley, came forward on November 23rd and told police that he had picked up a man answering the description of Lee Harvey Oswald the afternoon before. He said he saw Oswald walking south on Lamar Street from Commerce Street. The man stopped him and asked, "May I have a cab?" He took his fare to 500 North Beckley Avenue, unloading him at twelve-forty-five P.M. at the address the fare had asked to go to, although Oswald's rooming house was at 1026 North Beckley, five blocks north of where the cabdriver said he deposited his fare.

At 1026 North Beckley Avenue, the housekeeper, Mrs. Earlene Roberts, testified that on the night of November 21st, Oswald did not return to the rooming house. She saw him on Friday, November 22nd, about one P.M., and noted that he hurried into the house. She remarked on this to him, but he did not reply and was only in the house for approximately four minutes. He was in his shirt-sleeves but, as he went out, he was zipping up his jacket. Mrs. Roberts watched her lodger go outside and stand at the bus stop on the east side of North Beckley Avenue.

Oswald was next seen almost a mile away at the southeast corner of Tenth Street and Patton Avenue, moments before Patrolman J. D. Tippit was shot dead. Since it was daylight, Patrolman Tippit was alone in police car number ten, the normal police procedure for any patrolman working a residential district in the daylight hours. On November 22nd, at twelve-forty-four P.M., the police radio dispatcher on channel one ordered all downtown patrol squads to report to Elm and Houston streets, followed by a description of a suspect wanted for questioning in the murder of President Kennedy. But, at twelve-forty-five P.M., the dispatcher ordered Tippit, badge number seventy-eight, to go to the Oak Cliff area. At twelve-fifty-four P.M., Tippit reported that he was at Lancaster and Eighth streets, and he was told to be "at large for any emergency that might come in." At one-fifteen P.M., Tippit was cruising east on Tenth Street, eight blocks from where he had received his previous message. A few yards past the intersection of Tenth Street and Patton Avenue, Tippit stopped a man walking east along the south side of Patton. The man came over to the car in response to something Tippit said, leaned down, and talked to the officer for a moment. Then Tippit got out of the car and started to walk around the front of it. As he reached the left front wheel, the man pulled out a revolver and fired several shots, killing the patrolman. The man started back toward Patton Avenue, ejecting cartridges as he ran and reloading his revolver.

At least twelve witnesses observed a man with a revolver in the vicinity of the shooting of Officer Tippit. Taxi driver William Scoggins was eating lunch in his cab, which was parked on Patton Avenue, facing the southeast corner of Tenth Street and Patton. He saw the cruising police car stop and a man called over to it. Then he observed Tippit leave the car, heard three or four shots fired, and saw the patrolman drop to the ground. Scoggins got out of his cab and hid behind it as the man with the revolver came in his direction. The man took a shortcut across a yard through some bushes, but passed within twelve feet of the cabdriver.

Another witness was Domingo Benavides, who was driving a pickup truck west on Tenth Street. Crossing the intersection at Patton, he saw a policeman standing by the left door of his parked car, with a man standing at the right-hand side of the car. Benavides heard three shots and saw the policeman fall to the ground. He saw the gunman run to the corner, empty his gun, and throw some shells into the nearby bushes. Benavides went to the police car and used the radio in it to alert the police to the shooting at one-sixteen P.M. He also found two empty shells and gave them to Patrolman J. M. Poe when he arrived at the scene of the shooting. Since Benavides was not called to the police station to identify the man with the revolver, he never saw Oswald in the police lineup. However, he testified to the Warren Commission that a photograph of Oswald looked like the man who shot Tippit.

Mrs. Helen L. Markham, a waitress, was just about to cross Tenth Street at Patton. As she waited for the traffic to pass, she saw a police car stop a young man, who she observed pull a gun. Then she heard three shots fired. The man ran away, and Mrs. Markham ran toward the police car to find Patrolman Tippit lying in a pool of blood. She screamed and became hysterical, but she positively identified Oswald in a police lineup as the man she saw kill Tippit. Mrs. Markham's screams aroused Barbara Jeannette and Virginia Davis in their apartment in the multi-unit house on the southeast corner of Tenth and Patton. Running to the door, they saw a man with a revolver skirting across their lawn. Barbara Jeannette called the police. Later in the day Barbara Jeannette found an empty shell case near the house, and Virginia found another one. Ted Callaway and Sam Guinyard heard the shots from a used-car lot. Both saw a man coming south on Patton with a revolver in his hand. Four other males saw a white male with a revolver in the vicinity of the shooting.

At one-forty-five P.M., the police radio sent out a message that a suspect in the murder of Patrolman Tippit had gone into the Texas Theatre on West Jefferson. Fifteen police officers went to the theater, where Lee Harvey Oswald was apprehended. He was sitting in the rear of the theater on the main floor. Patrolman N. M. McDonald recognized him from the radio description and told the man to get to his feet. He did so, raising both hands; then he struck out at McDonald with his left fist. At the same time, he drew out a .38-caliber Smith and Wesson revolver with his right hand. There was a scuffle as three officers threw themselves on the man and took the gun from him. At one-fifty-one P.M., police car number two reported that it was returning to the Dallas Police Station with a suspect. There he met with Captain Fritz at two-fifteen P.M., and was intermittently interrogated for twelve hours.

Subsequently, Oswald was charged first with the murder of Patrolman Tippit and then with that of President John F. Kennedy. Oswald was detained in the Police and Courts Bureau in downtown Dallas pending his removal on Sunday, November 24th, when he was scheduled to go to the county jail to await his trial. Then at eleven-twenty-one P.M., on November 24th, in full view of millions of television viewers and the live witnesses of the press of the world, Lee Harvey Oswald was fatally shot in the stomach by a Dallas nightclub owner, Jack Ruby.

As the Warren Commission delved into the shadowy life of Lee Harvey Oswald, many startling facts emerged. Oswald was released from active service in the marines on September 11, 1959. He served at Atsugi in Japan intermittently from August 1957 until November 1958. Although he studied Russian there, when he took an aptitude test in Russian in February 1959, he was rated "poor." Oswald left the United States for Helsinki, Finland, on September 20, 1959, via La Havre, France, and London. On October 14th he was issued a Soviet tourist visa, number 403339, and left Helsinki by train for Moscow on October 15th. Two months and twenty-two days later, Oswald left Moscow to take up residence in Minsk, after announcing that he wished to relinquish his American citizenship at the American Embassy on October 31st.

From the time he left for Russia by train, Oswald kept what turned out to be an historic diary, which later became available for the Commission to study. In the diary, Oswald recorded the fact that he told his Intourist guide, Rima Shirokova, that he wished to renounce his American citizenship on the day he arrived in Moscow. The Russian Committee on State Security, better known as the KGB, interviewed Oswald. According to his diary, he attempted suicide when his application for Russian citizenship was first turned down. Medical records from Botkinskaya Hospital in Moscow, furnished by the Soviet Government, reveal that Oswald was treated there from October 21st to 28th for a self-inflicted wound on the left wrist. On October 31st, Oswald saw Richard E. Snyder (consul at the U.S. Embassy in Moscow) and informed him he wished to renounce his American citizenship, and was told that he would have to complete the necessary papers to effect this. He was allowed to remain in the country indefinitely, but he did not know he was accepted as a citizen of the U.S.S.R. until January 4, 1960. In November 1959 he had a five-hour interview with Mrs. Priscilla Johnson, an American journalist working in Moscow. According to his diary, Oswald resided in Minsk from January 1960 until June 1962, and the Commission viewed two photographs taken by American tourists in Minsk in August 1961, in which Oswald appears.

Oswald obtained a job at the Byelorussian Radio and Television Factory, where his pay ranged from seventy to ninety dollars a month. But he was also given five hundred dollars by the Russian Red Cross for his expenses when he left for Minsk; and his salary at the factory was augmented by seventy dollars a month, also paid by the Russian Red Cross. He also had an apartment at the modest rent of six dollars per month.

In February 1961, Oswald wrote to the American Embassy in Moscow, expressing a desire to return to the United States. In March, he met a nineteen-year-old Russian girl, Marina Nikolaevna Prusakova, a pharmacist, who had been brought up in Leningrad but was living with her aunt and uncle in Minsk. On April 30, 1961, Oswald and Marina were married and he kept up a lengthy correspondence with the American and Soviet authorities, requesting permission for he and his wife to leave the Soviet Union and return to the United States.

In February 1962, their daughter was born, and they began to prepare to leave the U.S.S.R. They departed from Moscow on June 1, 1962, receiving assistance in their traveling expenses from the U.S. Department of State, which gave them a loan of $435.70. Two weeks later they arrived in Fort Worth Texas, where they lived for a few weeks with Oswald's brother, Robert, and then with his mother. On June 26, Oswald was interviewed by the FBI, and agreed to inform them if there was any attempt to enlist him in intelligence activities by the KGB. He was interviewed again on July 16th, the same day that he started to work as a sheet-metal worker. The Oswalds moved into an apartment of their own in August.

October 1962, found Oswald leaving his job in Fort Worth and moving to Dallas. In Fort Worth, the Oswalds knew many Russian-speaking people who were good to them, helping them with food and clothes, and acting in a generally neighborly manner. Oswald was not as well liked as Marina, and there appears to have been some sympathy for Marina and her baby. Oswald is remembered for his increasing disdain for democracy and capitalism—if not for American society as a whole. In February 1963, the Oswalds met with Russian-speaking Ruth Paine, who was temporarily separated from her husband, Michael. She lived in the Irving suburb of Dallas with her two children.

On April 6, Oswald lost his job with a photography firm. Four days later, according to Marina's testimony, he attempted to assassinate Major General Edwin A. Walker, using a rifle he had ordered by mail a month earlier. She produced a note he had left in case he did not return. Following this incident, Marina suggested that her husband leave Dallas and go to New Orleans to look for work. Oswald departed on April 24, 1963. Ruth Paine invited Marina and the baby to stay with her in her Irving house. Early in May, Oswald obtained work, and Mrs. Paine drove Mrs. Oswald and the child to join Lee in New Orleans.

On July 19th, Oswald lost his job as a greaser of coffee-processing machinery and concentrated on his pro-Castro activities until August 9, 1963, when he was arrested for disturbing the peace while distributing pro-Castro leaflets.

Mrs. Sylvia Odio testified that Oswald visited her apartment in Dallas in late September with two other men who appeared to be Cubans but might have been Mexicans. One of the Cuban-types was called "Leopoldo," and Oswald was introduced to her as Leon Oswald. The men did not identify themselves with their real names. She concluded they had underworld connections and were using their "war names." She remembered that they came in from New Orleans and were about to leave on a trip to an unstated destination. The reason for the visit was that Mrs. Odio was a Cuban by birth, and the men knew that both of her parents were political prisoners of the Castro regime. The men thought that Mrs. Odio would help them prepare a letter to solicit funds for the Cuban Revolutionary Junta— an anti-Castro organization. Mrs. Odio fixed the date of the visit as either September 26th or 27th because she moved to another apartment on October 1st.

The Commission did not accept Mrs. Odio's evidence because of conflicting evidence that Oswald cashed his unemployment check in New Orleans on September 25th sometime between eight A.M. and one P.M. In addition, the Commission established that Oswald was traveling on a Continental Trailways bus on September 26th from Houston to Laredo. It was scheduled to arrive in Laredo at one-twenty P.M., on September 26th, and Mexican immigration officials produced records to show that Oswald crossed the border at Laredo to Nuevo Laredo between six A.M. and two P.M. on that day. The Commission requested that the FBI try to find the two men who were purported to have visited Mrs. Odio with Oswald. On September 16, 1964, the FBI located Loran Eugene Hall in Johnsondale, California. He said he was in Dallas in September 1963 and visited Mrs. Odio, accompanied by Lawrence Howard, a Mexican-American from Los Angeles, and William Seymour from Arizona. The Commission concluded that Lee Harvey Oswald did not visit Mrs. Odio and that she mistook William Seymour for him, since he was the only member of the group who spoke very few words of Spanish. Mrs. Odio had previously testified that the man introduced as "Leon Oswald" spoke very little Spanish.

On September 23rd, Mrs. Ruth Paine had driven to New Orleans to pick up Marina, the child, and the belongings of the Oswald family. They drove back to Mrs. Paine's house in the Irving suburb of Dallas, leaving Oswald to hopefully obtain employment again. The Commission learned that Oswald decided to go to Mexico City but, according to "The Warren Report," the evidence of Mrs. Odio was in conflict with other evidence proving that Oswald was indeed on his way to Mexico City. Oswald visited the Cuban and Russian embassies in the Mexican capital, first requesting permission to visit Cuba, and stating that he was en route to Russia. The Cuban officials would not issue a permit until they had proof that Oswald was actually going on to Russia. Failing to get visas for either country, Oswald returned to Dallas on October 3rd, where he rented a room from Mrs. Bledsoe, staying there until October 14th. He then moved to the North Beckley address, using the name of O. H. Lee. On the same day, Mrs. Paine heard from a neighbor that there was a vacancy for a clerk at the Texas School Book Depository, and Oswald commenced work there on October 16th. A second child was born to Marina on October 20th.

All the peregrinations of Oswald were carefully studied before he was captured at the Texas Theatre and subsequently accused of the murders of Patrolman Tippit and President Kennedy. Then Oswald himself was assassinated in November by Dallas nightclub owner, Jack Ruby. Indicted for the murder, Ruby was brought to trial and found guilty on March 14, 1964, when he was sentenced to death. The sentence was later commuted to life imprisonment. The Commission had examined 395 witnesses, taken sworn statements from another 63, quizzed yet another 94, had also assessed over 26,550 interviews, and amassed its evidence into 26 volumes—all in order to arrive at its conclusion that Lee Harvey Oswald *alone* was responsible for the assassination and that there was "no evidence of any conspiracy."

But was there?

4 | THE CONSPIRACY SCENARIO

The New York Times of February 25, 1976, carried the following four-and-one-half-inch Associated Press story on page sixteen:

CORONADO, CALIF., Feb. 24 (AP)—An independent medical investigator, confirming the findings of the Warren Commission, says only two bullets were fired at President Kennedy and both came from the gun of Lee Harvey Oswald.

The conclusion reached by Dr. John K. Lattimore, the first outsider permitted to look at the Kennedy autopsy photographs and X-rays, agrees with the Commission's finding that Oswald alone killed Mr. Kennedy on a Dallas street in 1963.

Dr. Lattimore, an expert on medical ballistics, is president of the American Urological Association and chairman of the Urology Department at Columbia University School of Medicine in New York City.

In an interview, Mr. Lattimore said last night, "If you look at the evidence, both bullets were re-

covered and both came out of Oswald's gun to the
exclusion of all other guns."

There you should have it—twelve years after "The
Warren [Commission] Report" and thirteen years after
the most heinous crime in America, the first outsider to
be permitted to view the Kennedy autopsy photographs
and X-rays agreeing with the Warren Commission that
"only two bullets were fired . . . and both came from the
gun of Lee Harvey Oswald." Wait a minute! *Both* bullets? If the two bullets that struck John Fitzgerald Kennedy at twelve-thirty P.M., on November 22, 1963, are
considered by Lattimore to be both bullets, what about
the third bullet? The same third bullet that led the
Commission, in its own words, "to conclude that there
were three shots fired"? And the bullet that "hit the
street" injuring "James T. Tague, who got out of his car
to watch the motorcade"? Where did the bullet go that
the Commission labored so desperately to include in its
report, the one they attributed the magical ability to
change its flight in mid-air to strike both Kennedy and
Governor Connally?

Lattimore, by his conclusion, may be apologizing for
the implausibility of having Oswald—an at-best fair
shot—hit his target two out of three times in the maximum time of 4.8 to 5.6 seconds with a faulty sight. Or
he may be apologizing for the incredible "Magic Bullet"
theory. But whatever he is doing, he is *not* agreeing with
the Warren Commission that "there were three shots
fired."

And if Lattimore's contention is that "both bullets"
(which struck Kennedy) were fired "from the gun of
Lee Harvey Oswald," a third bullet fired by a person or
persons unknown gives you at least a second gunman
and that most dreaded of thoughts: a conspiracy!

The Warren Commission had produced its report in
the hopes that it would satisfy Americans that Oswald
was the lone assassin of President Kennedy and that
there was no conspiracy. As an isolated case of murder,

this might have been acceptable; but then came the assassinations of Martin Luther King and Robert Kennedy, followed by the attempted assassination of Governor George Wallace. The scenarios all turned out to be written by the same hands . . . too well done, down to the smallest details, to be a coincidence. The assassin always appears to have worked alone, and commits the murder in a fit of rage against the victim. The lone assassin always keeps a diary and address book and is very placid when arrested. The FBI and CIA are called in to produce evidence. The due process of law then announces that there was no question of a conspiracy—just another nut doing his thing, and everyone should think nothing more about it.

The Zapruder film is probably one of the more important pieces of evidence concerning the assassination of President Kennedy. "The Warren Report" mentions this film, but it has a strange history. It was bought at once by *Life* Magazine, reportedly for the sum of $25,000. The purchase was guarded so jealously by the magazine that it was three months before the Warren Commission was able to view the original copy. During this period, FBI experts and the Warren Commission staff contented themselves with an inferior edited copy of the film. No member of the Warren Commission ever saw the original print, and only three of the seven members of the Commission viewed the inferior copy. In the early period of the assassination inquiry, the copy was obtained by Secret Service Agent Max Phillips in Dallas. He sent it along with a handwritten note to his superiors in Washington, D.C.: "Enclosed is an eight-mm. movie taken by Mr. A. Zapruder, 501 Elm Street, Dallas, Texas. Mr. Zapruder was photographing the President at the instant he was shot. According to Mr. Zapruder, the position of the assassin was *behind* Mr. Zapruder."

This important piece of evidence was one of those unfortunate errors that often beset the Commission. Frame by frame, the film was reprinted in volume eigh-

teen of "The Warren Report." Only two frames were
out of sequence, and they were the vital ones showing
the effect the head shot had on President Kennedy.
Because of the printing error and the reversing of
two frames, it looked as if the President's head went forward, when the true sequence of frames clearly shows
Kennedy's head thrown backward.

In the sequence of more than one hundred and fifty
frames, it is strange that the only printing error
concerns these two frames and this is what the three
members of the Commission saw. There are letters available in the National Archives concerning the Zapruder
film.

Office of the Director

United States Department of Justice
Federal Bureau of Investigation
Washington, D.C.

December 4, 1964
BY COURIER SERVICE

Honorable J. Lee Rankin
General Counsel
The President's Commission
200 Maryland Avenue, Northeast
Washington, D.C.

Dear Mr. Rankin,

You previously have been informed that this Bureau is in
possession of a copy of a film portraying the assassination
of President John F. Kennedy. The film being referred to
was taken by Adrian Zapruder who, after making a copy
available to the FBI, sold the film to *Life* Magazine. This
Bureau has not permitted the copy of the film to be
released outside of this Bureau without the concurrence of
the Committee.

The Central Intelligence Agency has inquired if the film
copy in possession of this Bureau can be loaned to that
Agency solely for training purposes. The showing of the film
would be restricted to Agency personnel. We have been
informed that the Central Intelligence Agency consulted with
Mr. Alfred Goldberg of the Commission who, according to
that Agency, has approved the loan of this film.

Unless advised to the contrary, this Bureau will make

available a copy of this film to the Central Intelligence Agency
on a loan basis and under the arrangement described above.

> Sincerely yours,
> J. Edgar Hoover

The FBI chief did not get the correct name of
Zapruder, referring to him as "Adrian" not Abraham.

A further letter proves to be very revealing. A
research worker, David Lifton, wrote to the FBI in the
name of a lady who knew about the reversing of the
frames. This was the reply:

United States Department of Justice
Federal Bureau of Investigation
Washington, D.C. 20535

> December 14, 1965
> AIRMAIL

Dear Miss ———

Reference is made to your letter dated December 6, 1965,
to Special Agent Lyndal L. Shaneyfelt regarding the labeling
of two of the Zapruder frames (numbers 314 and 315) of
Commission exhibit 885 in volume eighteen of the "Hearings
Before the President's Commission on the Assassination of
President Kennedy." You are correct in the observation that
frames labeled 314 and 315 of Commission exhibit 885 are
transposed in volume eighteen as noted in your letter.
This is a printing error and does not exist in the actual
Commission exhibit. For your information, the slides from
which Commission exhibit 885 was prepared are correctly
numbered and are being shown in their correct sequence.

The National Archives is aware of this printing error;
however, I do appreciate your interest in this matter.

> Sincerely yours,
> John Edgar Hoover
> (Director)

We can marvel that the CIA, no stranger to ambush
tactics, wanted a copy of this film "for training purposes"; and when we have gotten over that astonish-
ment, we can begin to worry that two vital frames were
transposed.

It is even more amazing that *Life* Magazine did not
part with its master copy of the Zapruder film for three
months after the assassination. It could have been con-

strued as withholding valuable evidence concerning a crime, a crime that was of major importance to the country. It could also have made a lot of money by showing the film in theaters throughout the world, but television studios seeking to show the film were visited by lawyers who threatened to sue. Time-Life Inc. did everything in its power to prevent the film from being screened anywhere.

In 1968, a book was published in Liechtenstein, where there are no libel laws. In *Farewell America,* the author says: "We were fortunate enough to obtain copies of this film from two different sources in the United States. One is a poor copy, the other of excellent quality. We have run through this film dozens of times. Certain of the photographs taken from it and published by leading magazines throughout the world have been retouched. Others were never published at all. These faked photographs and these cuts were the work of the photographic technicians of Time-Life Inc., who were acting on official instructions."

On whose instructions?

The author went on to say: "The unedited version of this very moving film utterly demolishes the official version of the assassination of President Kennedy put out by the Warren Commission. The Zapruder film belongs to history and men everywhere." We also studied an unedited copy of the Zapruder film and we studied it more than a dozen times. We saw it in slow motion and we stopped it frame by frame. It was a nauseating experience as we watched John Kennedy's head explode in a cloud of red blood lasting nearly a second; and we noticed that the President was thrust violently backward by the bullet fired by a gunman situated in front of the car, not the back. More nauseating, though, was the impact that so much trouble had been taken to produce a cover-up story to postulate the theory of the lone assassin and that a Government commission had placed its seal of approval on this theory. The memory of that unedited film, seen time and time again, will live with us forever.

The Time-Life company went to a lot of trouble to see that the film did not get into the wrong hands, and their efforts failed. When *Six Seconds in Dallas* was published in 1967, Time-Life sued the publishers for even using sketches of the Zapruder movie. The author, Professor Josiah Thompson, made a routine request for reproduction rights, but they were denied by the company.

If you do not care to believe the Zapruder film, there are other films of the assassination in existence, although one remained in the files of the United Press International Library in New York, gathering dust for more than eleven years. This is called the "Nix film," made by Orville O. Nix. Again, there is a clear view of the backward jerk of President Kennedy's head after the final shot. Three members of the Warren Commission viewed this film, yet Orville Nix himself was never called to testify to the Commission. However, according to a filmed interview with Nix, he believed the shots came from the grassy knoll. Although Zapruder and Nix are now dead, their films remain to contradict the finding of "The Warren Report." What they show is bad enough, but what they prove about the Warren Commission is even worse.

One-and-a-half hours after the assassination, NBC News reported that "the President was struck in the right temple by a bullet." Half an hour later this story was changed to "the President was wounded in the back of the head and on the right side of the head."

Mrs. Mary Muchmore, standing in the center of the triangle formed by Main, Houston, and Elm streets, also filmed the assassination. She sold her film to United Press International, and selected frames—but not the film in its entirety—were sold round the world. Once again the film shows the head of the President being jerked back with considerable force, indicating a shot from the front. And again, three members of the Commission viewed the film and neglected to call Mrs. Much-more as a witness. A witness to the assassination appears in one frame of the Muchmore film. This was Charles Brehm, who said that he saw "a portion of the President's skull flying slightly to the rear of the President's car and directly to its left." He was not called before the Warren Commission, even though his story is confirmed by a description of the final shot as seen by Associated Press photographer James Altgens.

If you want more films, there is the eight-mm. photograph taken by amateur photographer Robert J. Hughes. He took his photograph at twelve-thirty P.M., and it shows the motorcade turning into Elm Street under the Book Depository. At the corner of the sixth-floor window, there is an inanimate object, resembling a cat. But, in the window *next* to the corner one where Oswald is said to have fired his rifle, there is the clear figure of a man. The Warren Commission dismissed this photograph as lightly as a feather wafting in the breeze and relied on the report of the FBI agent who filed it: "From the photographs, there appears to be a person in the sixth-floor window." Without the specification of the "window next to the corner," an entirely different conclusion was inevitably drawn.

Situated on Houston Street at the time of the assassination, Mrs. Carolyn Walther was interested in the sixth-floor windows. She says she saw two men. One was holding a rifle with the barrel pointed down; standing beside him was another man. She could not see his face, but noticed he was dressed in brown. Although she told her story to the FBI, it never reached the Warren Commission. They were interested in knowing if she could identify Oswald, but were not interested in the fact that she had seen two men.

Mrs. Walther's evidence should have been considered in conjunction with the Hughes film, specifically in a detail of one frame of the film. It shows that the corner window is half-open and that the white shape in it moves. In the left-hand window next to the "assassin's window," there is another figure. For some eighty frames of this film, the figure can be seen but, at twelve-forty-two, twelve minutes after the assassination, there is no figure in the window. When *Life* Magazine published a frame of this movie, a remarkable bit of photographic exorcism had been performed. There was *no* figure in the window.

Mr. F. M. Bell also kept his eight-mm. movie camera rolling during the assassination. His film was never examined by anyone; nor was he interviewed. He was standing at the corner of Main and Houston streets. His film very clearly shows people throwing themselves on the ground and looking toward the grassy knoll and policemen beginning to run toward the knoll. The final frames show a flurry of spectators joining in the rush up the embankment.

The visit of a President to any city always brings out an enormous number of spectators anxious to have a personal record of the visit. Dallas was no exception. A request for film from these spectators would have meant a lot of work for investigators, but many of them would have shown the same scene as the movies of Zapruder and Orville Nix. It would have been worth the effort since it is doubtful that so many hundreds of films could have lied. They might have yielded more truthful and pertinent information than the pubic hairs of Lee Harvey Oswald and the mass of other trivia that the investigators placed before the Warren Commission.

After the assassination, most news sources adopted the official version of the events as soon as it became apparent that there was one. Despite the fact that the Dallas papers gave reports of no less than seven shots, the wire services agreed on three. The grassy knoll was dropped as the place where the shots came from, following the Secret Service report that all shots came from the right rear of the President. Numerous witnesses and the Dallas police themselves agreed that, although they first concentrated their attention on the railway yards adjacent to and to the rear of the grassy knoll, the

Texas Book Depository was quickly pinpointed as the "assassin's hideaway." Twenty percent of newspaper headlines referred to Oswald as the assassin without using the words "alleged" or "accused." Every negative adjective imaginable was applied to Oswald and flaunted on the front pages of newspapers. It is surprising how much was known about him so soon, since investigation into the background of a suspect generally takes time. Magazines quickly followed up with the story of only three shots, all coming from the Book Depository. There was a consensus of opinion that Oswald was the lone assassin. Despite this, rumors of conspiracy spread, and the Harris Poll indicated that over fifty percent of all Americans felt Oswald must have had help in assassinating the President.

The Warren Commission compiled a list of witnesses mentioned in various media reports, including Norman Similas, Robert Hilburn, R. Bothun, Ed Johnson, J. Broseh, Robert McNeill, Barbara Richardson, Peggy Burney, Alan Smith, Robert Clark, and J. Bell. The FBI contacted only one—Norman Similas, a Canadian visitor to Dallas. He claims he had a photograph taken during the assassination that showed no one was visible in the sixth-floor corner window. The film was lost by *The New York Times*, to whom he gave the photograph for processing, but the FBI investigated his background to see if he had a criminal record.

The list of witnesses who testified to the Warren Commission is short compared to those who could have given evidence. Of the ten eyewitnesses standing between the grassy knoll and the President's limousine, nine expressed their opinion that the shots came from the knoll directly behind them. Only one of these witnesses was called, Abraham Zapruder himself. The Commission never asked him where he thought the shots came from, but restricted themselves to asking him how much money *Life* Magazine paid him for the rights to the film. Eight eyewitnesses standing across the street facing the grassy knoll told investigators that they believed the shots came from the knoll, but only three testified before the Commission. Of twelve people on the triple underpass, ten thought the shots came from the knoll. However, the Commission only called upon two to testify in their hearings. Six people out of twenty-nine testified, leaving the vital testimony of twenty-three virtually ignored by the Commission.

Then there is the damning testimony of Marina Oswald, wife of the suspected assassin. She was the first witness called by the Commission. She was first summoned on February 3, 1964, and made three other appearances between February and September. Her evidence was accepted as gospel, although it was contradictory to the evidence of credible and disinterested witnesses. In addition, her evidence was unsupported by other corroboratory testimonies but, thanks to her, the Warren Commission concluded that Lee Harvey Oswald made an attempt on the life of Major General Edwin A. Walker and that he purchased and possessed a rifle that he stored in the house where Marina was living. Mrs. Oswald frequently reversed her testimony, especially about the use of aliases by her husband. She testified that Oswald began rifle practice in January 1963, but the rifle was not ordered until March, two months later. Charitably, the Commission reported, "she might have misunderstood her husband." If she did, they continued with the misunderstanding to the detriment of the character of Oswald. Marina Oswald may well have been a very frightened woman, especially if the FBI implied that she would be deported if her evidence did not coincide with what they wanted to hear as she later indicated was the case.

So far, it is possible to conclude that the Warren Commission was deliberately misled and, although this says nothing for its members' intelligence, such things are not unknown in legal circles. But, in its report, the Commission deliberately lied, as we can see from the transcript of an executive session, declassified as late as

1974. This evidence effectively destroys the link-pin that led to the Commission's "no conspiracy" conclusion.

In the executive session of January 27, 1964, the Commissioners saw a picture that had been taken at the autopsy of the President. It showed a bullet wound in the back, below the shoulder blade and to the right of the backbone. The Commissioners' report, released in September 1964, stated that the wound was at the base of the neck and presented a medical drawing that was clearly in error of the actual autopsy photograph. At this stage, the Commission must have been in a state of confusion on deciding how so many wounds could have been suffered by the President and Governor Connally when only three bullets had been fired. So the Warren Commission moved the back wound upward, stating that one of the bullets passed through the President's neck and had then gone on to pass through Connally's back, his wrist, and finally lodged in his thigh. Thus it established the theory of the single bullet, a truly magical one if we are to believe this; without that single-bullet theory, the findings of the Commission cannot be upheld. It is obvious that more than three bullets were fired, and, if this is so, it was impossible for Oswald to have fired them all, since only three cartridge shells were found on the sixth floor of the Book Depository. The "Magic Bullet" theory has intrigued marksmen and assassination theorists for years, but it obviously did not intrigue the Warren Commission enough to investigate it thoroughly.

The Warren Commission also described the Mannlicher-Carcano rifle found in the Depository as an accurate weapon. Italian soldiers in World War II laughingly describe this rifle as "the humanitarian weapon." They knew of its inaccuracy due to poor design and the way in which the firing pin could sometimes blow out into the face of the shooter. The lone-assassin theory begins to fall apart even more when we consider this rifle, accepted by the Warren Commission as the death weapon. The rifle was sent for testing to the Infantry

Weapons Evaluation Branch of the Ballistics Research Laboratory of the Department of the Army. Before it could be fired, the telescopic sight had to be rebuilt, and three light metal shims were added to correct deficiencies in the azimuth and elevation. A gunsmith insisted the shims had to be added because the scope, as received, was set up for a left-handed man. No one was anxious to test the weapon even with the modifications because the original $3 rifle, later priced at $12.78, had a rusty pin that might break. Oswald was right-handed and, even with limited intelligence, it might be presumed that he would have obtained a scope suitable for a right-hander. Both were available from Klein's, the Chicago-based company where he purchased his rifle—if, of course, he did purchase it, and again we have Marina's evidence that this is the whole truth.

Three "masters" of the National Rifle Association tested the weapon. All found it difficult to open the bolt. Ronald Simmons, chief of the Infantry Weapons Evaluation Branch, told the Commission: "As a matter of fact, Mr. Staley [one of the marksmen] had difficulty in opening the bolt at his first firing exercise." None of the three marksmen, masters of the skill and technique of shooting, could duplicate, or even approach, Oswald's feat of marksmanship. They fired at a standing target, and none of the six shots fired by each of them struck the neck or head of the target—even with each marksman taking as long as he liked before firing the shot. Oswald had only eight-tenths of a second to take aim and fire at a moving target!

Despite this evidence, "The Warren Report" stated: "The various tests showed that the Mannlicher-Carcano rifle was an accurate rifle and that the use of a four-power scope was a substantial aid to rapid, accurate firing."

There are numerous unfavorable reports on this rifle in the trade magazines and the expert opinion of the weapon is poor. Jack O'Connor, in his *Rifle Book,* described the Mannlicher-Carcano as "terrible." The

October 1964 issue of *Mechanix Illustrated* described the rifle as "crudely made, poorly designed, dangerous and inaccurate, unhandy, crude and unreliable on repeat shots, had safety-design faults."

In his choice of this rifle, Oswald seems to have had singularly bad taste and was pushing his luck very hard if he hoped to accomplish his purpose. In Oswald's last-known evaluation, he was described as a poor shot, scoring only one point above the minimum requirement for marine qualification. The date of that evaluation was May 1959. Within four years, he must have made remarkable progress, as he did with learning the Russian language.

When Oswald's belongings were examined and his apartment searched, no ammunition was found and none was ordered when the application was made to buy the rifle. Only one shop in the Fort Worth-Dallas area stocked suitable cartridges for the Mannlicher-Carcano, and no one could recollect Oswald purchasing any. The rifle found at the Book Depository was well-oiled and clean, but no cleaning materials were found. We can presume that the search of Oswald's possessions on his person and in his apartment was thorough because the police inventory lists "a label with King Iscar kipper recipes," another instance of the mass of trivia that was collected as evidence. If Marina Oswald had not come to the aid of the Commission, no one would ever have known that Oswald practiced with his rifle. Yet the picture presented of Oswald in the Commission report is that he was a resourceful marksman and took only four rounds of ammunition with him to the Book Depository, using only three, each one finding its mark on the moving target.

Not only does Oswald emerge as a remarkable marksman, but he must also have been very swift on his feet. According to testimony, he was seen on the second floor of the Depository within eighty seconds after the assassination and was apparently not out of breath after presumably hiding the rifle on the sixth floor and running down four flights of stairs. He was also nonchalant. Instead of fleeing the scene of the crime immediately, he drank a Coca-Cola and left the building at a slow pace, not by the back entrance but by the front door where there were many policemen and a large crowd. His veins must have been filled with ice water.

Oswald's departure from the Book Depository was not officially noticed for at least half an hour. He became a suspect only after the police found the rifle hidden away behind packages on the sixth floor. The time then was one-twenty-two P.M., but a police dispatcher sent out this message at one-forty-six P.M.: "We have a man that we would like to have you pass this on to at the Criminal Investigation Division to see if we can pick this man up. CHARLES DOUGLAS GIVENS, G.I.V.E.N.S. He is a colored male, a porter that worked on this floor up here. He has a police record and he left."

The Warren Commission is silent on this issue, and it does not explain why Captain Fritz did not broadcast a description of Oswald at one-twenty-two P.M., when he found Oswald was missing. Instead, Fritz stopped to see Sheriff Decker, then went to the Police Building before setting out to look for Oswald at the address where Marina and the children were residing.

The Secret Service agents emerge as a group of bumblers during their visit to Dallas. Many of them were out painting the town red the night before the assassination. The only black member of the Secret Service at the time remarked on this, and was released from the Service shortly afterward. When Dallas Police Sergeant D. V. Harkness arrived at the rear of the Book Depository at twelve-thirty-six P.M., he found some Secret Service agents milling around, but it was he who sealed off the building. Although there were plenty of Secret Service men around, including some on the grassy knoll and in the railway yards, there is some doubt as to whether everyone who said he was a Secret Service agent was indeed a member of the agency. Oswald, in his first interview after his arrest, said that as he was leaving the Book Depository, two men intercepted him at the door, identified themselves as Secret Service agents, and asked for the location of a telephone. "The Warren Report" states that Secret Servicemen assigned to the motorcade "stayed at their posts during the race to the hospital. None stayed at the scene of the shooting and none entered the Texas School Book Depository at or immediately after the shooting. Forrest V. Sorrels, special agent in charge of the Dallas Secret Service office, was the first Secret Service agent to return to the scene of the assassination approximately twenty or twenty-five minutes after the shots were fired."

The Secret Service report presented to the Warren Commission also states that none of its agents were then present, so it is logical to presume that men armed with false credentials were at the assassination scene. The Commission could have assumed that this indicated a well-planned conspiracy at work.

The twenty thousand pages of "The Warren Report" included photographs of Russian scenery, dental charts of Jack Ruby's mother, postcards showing bullfights, a study of Oswald's pubic hairs, and hundreds of FBI, Dallas police, and Secret Service reports, but there was no room for Commission document 354. It was stored in the National Archives and mentions that a Mr. Jack Brian, detective, Dallas Police Department, stated that he interviewed Mr. James Powell of Army intelligence. He was trapped in the Book Depository when the doors were sealed. Mr. Powell stated that he was watching the motorcade from a position near the corner of Houston and Elm streets, the site of the assassination. He heard shots and then joined the group of sheriff's deputies heading toward the rear of the Depository. He worked with the sheriffs for about eight minutes, then entered the front door of the building in search of a telephone. There is no mention of James Powell's name in "The Warren Report," and we can only wonder if this was the man Oswald saw and spoke to on his way out to his own appointment with destiny.

Thirteen people were arrested after the assassination, none of them mentioned in "The Warren Report." One person was arrested in front of the Depository, two in the Dallas Texas Building at the corner of Elm and Houston streets, and three in the railway yards behind the grassy knoll. Before his arrest in the Dallas Texas Building, there is a photograph in existence showing Eugene Brading in front of the School Book Depository Building. He was a California convict on parole, but no one at the Dallas Police Station bothered to fingerprint him or investigate his background. He gave his name as Jim Braden and said he was in Dallas on oil business.

When Oswald was arrested at the Texas movie house, he called to a witness of the event, Johnny Brewer, "I am not resisting arrest." At the police station, he was warned by Sergeant Gerald Hill that there would be photographers and reporters and that he could hide his face if he wished. Oswald replied: "Why should I hide my face? I haven't done anything I'm ashamed of." At seven-fifty-five P.M., on November 22nd, Oswald told reporters: "I'm just a patsy . . ." After ten hours in custody and being interviewed, no tape recordings or stenographic records exist of anything Oswald said to the nineteen investigators who talked with him.

On November 18th, President Kennedy visited Tampa and Miami. The Miami police cancelled his proposed motorcade because earlier in the month they had taped a telephone conversation between an informer and Joseph Milteer, a member of the right-wing, extremist National States Rights Party. On the tape, Milteer boasted that the best way to "get the President was from an office building with a high-powered rifle." Furthermore, he said, "They will pick up someone within hours afterward if anything like that would happen, just to throw the public off." The Miami police informed the FBI and the Protective Research Section, the branch of the Secret Service responsible for the safety of the President. These services, nevertheless, saw little that would warrant extra precautions during the visit of the President to Dallas, the "City of Hate." Yet, on November 20th, Dallas Police Chief Jesse Curry appeared on television and warned that the police would take action if there was any improper conduct during the visit of the President. Later, he revealed that there were thirteen groups under police surveillance, and one of them was the National States Rights Party. On November 15, 1963, the San Antonio office of the Protective Research Section was advised by telephone from the FBI headquarters in Washington that "a subject interviewed by them on November 14th stated that he was a member of the Ku Klux Klan and that during his travels throughout the country, his sources informed him that a militant group of the National States Rights Party plans to assassinate the President and other high-ranking officials." That should have been enough to make sure that the bulletproof bubble top was put on the President's limousine. However, it was left off, even though the weather had been inclement that morning, but cleared considerably by the afternoon. The route for the motorcade was changed, and the new route provided a perfect site for an ambush. But no one checked out "why" the route was changed or by whom.

Oswald carried duplicate identification cards when he was arrested, which would have been enough to suggest that he was in some type of undercover work while posing as a Communist. However, the sagacious members of the Commission concluded that A. Hidell was a fictitious person created by Oswald. Again, the helpful Marina came to their aid, testifying that Oswald threatened to beat her up if she did not sign her name A. J. Hidell on the "Fair Play for Cuba Committee" membership card.

Two photographs of Oswald were found by the police that Oswald stated were fakes. We have seen these photographs, and they look as if Oswald's head had been superimposed on the body of another person, and there is a shadow under the nose that is inconsistent with the other shadows in the picture. Like the magic bullet, the theory of light and shadows also defies logic. Besides, the head in the picture seems out of proportion, and we learned from a photographer that when a head is superimposed on a body, the cut has to be made around the chin. So the head is always bigger than it would be on a normal picture. Several skilled photo analysts came forward to give their opinion that the photographs were composites. California photographer Fred Newcombe saw the two photographs of Oswald and noted that, while Oswald had a cleft on his chin, Oswald's face in the photograph taken with his rifle had no such cleft. The ring worn on his hand in the photographs was on the wrong hand. . . . Oswald was known to have worn his ring on the opposite hand.

Who was responsible for giving composite photographs to the Warren Commission? And why has a third one *just* been unearthed by Senator Schweiker of Pennsylvania when Marina had testified she had burnt all other pictures of her husband?

Oswald's work background is interesting. When he returned from Russia, he started as a trainee in a photography company. He was dismissed in April 1963, because he was not able to produce photographic work with sufficient precision. But the Warren Commission concluded that through this work he might have been able to forge some of his identification documents on the equipment available to him at this company. During his sojourn in New Orleans, Oswald worked for the William B. Reily [Coffee] Company from May until July 1963. He was hired by Alfred Claude, who went to work for the Chrysler Aerospace Company the same month Oswald left his job. Then Emmett Barbee, Oswald's immediate supervisor, left the coffee business to start a new career with the National Aeronautics and Space Administration. A few weeks later, Oswald's workmate, John D.

Branyon, also went to work for NASA; and yet another co-worker left to join the Chrysler Aerospace Division, a NASA contractor. Any one of these men could have given testimony about their association with Oswald, but only Barbee was called. Oswald himself had told a friend in the garage adjacent to the Reily Company that he would like to work for NASA. It is hard to believe that NASA would have considered employing a former defector to the U.S.S.R., considering the secrecy of most of its work. NASA is now rumored to be infiltrated by the CIA, and it is possible the workmen who knew Oswald went on to better things as the price for silence.

The idea that there may have been two men using the name of Lee Harvey Oswald is no longer considered an impossibility. If this is so, then we have another link with Oswald as the patsy set up as part of a conspiracy. In September 1963 a Lee Oswald was in New Orleans but, another Oswald was practicing at the Dallas Sports Drome rifle range and showed himself to be a good shot. Someone identifying himself very determinedly as Lee Harvey Oswald appeared at the Dallas Downtown Lincoln-Mercury salesroom on November 9th. This Oswald told an employee that he was about to come into some money and planned to return to Russia. Assistant Sales Manager Frank Pizzo, seeing photographs of Oswald, the so-called lone assassin, said that the hairline of the Oswald who came to his place of business did not match with the hairline of the real Oswald. Furthermore, the man who visited Pizzo's establishment took a car out to test drive and Oswald could not drive!

Then we have the conflicting evidence of Sylvia Odio who swears that Oswald visited her when the Commission accepted evidence that Oswald was in Mexico City. The question is still in doubt that it was Lee Harvey Oswald who was indeed in Mexico City, and there are now some sinister connotations about this visit. It does not help that E. Howard Hunt, now convicted as a Watergate burglar, was the CIA station chief in Mexico City at the time of Oswald's doubtful visit. Hunt's activities in and from 1963 remain a clandestine secret, but his name cropped up again after the attempted assassination of Governor Wallace. Charles Colson, aide to Richard Nixon unofficially but believed by some to have been the highest-ranking CIA officer in the White House, instructed Hunt to go to the apartment of Arthur Bremer, the man captured after the assassination attempt.

The dirty tricks of the Nixon regime were probably geared to the activities of E. Howard Hunt even as far back as 1963 and, if they were, then we have to acknowledge the possibility of one Lee Harvey Oswald being set up as a patsy by one of the Government establishments. Professor Richard Popkin's theory of two Oswalds may not be so wrong, after all. Hunt has already presented several versions as to where he was on November 22nd, and lies are now known to be quite common to members of the CIA. When the three "tramps" were arrested in the railway yards behind the grassy knoll, there is no record of their names, and this has continued to intrigue researchers who think they *might* have been Hunt, Bernard Barker, and Frank Sturgis. Criminologist Charles V. Morton of the Institute of Forensic Sciences in Oakland, California, states that the lack of clarity in the photographs available was insufficient to provide an absolute basis for an opinion.

Who were the three tramps, and why were their names not recorded? If they were not Hunt and his friends, at least we should know who they were.

As the motorcade moved slowly on its way to the Dallas Trade Mart where the President was to speak, just a few blocks ahead of the approaching motorcade two spectators on Houston Street saw a man cradling a gun at the sixth-floor window of the Book Depository. With him was another man, and the spectators recalled that the gunman never moved but kept his gaze focused on the grassy knoll. They presumed the two men were Secret Service agents. We think that the gunman in the

Book Depository fired a shot that was a signal for gunmen hidden by the trees separating the grassy knoll from the car park in front of the railway yards. In the railroad control tower, Lee Bowers, Jr., noticed three cars slowly cruising through the area before the assassination. Two had out-of-state license plates, but the driver with Texas plates "appeared to have a mike or telephone in the car." Bowers recalled that the third car left the area at twelve-twenty-five, five minutes before the shooting began. An assassination team trained in superb marksmanship would have needed some form of radio contact. They had to complete their job on time and before the Secret Service had time to act. They would also need stooges on the grounds to deflect attention. A man wearing green army fatigues had an attack of epilepsy on Elm Street. No one knew who he was. Police, sheriff's men, and spectators ran toward the grassy knoll where a man *acting* as a Secret Service agent was discovered. The Warren Commission conceded that there were no Secret Service men in that area.

Who were the bogus agents?

The President was mortally wounded, spinning backward into his seat, with a third of his brains blasted out. Pigeons flew out of the trees that fringed the grassy knoll, and spectator Jim Tague, standing near the triple underpass, felt warm blood on his face. A bullet had hit the pavement at his feet, and a fragment of it had wounded his cheek. Another spectator, S. M. Holland, ran behind the trees and found numerous cigarette butts on the ground. A puff of smoke from the trees attracted his attention. A policeman spoke to a man who presented Secret Service credentials and was allowed to depart.

The President was assassinated, but where were the assassins?

Coolly playing for time when the "patsy" was picked up, they could leave the town as quietly as they had arrived. There were plenty of witnesses, and about to blossom into the wilderness of doubts were the men designated to examine witnesses of the assassination and seek the truth for all the world to know.

The Warren Commission was waiting in the wings while the last touches to this scenario were being applied. The opening scenes of the scenario had gone well, produced and executed with a masterly dramatic sense of timing. Many of the critics left at the end of the first act and could not believe the accounts of the second act that kept up the pace of the assassination, and the third act that, through improvision, almost stole the show at the last moment. By then the critics were too exhausted and too confused to readily understand the social, moral, and political connotations of the scenario in Dallas.

It was some time before the critics got their second wind and began to dissect the scenario, scene by scene. By then, it was almost too late. Exhilarated by success, the scenario writers produced an encore, and yet another.

As the high-noon sun burned out the last haziness of what had promised to be a damp day in Dallas, Mrs. Acquilla Clemons and Frank Wright saw two men standing near a patrol car. They watched a police officer get out, and Frank Wright saw the man fall to the ground, shot to death. One of the men got into a waiting car and drove away. Officer Tippit was dead as the search went on for the assassin of President Kennedy. There were plenty of witnesses to the murder of Tippit, including Domingo Benavides who got a good view of the killer. The name Benavides was to surface again when Martin Luther King was murdered. Warren Reynolds also saw the killing and the killer fleeing the scene. Strange things began to happen to these witnesses as time dragged on and the Warren Commission convened. Neither Mrs. Clemons nor Wright were called to testify. Wright spoke to independent interviewers and stated that what came out on television and through the news was not what he saw. Mrs. Clemons was interviewed by

FBI agents and a man who visited her two days after the shooting. "He looked like a policeman," she told author Mark Lane. "He wore a gun and told me it was best if I did not say anything to anyone because I might get hurt."

In February 1964, Eddy Benavides, who closely resembled his brother, Domingo, was fatally shot in the head. Two weeks later, Domingo's father-in-law was shot while he was at home. Both Domingo and his father-in-law think that Eddy's death was a case of mistaken identity . . . that it was he who was being sought, and he spoke of threatening phone calls telling him to keep quiet. Warren Reynolds was not interviewed by the FBI until two months after he witnessed the murder of Officer Tippit. Two days after the interview, he was shot in the head by a bullet from a .22-caliber rifle, but he survived.

Three weeks after he got out of the hospital, a stranger tried to pick up his ten-year-old daughter and force her into a car. Such tactics achieved the desired result. In July 1964, Reynolds changed his testimony and positively identified Oswald as the man he saw at the scene of Tippit's murder. Only six months earlier, he had told the FBI that in no way could he connect Oswald with either of the two men he saw. No mention of the attack on Reynolds's life appears in "The Warren [Commission] Report."

The year after the assassination of President Kennedy was a year full of missing witnesses who were gradually eliminated by violent means. If there was a "Kennedy Curse" in existence, it stretched out from his clan to embrace dozens of innocent people who were in the right place at the wrong time. Seventeen witnesses on the peripheral of the terrible events in Dallas on November 22nd met equally terrible and violent deaths.

The assassins walked on the streets of American cities . . . in Los Angeles, Miami, and Las Vegas . . . exotic cities, where they knew that people in crowd scenes were always expendable. It is the producers who reap the profits and live to enjoy them.

Act III of the conspiracy scenario took forty-eight hours to get going. Jack Ruby walked into the basement of the well-guarded Dallas Police Headquarters and calmly shot Lee Harvey Oswald as he was about to be transported by armored car to jail. On the surface, it was as simple as that but, beneath the surface, there was a cauldron of intrigue bubbling away. How did Jack Ruby get into the basement when the entrance and exits were guarded by police officers, awaiting the arrival of the armored car? A diversion was created when a police officer got into a police car and drove it up the entrance ramp, causing the officer guarding it to step into the street to allow the cruiser to enter Commerce Street. It was enough time for Jack Ruby, having stopped off to send a telegram at the nearby Western Union office, to slip quietly down the ramp and into the parking area of the basement.

Eleven years after the assassination of Lee Harvey Oswald, Sybil Leek visited the basement. In the ensuing years, many people wondered how Ruby got into the closely guarded area. She went to the guardrail alongside the entrance ramp, some twenty yards away from the spot where Oswald had a momentary flash of recognition as he saw the man who was about to eliminate him. Eleven years ago, there were television cameras, newspaper men, and a cordon of police at the bottom of the ramp. However, there is a point where the railing is slanted and there is a low point where a fat, fiftyish man could conveniently hop over as the eyes of the people in the basement are riveted on a higher point, watching the strange behavior of a police cruiser exiting through the entrance ramp. In the thousands of pages written about Jack Ruby's confrontation with Oswald, there was never a word written about the cruiser that took the wrong way out. But, Bob Shaw, supervisor of information for the Dallas Police Department, knew about it and also knew that the officer in the car was quietly "sent to the country," where no one could interview him. It was easier to forget the whole business rather than make waves. Only the shock tactics brought about by Sybil's clear statement of what she saw psychically allowed Bob Shaw to remember the events. His words were heard by reporter Malcolm Abrams, who had accompanied Sybil to Dallas, and a tape recorder provides tangible evidence of Shaw's surprised, blurted-out explanation.

Of the seventy or more policemen in the basement during the ten minutes before the shooting of Oswald, no one came forward to say he had seen Jack Ruby make his entrance. A few members of the Warren Commission wondered if he might have received any assistance from the police in gaining entry, but an affirmative answer would have meant a fresh evaluation of other evidence. Predictably, the Commission report gave no indication that Ruby received any assistance in obtaining entrance to the basement. What happened to the testimony of the guard on duty at the Commerce Street entrance? No one at the time asked why a police cruiser should deliberately take the entrance ramp instead of the exit one. At first, Ruby refused to give any explanation himself but, on December 21st, he said he walked down the Main Street ramp at eleven-seventeen A.M., after he had dispatched a money order from the Western Union office. The shooting took place at eleven-twenty-one A.M. Although this was the quickest route to the basement, Ruby could have walked from the Western Union office to the Commerce Street ramp well within the four minutes needed to bring him up to the estimated time of the murder. R. E. Vaughn, the policeman on duty at the exit ramp leading to Main Street, was interviewed and stated he saw a man come down the ramp three or four minutes before the murder, but he did not question the man. However, the other officer on guard at the head of the Commerce Street entrance made no statement at all or, if he did, it did not reach the members of the Warren Commission.

The shooting of Oswald was the result of the failure of the Dallas Police Department to take precautions to adequately guard their important prisoner. If Ruby made up his mind to kill Oswald, he must have done it while at his apartment and then stepped out, complete with the necessary weapon to achieve this. He must also have known that there would be security measures to guard Oswald. Alternately, he could have received a tip-off that Oswald was to be brought outside the police station within a specified time, and there was evidence that good timing helped to achieve the murder. The name of one of the two officers escorting Oswald from the third floor to the basement is not given in the list of witnesses examined by the Warren Commission, but with Detective James R. Leavelle was Joe Cody, the nephew of Ruby's Chicago friend, Allen Cody. There was a last-minute plan to transfer Oswald to jail by an unmarked police car, although an armored truck was originally specified. The change of plan was effected without informing Captain Fritz, who was told of the arrangement shortly before eleven A.M.

Who initiated the change of plan . . . and who told Captain Fritz about it? These questions were not cleared up in "The Warren Report."

The Warren Commission, fed a palatable diet of regurgitated information by the FBI and other Government agencies, could find no evidence linking Oswald with Ruby. Among other links they had was the fact that both Oswald and Ruby were expendable in the conspiracy scenario, but the tenuous links of association went back long before Ruby confronted Oswald in the basement. They moved in the same circles, and witnesses could have been interviewed who could testify that Oswald and Ruby, while not being buddies, certainly knew each other. Maniacs plan killings and no more; however, conspirators plan killings and cover-ups by creating a maze of decoys and dead ends to make the seekers of truth dizzy with deception. Along the line, there are human sacrifices, and the destinies of Jack Ruby and Lee Harvey Oswald were linked both as patsies and sacrifices. Those creating the conspiracy scenario and the cover-up had to be appeased, like the ancient pagan gods, and blood sacrifices have always been a part of such appeasement.

Lee Harvey Oswald had to die.

Jack Ruby was the instrument of death.

Jack Ruby had to die.

5 | THE FBI SCENARIO

The members of the Warren Commission relied a great deal on the FBI to interrogate witnesses and supply them with information. At that time, the FBI was beyond reproach with J. Edgar Hoover standing righteously at the helm. Television and movies glamorized the dedication and integrity of the men in the FBI, and it seemed that they were a chosen race of men, set apart from mere mortals.

Like tenacious terriers, they sniffed out clues, followed up information, and finally brought the right person to court, where he was given the benefit of American law: a man is regarded as innocent until he is proven guilty, then must pay a just price for his crime.

It seemed that we all accepted the unspoken rule that when the FBI finished with an investigation and a suspect was indicted, all evidence had been well sifted, and all witnesses interrogated under strict lines of correct procedure, after which the public prosecutor prepared his case. Throughout the world, the agents of the Federal Bureau of Investigation were known to be upright, honorable, and fearless. It seemed as if no major legal case in the United States was ever solved unless the FBI had been called in to supplement local-police investigation. There was an aura of invincibility about J. Edgar Hoover's men, and the general public presumed that only those with something to hide were afraid of the FBI.

Most Americans knew Hoover as "The Director," a perfect hero in an imperfect time, who had personally ferretted out and arrested many of those referred to as "Public Enemy No 1." *The New York World-Telegram* wrote, in an editorial: "Pick a small boy these days and ask him whom of all the people in the world he wants to be like, and ten-to-one he will reply, 'J. Edgar Hoover.' " Such was the esteem in which the FBI and "The Director" were held. But that was before 1963.

Before 1963 few faults could be found with the FBI beyond an overenthusiasm for work, determination to protect the public from criminals, and dedication to the high standard of principles pontificated upon by the chief of the bureau, J. Edgar Hoover. But Hoover and the FBI seemed obsessed with a "Communist conspiracy" and didn't even acknowledge, in the words of Hoover, the "existence of a so-called Mafia."

The FBI was supposed to be the conscientious eyes and ears of America, the guardians of all that meant law and order. We thought the bureau was composed of men with superior brains, a regular think-tank of very special law-enforcement officers. And if J. Edgar Hoover sometimes seemed too autocratic, too much the patriotic father of his special breed of men, we were all inclined to forgive this as the cause of law and justice in this country, which was so in tune with all the Constitution stands for.

Today more than three-quarters of the population of America wonders how deeply Lee Harvey Oswald was involved with the FBI.

From the very beginning, the Warren Commission had decided on the lone-assassin theory. Unable to

afford its own staff of fact-finding investigators and
provided none by the Congressional Charter that
established the Commission, some Commission members—especially Congressman Hale Boggs and Senator
Richard Russell—were concerned that the evidence supplied by the FBI had already been tainted and slanted
by the Bureau's conclusion that Oswald did it alone.
Normally, the FBI would present a so-called "objective"
evaluation of material. Instead, the Commission received
the whole thing, delivered, sealed, bound, and concluding that Oswald fired the shots that killed the President.
As far as the FBI was concerned, it had done its job.
Rather than telling the Commission, "Here is the evidence, now you evaluate it," it said, "Tell the American
people what happened since it is your job as the Warren
Commission."

While it appeared that the FBI was doing its job, it
was in reality feeding distorted information to the Commission. And that is what the American people got in
the final report.

To understand today how it was possible for the FBI
to operate in such a manner, we must go back into the
history of the FBI itself in order to find a pattern for its
behavior. If the seemingly subtle way in which the FBI
handled the Warren Commission members and manipulated the law to suit its own purposes seems out of the
ordinary, all one has to do is look at its historical prec-
edents. The FBI has always played its part in helping
powerful men into positions where they could best be
useful to businessmen through political rein-pulling. Go
back to 1880 when Mark Hanna became known as "The
Lord of the Great Lakes." He was the archetype of a
breed who knew that if politics could be controlled, it
could work efficiently for a group of ambitious businessmen. They were aware that money and power could
control the country, but they also needed the cooperation of a law-enforcement body to give the right aura
of respectability. It was Hanna who masterminded the
plan to get William McKinley into the White House;

and he was helped by his favorite lieutenant, William Daugherty, who was later appointed Attorney General. When his old boss, Hanna, was accused by a Congressman of offering $1,750 to buy his vote, Daugherty rose to the occasion and refused to answer any questions. The figurehead of big business, President McKinley, was assassinated by a Polish-American anarchist named Leon Czolgosz, who confessed an urge to kill a "great leader."

Hanna himself had ambitions to become President but died from an attack of typhoid fever in February 1904, before he could achieve his goal. His chief henchman, William Daugherty, lived and he in turn had his own favorite lieutenant, William Burns. Aided by Daugherty, he became the head of the Bureau of Investigation, later known as the FBI. Through the offices of Daugherty and Burns, crime increased and became a paying proposition for businessmen. And the FBI, then as now, could make or break any politician—even a President. England had its king-makers, America had its President-makers, and both relied on success through political string-pulling linked with a malleable department of law enforcement, enabling power and money to walk hand-in-hand undisturbed.

Lee Harvey Oswald had been in contact with FBI officials several times. When he returned from Russia, he was debriefed by them, according to CIA Director William Colby. When he was arrested in New Orleans, he asked to see an FBI agent, although he was charged with a simple matter of disturbing the peace that merited a small fine of ten dollars.

(This minor fracas came about when Oswald was accosted on a New Orleans street by José Brenier, the same José Brenier whom Oswald had approached to recruit men for the anti-Castro committee, as he handed out Fair Play for Cuba leaflets. After audibly telling Brenier, "Hit me here, José," both Oswald and Brenier were arrested for disturbing the peace. Brenier was released without being charged, and Oswald was released after "seeing the FBI" and paying his ten dollars. If one commits a minor misdemeanor, is arrested by the local police, and insists on seeing an FBI officer, it is unlikely an agent would appear as appeared for Oswald when he was arrested in New Orleans; and when he was arrested again in Dallas, we have no doubt Oswald thought the FBI would help him out again as it had done in New Orleans.)

When picked up, he had the private telephone number and address of FBI Special Agent James P. Hosty, Jr., with him. Hosty had visited the Paine house several times and had even ventured inside it in Oswald's absence! After the assassination, Hosty was moved out of Dallas so fast by the FBI that he did not have time to sell his house—nor answer questions.

The idea that Oswald might have been an FBI informant was immensely troubling to the Commission, since the Bureau insisted from the first that Oswald was the lone assassin and therefore not part of a conspiracy. Lee Rankin said, "The FBI wanted the Commission to fold up and quit"; and there were many unofficial as well as official meetings of the Commission in which Congressman Boggs and Senator Russell were concerned about the FBI's persistence in their allegations of Oswald's guilt. It was an easy way out for anyone concerned with the assassination. With Oswald dead and the Commission empowered to get at the truth as quickly as possible, they were hurried and harried to get the final report out as soon as possible and put the mind of everyone in America at rest—particularly before the 1964 Presidential election. With a dead gunman accused and then with the guilt placed firmly on this one man, it was a neat way to resolve the matter.

It was Lee Rankin who tried to put everything in perspective at a closed-door meeting of the Commission on January 22, 1964, called by Chief Justice Earl Warren. He advised the Commission members that the attorney general of Texas had information suggesting that Lee Harvey Oswald might have been acting as an FBI undercover agent. This meeting lasted from five-twenty

P.M. until seven P.M., at the Commission headquarters. The minutes of this meeting are not listed in the official "Inventory of the Records of the President's Commission on the Assassination of President Kennedy," which was issued by the National Archives in 1973, ten years after the assassination. Marion M. Johnson, custodian of the Kennedy records, told *The New Republic* that the minutes of the January 22, 1964, meeting were not listed because they had not been "discovered" when the catalogue was completed in 1973.

The minutes were finally declassified on March 14, 1975. The quality of the transcript is poor, with words missing and others misspelled and the identity of the speakers not always clearly indicated. This declassification probably took place when Waggoner Carr, who was attorney general of Texas from 1963 to 1964, charged that the Commission failed to meet his request that a check be conducted on all FBI and CIA informants who were in Dallas immediately before the assassination of President Kennedy. It was these charges that focused the spotlight on the strange and difficult relationship between the Warren Commission and FBI Director J. Edgar Hoover throughout the investigation. It was Waggoner Carr who also caused the meeting to be convened on January 22, 1964, when the information given so astounded the Commission that Allen Dulles, the former CIA director, seriously proposed that the minutes be destroyed.

It is possible that the minutes did not appear in the official inventory because the Commission thought the minutes had indeed been destroyed—but there was a great deal of carelessness in the filing of the mass of documents. It was easy enough for the minutes to have been slipped in with other papers and then when recognized as being dangerous, carefully pushed aside, hoping that no one would ever refer to them again. Their contents throw some light on the secondary doubts then assailing the members of the Commission.

Mr. Rankin: Mr. Waggoner Carr . . . called me at eleven-ten this morning and said that the word had come out—he wanted to get it to me at the first moment—that Oswald was acting as an FBI undercover agent, that they had the information of his badge—which was given as number 179—and that he was being paid two hundred dollars a month from September 1962 up through the time of the assassination. I asked what the source of this was, and he said that he understood the information had been made available so that defense counsel [Melvin Belli] for Ruby had that information, that he knew the press had the information, and he didn't know exactly where Wade [Dallas district attorney who tried Ruby case] had gotten the information but he [Wade] was a former FBI agent.

That they, that is, Wade before, had said that he had sufficient [evidence] so that he was willing to make the statement.

I brought that to the attention of the Chief Justice immediately, and he said that I should try to get in touch with Carr and ask him to bring Wade up here, and he would be willing to meet with him anytime today or tonight to find out what was the basis of this story. I tried to get Carr, but he was out campaigning in Texarkana so . . . it took him quite awhile to get back to him and talk to him. I just got through talking to him, and he told me the source of the information was a member of the press who had claimed he knew of such an agent, that he [Oswald] was an undercover agent, but he now is coming with the information as to his particular number, and the amount he was getting, and the detail as to the time when the payments started. Wade said he [himself] as well as him [the member of the press] did not know the name of the informant, but he could guess who it was, that it was given to his assistant, and he was sure that he knew, and he said he was trying to check it out to get more definite information.

Carr said that he could bring Wade in sometime the first of the week but, in light of the fact that it was this man of the press and that they did not think it would be broken by the press immediately, although there had been all kinds of stories down there but Carr said there were some twenty-five to forty different stories about this being the case . . . but this was the first time that he got something definite as to how they were handling it or how it could be handled by himself. But I was concerned about an undercover agent. He thought that the press would not bring the story without some further proof, and they are working on that now, he said. So he thought that if he brought Wade back on Monday or Tuesday, that that would still take care of any major problem. When he first told us, he said the press had it, and he was fearful because he hadn't even gotten this from Wade. He got it from another man that the press would bring it before we could know about it, and the Commission would be asked all kinds of questions without having information about it. Now he said Wade told him that the FBI never keeps any records of names. . . .

CONGRESSMAN BOGGS: There is a denial of this in one of these FBI records, as you know. . . .

SENATOR COOPER: In this file we had yesterday, one of the lawyers for this fellow who claims to represent . . . Oswald or one of them, Ruby, told about this, do you recall it, he said it was being rumored around.

MR. RANKIN: Yes, it was being rumored that he was an undercover agent. Now it is something that would be very difficult to prove out. There are events in connection with this that are curious, in that they might make it possible to check some of it out in time. I assume that the FBI records would never show it and, if it is true, and of course we don't know, but we thought you should have the information. . . . And Mr. Carr said that they . . . thought that they knew why the FBI was so willing to give some of these records to the defense counsel . . . he said a number of these records were furnished by the Texas authorities, and that they should not be given up to the defense counsel, and that the reason he thought that they were so eager to help Ruby was because they had the undercover, that Oswald was the undercover agent and had the number of his badge and so much, he was getting two hundred dollars a month and so forth, and that was the way it was explained as his justification to the court as a basis for determining the records and that that was the excuse the FBI, the reason the FBI had for being so eager to give the records up. That is the way it was developed. . . . I did talk to Jaworski [Leon] and he said he didn't think Wade would say anything like this unless he had some substantial information in back of it, and he [Jaworski] thought he [Wade] could prove it, because he thought it would ruin many politics, in Texas, to be making such a claim, and then have it shown that there was nothing to it. . . .

CONGRESSMAN FORD: How long ago did they get a feeling that there was some substance to the rumors that apparently had been—I just assumed, and I didn't ask them that, that Carr called me and seemed to be in a matter of great urgency at eleven-ten this morning, and that he was fearful that they would bring in the papers before we would even get to know about it, and that is the way he was talking and acting about it.

SENATOR COOPER: He felt there was. . . . He didn't know the name of the informant?

MR. RANKIN: No, he did not.

CHAIRMAN: What then would lead him to think it had substance?

MR. RANKIN: Well, he said that the reason he thought it might have substance was because Wade had heard these rumors constantly. . . .

SENATOR COOPER: How would you test this kind of thing?

MR. RANKIN: It is going to be very difficult for us to be able to establish the fact in it. I am confident that the FBI would never admit it, and I presume their records will never show it or, if their records do show anything, I would think their records would show some kind of a number that could be assigned to a dozen different people according to how they wanted to describe them. So that it seemed to me if it truly happened, he did use postal boxes practically everyplace that he went, and that would be an ideal way to get money to anyone that you wanted as an undercover agent, or anybody else that you wanted to do business that way with without having any particular transaction.

CONGRESSMAN FORD: There might be people who would see what was going on with that particular box, because the postal authorities do watch; they have means of watching in many places that no one could see. They can watch the clerks as to what they are doing in these boxes, and they can watch the individuals who are going in and out. They do that only when they have an occasion to be suspicious, but they might, in watching for somebody particularly; they might also see other things that they just have to note. That is a possibility.

At this juncture, the Commission tried to understand why the FBI might ever have employed Oswald in any capacity and why Oswald's name was on the FBI's New Orleans office security-file index. Here Dulles volunteered his CIA background to help search for possible reasons.

MR. DULLES: What was the ostensible mission? I mean when they hire somebody, they hire somebody for a purpose. It is either. . . . Was it to penetrate the Fair Play for Cuba Committee? That is the only thing I can think of where they might have used this man. It would be quite ordinary for me because they are very careful about the agents they use. You wouldn't pick up a fellow like this to do an agent's job. You have got to watch out for your agents. You really have got to know. Sometimes you make a mistake.

CONGRESSMAN FORD: He was playing ball, writing letters to both the elements of the Communist parties. I mean he was playing ball with the Trotskyites and with the others. This was a strange circumstance to me.

MR. DULLES: But the FBI get people right inside, you know. They don't need a person like this on the outside. The only place where he did any [thing] at all was with the Fair Play for Cuba Committee.

CONGRESSMAN BOGGS: Of course, it is conceivable that he may have been brought back from Russia, you know.

MR. RANKIN: If he was in the employ from 1962, September 1962, up to the time of the assassination, it had to start over in Russia, didn't it, because didn't he get back in February? . . .

MR. DULLES: They have no facilities; they haven't any people in Russia. They may have some people in Russia, but they haven't got any organizations of their own in Russia. . . . They might have their agents there. They have some people, sometimes American Communists who go to Russia under their guidance and so forth and so on under their control. . . .

MR. RANKIN: One of the strange things that happened, and it may have no bearing on this at all, is the fact that this man who is a defector, and who was under observation at least by the FBI, they say they saw him frequently, could [be] with a passport that permitted him to go to Russia. From my observations of the case that have come to us, such passports are not passed out with that ease.

MR. DULLES: I think you are wrong on that . . . because the passports are issued valid for anywhere except specified countries. . . . But any American, practically any American, can get a passport that is good for anywhere. An American can travel, and Russia is one of the countries you can now travel to. . . .

CHAIRMAN: I think our general counsel and I both have some experience in cases that have come before our court which would indicate that that isn't exactly the fact. . . . They have great difficulty, some of them, in getting a passport to go to Russia.

CONGRESSMAN BOGGS: Particularly for someone who has any Communist . . .

MR. RANKIN: The State Department knew he was a defector. *They* arranged for him to come back. [Emphasis added. In September 1963, Oswald got a passport in New Orleans in *one day* after his application, when his previous actions should have raised questions and even a red flag.]

MR. DULLES: But it doesn't get passport files or the passport records. They are issuing hundreds and thousands of passports. They have their own particular system. . . . They don't run around from the time a man comes in. If they don't find any clue, and they don't according to our record here, they don't find any warning clue in his file—they should have a warning clue in his file.

SENATOR COOPER: That is what they admitted, that they had not supplied the warning.

MR. DULLES: And the Passport Office doesn't on its own usually go around and inquire. They wait until it is assigned there. Then they follow it up.

SENATOR COOPER: This may be off the point a bit, but as I

reread the report, the chronology of the FBI checks on Oswald, they knew that he had gone to Texas. They learned from Mrs. Paine. They knew where Mrs. Oswald was living. They talked with her. They knew where he was working. . . .

CONGRESSMAN BOGGS: You will find the report from the FBI dated back last summer, and months before that and then months after that. . . .

MR. RANKIN: They had a report on many, they had an agent go and see him when he was in prison . . . in New Orleans . . . and he lied to them before the police. He said his wife was a Texas girl, and he married her in Texas, and a whole string of stuff, and in Dallas they had a report prior to that that was definitely contrary to it.

CONGRESSMAN BOGGS: The fellow [Edward] Butler who works for the . . . organizations . . . to disseminate and tie Communist propaganda to Latin America is the one who confronted him on the streets in New Orleans. . . . Butler says that this was the first time that they established that he had been in Russia and that he had defected at one time and then returned. You have undoubtedly in your files . . . that tape that was made . . . in New Orleans. . . . On that tape . . . he gives the normal Communist line, reaction to everything.

SENATOR COOPER: How do you propose to meet this situation?

CONGRESSMAN BOGGS: This is a serious thing.

The allegation that Oswald might have been an FBI informer became immensely troubling to the Commission in the light of the Bureau's insistence from the very outset that he was the lone assassin and that there was no conspiracy. The discussion in the Commission made it clear that suspicions were developing that the FBI may have been convinced of Oswald's guilt as the lone gunner because it knew him as an employee. It was a devastating thought. The Commission was so aghast that Dulles even suggested that the record of their session be destroyed. At that stage, the disposition of the Commission seemed to be to conceal evidence, if it actually developed into evidence, to spare the nation an intolerable truth. Rankin sought to place it all in perspective.

MR. RANKIN: I thought first you should know about it. Secondly, there is this defector too that is somewhat an issue in this case, and I suppose you are all aware of it. That is that the FBI is very explicit that Oswald is the assassin or was the assassin, and they are very explicit that there was no conspiracy, and they are also saying in the same place that they are continuing their investigation. Now, in my experience of almost nine years, in the first place it is hard to get them to say when you think you have got a case tight enough to convict somebody, that that is the person that committed the crime. In my experience with the FBI, they don't do that. They claim that they don't evaluate, and it is uniform prior experience that they don't do that. Secondly, they have not run out of all kinds of leads in Mexico or in Russia and so forth which they could probably . . . they haven't run out all the leads on the information and they could probably say—that isn't our business. . . . But they are concluding that there can't be a conspiracy without those being run out. Now that is not [normal] from my experience with the FBI. . . . Why are they so eager to make both of those conclusions . . . the original report and their experimental report, which is such a departure. Now that is just circumstantial evidence, and it doesn't prove anything about this, but it raises questions. We have to try to find out what they haven't said that would give any support to the story, and report it to you. . . .

The transcript becomes unclear at this point in identifying the speakers participating in the discussion as to which FBI official would know whether Oswald had, indeed, been an undercover agent. Rankin, replying to questions, said that Alan H. Belmont, whom he described as being in the FBI's Special Security Division, would know "every undercover agent."

MR. RANKIN: . . . . When the Chief Justice and I were just briefly reflecting on this, we said if that was true and if it ever came out and could be established, then you would have people think that there was a conspiracy to accomplish this assassination that nothing the Commission did could dissipate.

CONGRESSMAN BOGGS: You are so right.

MR. DULLES: Oh, terrible.

CONGRESSMAN BOGGS: Its implications of this are fantastic, don't you think so?

CHAIRMAN: Terrific.

MR. RANKIN: To have anybody admit to it, even if it was the fact, I am sure that there wouldn't at this point be anything to prove it.

MR. DULLES: Lee, if this were true, why would it be particularly in their interest—I could see it would be in their interest [the FBI's] to get rid of this man but why would it be in their interest to say he is clearly the only guilty one? I mean I don't see that argument that you raise particularly shows an interest. . . .

MR. RANKIN: They would like to have us fold up and quit.

CONGRESSMAN BOGGS: This closes the case, you see. Don't you see?

MR. DULLES: Yes, I see that.

MR. RANKIN: They found the man. There is nothing more to do. The Commission supports their conclusions, and we can go on home and that is the end of it.

MR. DULLES: But that puts the burden right on them. If he was not the killer and they employed him, they are already it, you see. So your argument is correct if they are sure that this is going to close the case, but if it doesn't close the case, they are worse off than ever by doing this.

CONGRESSMAN BOGGS: Yes, I would think so. And, of course, we are all even gaining in the realm of speculation. I don't even like to see this being taken down.

MR. DULLES: Yes. I think this record ought to be destroyed. Do you think we need a record of this?

MR. RANKIN: I don't, except that we said we would have records of meetings and so we called the reporter in the formal way. If you think what we have said here should not be upon the record, we can have it done that way.

MR. DULLES: I am just thinking of sending around copies

and so forth. The only copies of this record should be kept right there.

CONGRESSMAN BOGGS: I would hope that none of these records are circulated to anybody. . . .

Five days later, the Commission was still agonizing over ways to approach J. Edgar Hoover on the subject of Oswald. It was caught between its concern that Hoover's written denial of Oswald's alleged employment in his bureau would not be believed by the public and its own fear of antagonizing the great man himself. The Commission seemed to have been afraid of Hoover, whose national popularity and reputation were frequently referred to. (According to Dallas Police Chief Jesse Curry: "The FBI was very jealous of its reputation, and J. Edgar Hoover was fanatic about it and didn't like to admit they made any mistakes." Curry went on to say that the FBI "had prior knowledge that Oswald was in Dallas.")

In view of Waggoner Carr's evidence and allegations, it would have been easier to prove that Oswald was in the FBI than to prove the negative. Allen Dulles, drawing on his own experience, expressed doubt that even if it was true, Hoover would ever admit it, stating that he would never have told the truth about any of his own agents even under oath. The Commission recognized that it was wholly dependent on the FBI, and it became more and more clear that the FBI was determined that the Commission should simply endorse its own premise that Lee Harvey Oswald was the lone assassin.

To complicate matters, Jack Ruby's lawyers had asked the FBI for material to prepare their case, but the request was turned down by Dallas County District Attorney Henry Wade at the request of the FBI. The Commission solved the dilemma by deliberately setting up an alibi for J. Edgar Hoover and the FBI. Commissioner McCloy expressed exasperation with the Commission's utter dependence on the FBI to supply evidence and

thought that the Commission was being inexorably
pushed to accept the Bureau's determination to have
Lee Harvey Oswald found as the lone assassin.

While the Commission had numerous reports from
the FBI, it could not be sure that it had everything, and
Lee Rankin expressed his suspicions about this . . . suspicions that were to be proved true in 1975. He also noted
that it was a "curious factor" that the FBI agents did
not approach Oswald after an interview with him in August 1963, yet they did approach and talk to Marina
Oswald and Ruth Paine in October. It was a result of
this talk with these women that Oswald wrote a
threatening letter to the FBI; however, the Warren
Commission did not know about it at the time of its
meetings nor of FBI agent Hosty's "close relationship"
with Oswald. And if the FBI did not proffer the information, neither did they seek Oswald out after this final letter. If the FBI was interested in preventing a
crime, it is likely that an interview with Oswald de-
manding an explanation for his threatening note might
have deterred the assassination.

The Commission was constantly forced to weigh the
evidence of Marina Oswald against that of others, but
never got down to evaluating it. Lee Rankin recalled
that Oswald was interviewed for two hours by the FBI
when he and his family returned from Russia, and was
very disturbed that the Commission had no record of
the gist of this conversation.

Senator Russell summed up the dilemma very suc-
cinctly: "It seems to me that we have two alternatives.
One is that we can just accept the FBI report and go on
and write the report based on their findings and supported by the raw material they have given us, or else we
can go on and try to run down some of these collateral
rumors that have just not been dealt with directly in
this raw material that we have. . . ."

"I think we must do the latter. . . ." said Congressman
Boggs.

But the final report showed that the Commission took

the first alternative, probably because it was unable to stand the pressure applied by the FBI and the thought of J. Edgar Hoover's terrible wrath.

Another fact disturbing to the Commission was that the FBI knew about Oswald in Russia and Mexico City. However, the evidence passed on by the FBI was surprisingly sparse, and the Commission members felt it should have been augmented. Of course, it never was . . . there was just enough meat in it to prove that Oswald was a less than likable character with no love for the United States. It was just enough evidence to force the Commission into accepting their preconceived idea that Lee Harvey Oswald was the lone assassin and not part of a conspiracy.

The FBI knew that Oswald had visited the Soviet Embassy on October 10, 1963, and that he wanted to return to the Soviet Union. Under the existing Bureau operating procedures, they *should* have followed up on any unexplained visits (called "bogies" by the FBI) by an American citizen to Communist embassies—particularly someone who had defected once. They did not! Why? Because he was already under FBI surveillance? Or because he was one of their undercover men?

We do not suggest that anyone in the FBI sat down one day and decided to assassinate the President; however, we firmly believe that the FBI not only told falsehoods to the Commission but participated in a cover-up by withholding evidence.

For the assassination of President Kennedy is a tragedy in two parts: first, the act itself and then the possibly more diabolic act of covering up the evidence— an act almost too sinister to think about. The scenario of the FBI is one that poses a threat to everyone in the United States for, in not presenting the full evidence, the FBI ceased to be the guardians of law and order and became instead accomplices—witting or unwitting—in murder. Worst of all, with the cover-up story of the FBI, we are left with the possibility that an assassin, or assassins, are still alive and may have continued with their destructive acts in the succeeding assassinations of Martin Luther King and Robert Kennedy and the attempt on Governor Wallace.

We now know that Lee Harvey Oswald wrote a threatening letter to the FBI two days before the assassination of the President, but the FBI covered it up for twelve years. The threatening note did not result in Oswald being placed under surveillance. Officials and agents of the FBI have told contradictory stories about their roles in the destruction of the threatening letter written by Lee Harvey Oswald. The Justice Department decided not to seek an indictment because, a spokesman says, the statute of limitations has barred prosecution of whoever issued the order to destroy the letter. The question is: who issued the order and why was the letter destroyed two hours after Oswald himself had been murdered by Jack Ruby? These questions will never be answered or even fully explained because one or more of the six FBI men who knew of the letter appears to be quite capable of lying to any investigators. An agent who destroyed the letter says he did so at the direction of his superior. Was this superior J. Edgar Hoover himself?

The note, personally delivered to the Dallas office of the FBI at 114 Commercial Street, threatened to "blow up" the office if the FBI didn't "lay off Marina" (Oswald's wife) and stop questioning her. Moreover, a teletype message that went out on the FBI's normal-movement overnight wire to the Mobile, New Orleans, and Dallas local offices on November 17th read: "Threat to Assassinate President Kennedy in Dallas, Texas, November 22nd–23rd, Miscellaneous Information Concerning . . ." The text went on to say, "Information has been received by the bureau that a militant revolutionary group will attempt to assassinate President Kennedy on November 22nd–23rd during his trip to Dallas, Texas. . . ." Why wasn't the fact that such a Telex was transmitted to its regional offices by FBI headquarters revealed to the Warren Commission?

(History repeats itself in a similar set of circumstances in 1975 when Sara Jane Moore of San Francisco sent a note to the local FBI office telling them that she feared she would have to shoot President Ford. She was not kept under surveillance, and even managed to get within shooting distance of the President.)

We can have no doubt that the FBI, following the precedent set when it came into existence, was as much interested in politics as in solving crimes.

In the 1950s a change came about, and the FBI became a Government body obsessed with looking for subversive activities to the exclusion of other criminal elements. Their counter-intelligence program was started to "stop the rise of a black messiah" and to "create a pervasive atmosphere so that even if there was not an agent behind every door, people would believe there was."

The FBI made it known that one of its functions was to stop radical groups such as the Ku Klux Klan, the Communist party, black movements, and the anti-war movements. There are numerous apocryphal stories that from 1950 on there were more FBI counter-intelligence agents in radical cells than members—and without them making up the bulk of the attendees, there would have been no movements. The "Cointel" (or Cointel-pro) was a covert FBI program that operated in Hoover's later years to crush, by whatever means possible, anyone whom Hoover disliked.

Cointel activities included: anonymous letters to wives of civil-rights sympathizers hinting at infidelities (causing some marriages to break up); attempts to cause warfare and disharmony among black activist groups; and the best-known instance of sending a letter to Martin Luther King, intimating that suicide would be the "best" way out. One former FBI agent indicated that the Bureau had "planted" the two famous composite pictures of Oswald posing with the supposed murder weapon to be found by Dallas detectives the following day. This was in order to reinforce the FBI's case that Oswald was "the [lone] assassin."

It is now known that the FBI conducted a six-year effort to discredit Dr. Martin Luther King, maintaining electronic surveillance, attempting to prevent a university from conferring an honorary degree on him, and trying to stop a personal interview with the Pope. They also once sent him a tape recording with several unsavory incidents that they had picked up from their telephone taps and room bugs. For, in obtaining permission from then Attorney General Robert F. Kennedy to "electronically eavesdrop" on King to discover if subversives were in fact part of the Southern Christian Leadership Conference membership, they had expanded the three wiretaps authorized to a total of over sixteen unauthorized and illegal taps. And not only did they possess incriminating information on the private life of Dr. King, but also on the private lives of others, including Muhammad Ali and any others who might have called or been called by King. The tape they sent King of the supposed unsavory discussions with women, who evidently were a large part of King's life, was accompanied by a letter that threatened Dr. King: "There is only one thing left for you to do. You know what it is. . . . You are done! There is but one way out for you." King had always regarded this as a heavy-handed attempt by the FBI to drive him to suicide. It was hardly the stance or the character of an organization charged with the maintenance of law-and-order and of providing the Warren Commission with documents that were supposed to be fact-finding in their nature and *lead* them to discover the real killer of President John F. Kennedy.

Much of the material discussed by the Commissioners still remains classified, including the actual Commission transcript, which would make very different reading from the official version quickly put out in book form by the self-righteous *New York Times*. As long as so many documents remain secret, the idea of the lone assassin

can be more easily sustained and the FBI's initial desire
to see that no conspiracy existed will be much more difficult to prove. The Kennedy records add up to 360 cubic
feet of material, and much of it remains uncatalogued
in the public inventory. According to Senator Richard
Schweiker, 152 Warren Commission documents still remain classified in the National Archives and include
107 FBI and 23 CIA reports. There is no use in saying
that this is in the interests of national security, because
the security of the nation was sorely afflicted when bullets sent President Kennedy to his death. Chief Justice
Earl Warren, from the beginning of the investigation,
was against the Commission hiring its own investigators
or obtaining subpoena powers. Everyone was worried
about his own prestige; but underlying this was also the
worry that an independent investigation might interfere
with the Jack Ruby murder trial scheduled for February
1964. Senator Russell, Congressman Boggs, and Mr.
McCloy demurred when Earl Warren firmly refused to
go along with the idea of independent investigators; so
the burden of producing evidence inevitably fell to the
FBI and CIA.

Leaks of the findings of the FBI continued to filter
through the media, adding further to the annoyance of
Senator Russell. And the delay of the FBI in presenting
its documents directly to the Commission was the beginning of a sub rosa but sustained feud between Russell,
Boggs, and McCloy and the FBI, a feud that added significant color to the eventual proceedings. Undoubtedly,
it was advantageous for the FBI to allow leaks to the
press and so induce Commission members to keep their
news confined to the idea of the lone-assassin theory.
When the FBI finally presented its material, it was
voluminous. Members got their reports in a huge box
and did not keep them under security because, despite
the enormity of the material, there was little in it that
had not already appeared in the press. Because of the
difficulty in reading the handwriting, Oswald's diary was
typed out by the FBI. The diary was found by the FBI

right after the assassination, but it was not released to
the Warren Commission until January 1964.

The ability or inability of the FBI to produce
documents and findings adequately was the recurrent
topic in most of the secret meetings held by the Commission. Lee Rankin felt a small staff was needed to act in
direct liaison with the FBI "because we might not get
all we needed by just going back to the FBI and other
agencies because the report has so many loopholes in it.
Anybody can look at it and see that it just doesn't seem
like they are looking for things this Commission has to
look for in order to get the answers it wants and is entitled to. . . ."

The FBI reports rarely agreed with the reports from
other agencies. One area in dispute was the speed at
which the Presidential car was traveling at the precise
moment the bullets were fired. Hale Boggs said: "What
is really significant is whether the man lived or died. If
the car speeded up, he probably would still be alive today." It has always been a mystery why the Presidential
car did not break speed immediately after an indication
of trouble . . . it would have been the normal instinct of
most drivers. In the attacks on President Ford in 1975,
he was quickly moved from the scene.

It was some years after the assassination before it was
asserted that Oswald had a reference number in the FBI
list of personnel and that he was paid two hundred dollars a month as an informer. But the Commission had
the testimony of Oswald's mother that she suspected her
son worked for the FBI and, despite Mr. Hoover's firm
denial in writing that anyone at the FBI knew Oswald,
in one secret session Mr. McCloy said: "Now there is
put in our hands a document that shows he was paid a
certain sum of money. Maybe we would have to go further than that, but I think it would be incumbent upon
us to ask the head of the agencies whether or not this
man was an employee."

However, the stature of J. Edgar Hoover silently pre-
vailed over the proceedings, and he had said that the

FBI knew nothing about Oswald. Having rejected the idea of independent investigators at the first meeting, the Commission was inexorably locked into accepting everything the FBI said. And it said what it wanted the Commission to believe, and that was an official acceptance of the lone-assassin theory. The Commission pondered about the lack of evidence connecting Oswald with specific groups. The FBI was supposed to check this out thoroughly, but it never did. The date when Oswald's income from the Red Cross in Russia was terminated was never determined. As Rankin remarked: "That entire period [in Russia] is just full of possibilities for training, for working with the Soviets and its agents." If Oswald was a trainee in Russia for espionage, the FBI should certainly have known about it. Every time the Commission needed more information from the FBI, it drew a blank. It is no wonder that the Commission finally came up with the confirmation of the lone assassin who was not part of a conspiracy.

Despite the FBI's insistence that the Warren Commission should not be concerned about the possibility that Oswald had affiliations with the FBI, more and more information is available today to indicate that he was in close contact with them and was indeed a paid informer. The suspicions and convictions of the members of the Warren Committee were put to rest, and they became an integral part of the massive cover-up when they signed their names to the final report.

In the signing of the final report, in which all Commission members had to be in agreement, it is interesting to note that Russell and Boggs were not willing to sign for several days. In the end, they did. Both Russell and Boggs are now dead . . . the latter in a mysterious plane disappearance in Alaska. The dissenting voices were silent, as were so many others who could have helped in the investigation.

It paid for the Commission to put their heads in the sand. Sometimes the thing most feared goes away but, in the case of the Kennedy assassination, it didn't. The specter of Lee Harvey Oswald as an FBI informant is more than just a suspicion.

J. Edgar Hoover was the main reason why the Commission was somewhat at a loss to explain the "Magic Bullet" and the bullet fragments. In a letter to the Commission, not included in the original twenty-six volumes of evidence and testimony, Hoover revealed that the "Magic Bullet" and bullet fragments were subjected to a spectrographic analysis. That test, Hoover stated, was inconclusive, and the Commission had to take his word for it. There was also an additional test, a neutron-activation analysis, a highly sophisticated technique that measures the differences in material that has been bombarded with radiation down to parts of a billion and sometimes even less. Blandly, Hoover stated that while *minor variations* were found between the fragments taken from the body of the President and those from Governor Connally, those differences were not worth considering. It sounded fine, but the truth is that *any* difference, however minute, is not only sufficient but meaningful and might even cast new light on the assassination.

For, unless atoms changed their structure that day in Dallas, Kennedy and Connally were wounded by separate bullets. Had the Commission really gone into this analysis, the entire report would have been very different. Why was this vital letter not included somewhere in the twenty-six volumes of evidence put out by the Commission?

In fact, all physical evidence linking Oswald with the assassination was inconclusive. A paraffin test showed traces of nitrates on his hands but not on his cheek. This test was dismissed by the FBI and subsequently the Commission as unreliable. Even the partial palm print on the rifle was not proved to be that of Oswald. It was the FBI's duty to come forward with this information—and they did not!

Charles Givens, one of Oswald's co-workers at the Depository, was interviewed by the FBI immediately after the assassination. At first, he told the FBI that he saw Oswald on the first floor of the Depository forty minutes before the assassination. Six months later, on April 8, 1964, when interviewed by David Belin, Givens changed his testimony, recalling that he had forgotten his cigarettes and had gone to the sixth floor, where he saw Oswald. Of course, it was much more damning evidence against Oswald to have been seen on the all-important sixth floor just before the assassination than to recollect that he was on the first floor.

Another amazing fact is that Dallas Police Captain Fritz, known to be a very thorough interrogator, kept no notes of his original interviews with Lee Harvey Oswald and that the small room where the interviews took place was swarming with FBI men. At the autopsy of President Kennedy, Francis X. O'Neill, FBI agent, was present throughout. His description of the wound in the President's back conflicts with the official autopsy report, as does that of James W. Sibert, also an FBI agent. In view of the conflicting descriptions of the wound in the President's back given by other FBI agents and the autopsy surgeons, it is noteworthy that other members who were present were not asked to testify. These include agents O'Neill and Sibert and the President's personal physician, Admiral George Burkley. Then there was John T. Stringer, a medical photographer. One roll of his film was taken from him by an FBI agent and exposed. The four funeral-home workers who prepared the body for burial were never interviewed. Richard E. Johnson, a Secret Service agent, was handed the "Magic Bullet" found on the stretcher by O. P. Wright, chief of personnel at Parkland Hospital. Wright was not called to testify, either. And the stretcher on which it was found was neither that of President Kennedy nor that of Governor Connally—but of a black child who had just come into Parkland for facial surgery!

If the Commission had been able to conduct its own investigation without relying on the FBI, it might have talked to Dallas policemen such as W. R. Westphal. He

investigated Oswald's old address at Elsbeth Street,
which the police knew about, although they claimed to
have no record on Oswald before November 22, 1963.
How did they know so quickly after the assassination
that Oswald had an association with Elsbeth Street?

Many witnesses testified to the Commission that they
were in the Texas Theatre when Oswald was arrested,
but ten witnesses also on the scene of the arrest were not
called. The caterer at the Book Depository who sold
lunches to employees might have testified that he knew
Oswald and might even have sold lunch to him on the
day of the assassination. "The Warren Report" credits
Captain Westbrook with finding Oswald's jacket discarded near the scene of the Tippit murder but, according to the Dallas police radio log, this jacket was
found by "No. 279." No effort was made to trace this
unknown man. Nor were post-office employees questioned at the main office where Oswald maintained Box
No. 2915. The inmates of the county jail were allowed
to watch the motorcade from a window, and it is possible that one of them may have noted something significant happening at the sixth floor or at any other window
of the Book Depository. They were in a good position to view the tragic events. There was also an Aber-
deen gunsmith who could testify that the scope on the
assassination rifle was installed for a left-handed man.
Oswald was right-handed and, by establishing this fact
from an authority on guns, the next step might have
been to ascertain if Braden-Brading, or any of the three
tramps picked up by the police, were left-handed. (And
whether the Japanese scope hindered the sighting of the
rifle, and indeed made it impossible to fire accurately
from a distance might also have been checked out.)

The members of the Commission who found loopholes in the vast amount of FBI documents were
right: everything that was submitted seemed to deliberately foster the idea of the lone assassin. However, there
were enough leads to have been followed up. The
chances are that if any six of the numerous leads had

been followed up, the Commission must have come up with the fact that the assassination was a conspiracy.

On June 3, 1960, Hoover sent a letter to the State Department warning that someone posing as Lee Harvey Oswald in Russia might try to get hold of Oswald's passport. How did Hoover know anything about Oswald at this date? Also in the letter was an FBI report from Dallas dated May 12, 1960, in which Oswald's mother, Marguerite C. Oswald, said she was worried about the safety of her son. She had written to him in Russia but had not received any replies . . . all letters had been returned to her. The State Department added a notation, issuing orders that Oswald's passport would not be returned to him through the Russian postal system but only in person; and the passport was actually handed over to a man calling himself Oswald in July 1961. Neither the Hoover memo nor the State Department notes were included in the Warren Commission file on Oswald, and the question arises as to why this information was suppressed. It certainly proves once more that the FBI knew more about Oswald than they wanted the Warren Commission to know.

The Warren Commission took care to include a section that indicated that Oswald and his assassin, Jack Ruby, were not part of a conspiracy (and that there was "no evidence of a conspiracy") . But the definition of a conspiracy could mean two people getting together to commit a foul deed. Did Ruby know Oswald? This is one of the main link-pins to proving that the two, if they did know each other, were working toward the same goal . . . that is, the death of President Kennedy.

We now have enough evidence to prove that Oswald was well known to the FBI and was paid a regular sum of money for information. In addition, we have some definite facts indicating that Jack Ruby was also on the payroll of the FBI. The late FBI director, J. Edgar Hoover, on June 9, 1964, wrote to Lee Rankin, general counsel of the Warren Commission, and described the relationship between Ruby and the agency; yet the letter, again, was never made a part of the Commission's report. It was found tucked away in the National Archives and made available to Lou Staples, a Dallas newspaperman. The three-page letter, Commission Document 1052, was left out of the report. Rankin requested information from the FBI on Jack Ruby and ten other people.

Certain information regarding the contact of Special Agent Charles W. Flynn with Jack L. Ruby on March 11, 1959, was acknowledged. Hoover confirmed that Agent Flynn, operating out of the Dallas FBI office, contacted Ruby "in view of his position as a nightclub operator who might have knowledge of the criminal element in Dallas." Hoover went on to say in his letter: "The purpose of the contact was to determine whether or not Ruby did have such knowledge and, if so, if he would willingly furnish information to this Bureau." On being approached by Flynn, Ruby "expressed his willingness to furnish such information. A personal description of Ruby was obtained by Special Agent Flynn on this occasion of contact on March 11, 1959, but no information or other results were obtained." If no further information was obtained, it seems strange that Ruby was contacted by the FBI on at least eight known occasions between March 11, 1959 and October 2, 1959.

Special Agent Manning Clements of Dallas added to the description of Ruby six days after the assassination of Oswald and noted that Ruby was "a known Dallas criminal." We now know that Ruby was well known to underworld personnel in Chicago before he came to Dallas; apparently, his activities had not stopped. It is difficult in the light of Clement's letter to see Ruby as the patriotic little man who, on the spur of the moment, decided to eliminate the suspected killer of President Kennedy. It becomes even more impossible to see Ruby as a nonentity if we go back to the late 1940s when an inconspicuous California Congressman, Richard M. Nixon, suddenly made headlines as a member of the House Un-American Activities Committee. At that time, a Jack "Rubenstein" of Chicago was a regular informant of

Nixon's. (Jack Ruby changed his name from Rubenstein when he left Chicago to become Jack Ruby of Dallas.) Ruby was known to have mixed freely with Dallas police and was called a "police buff," but friends in Chicago are definite in their opinion that Ruby was not the sort of man to be a "police buff." If he ran around with policemen, it was because there was something in it for him. Perhaps Attorney Hunter was thinking of presenting evidence that Jack Ruby was an FBI informer when he told friends he had an ace up his sleeve that he would throw out at Jack Ruby's second trial; however, we'll never know for sure since he died mysteriously weeks later.

The Warren Commission paid no attention to the claims made by a Dallas attorney who told the FBI he heard Oswald and Ruby discussing a plan to assassinate Governor Connally. This conversation allegedly took place on October 4th, the day after Oswald returned from Mexico and the venue was Ruby's nightclub, the Carousel. Under any other circumstances, except a deliberate cover-up, this evidence should have been checked and rechecked by a commission dedicated to producing the truth of the assassination. Again we come back to the testimony of Dallas County Deputy Sheriff Roger Craig, who saw a light-colored Rambler station wagon pick up Lee Harvey Oswald from the steps of the Book Depository. Ruby was known to have owned a similar type of car that Mrs. Ruth Paine, Oswald's Russian-born friend and landlady, sometimes borrowed!

If Jack Ruby had come up for a second trial in December 1966, it is likely that Dallas District Attorney Henry Wade would have brought out a great deal of evidence linking Ruby with Oswald. In January 1967, Jack Ruby was dead, and several tons of documents were hauled away to a secret warehouse. The state did not pursue the conspiracy theory at Ruby's trial, and Wade had a couple of reasons why this was not done. First, millions of television viewers had witnessed the slaughter of Oswald by Jack Ruby. The only thing to prove, in order to effect a sentence of guilty, was that Jack Ruby premeditated the deed. Ruby admitted as much to the police. Secondly, there was a needless risk involved in going the conspiracy route, and it was not needed when Ruby had already admitted to the murder. Yet another reason could have been pressure from the FBI, which urgently desired the lone-assassin theory be upheld.

Then the Texas Court of Criminal Appeals reversed the Ruby conviction, striking out any future use of the testimony of Police Sergeant Patrick Dean, who stated that minutes after the shooting of Oswald, Ruby orally confessed that he had planned the murder. Ruby's death removed any chance of a court trial. Had there been a new trial, six new witnesses would have come forward, and the gist of their testimony would have been that Oswald and Jack Ruby knew each other . . . not only in Dallas but in New Orleans and Cuba.

The association of Ruby and Oswald could have been the result of a conspiracy initiated by Cuban exiles to overthrow Fidel Castro; and money may have been paid to Ruby and Oswald to motivate them to be part of this plot. There are plenty of witnesses now available to link Ruby and Oswald together in a series of meetings in bars, restaurants, and business places. Both had rented post-office boxes side-by-side at a sub-station, and the housekeeper at Oswald's rooming house was the sister of one of Ruby's business associates. Both men lived within walking distance of each other, and Oswald is now known to have dated a stripper employed by Ruby at the Carousel Club, where a cab deposited him on a regular basis. The girl, who was of Mexican origin, disappeared a few days before the assassination. It is conceivable that Ruby and Oswald knew each other, but no one followed up the leads that could have proved this—certainly not the FBI!

Several witnesses testified at the Warren Commission that they saw Oswald and Ruby together on a number of occasions. The interesting thing about these witnesses is that in every case their testimony was discredited either by Ruth Paine, who always swore that Oswald was elsewhere than the place and date when a witness said he had been seen, or by the FBI, which produced evidence to cast doubt on the credibility of the witnesses. If witnesses were interrogated before appearing in front of the Commission, why bring so many forward and then find that their testimony could be contradicted and destroyed by Ruth Paine and the FBI?

Jack Ruby throughout his life seems to have been singularly unfortunate in his choice of associates. On October 24, 1947, Paul Roland Jones, a friend of Ruby's sister Eva Grant, was arrested for violating the Federal narcotics statutes. Five days later, Jack and Hyman Rubenstein were interrogated in Chicago by agents of the Bureau of Narcotics. The brothers admitted knowing Jones but denied knowing anything of his activities in narcotics. In 1954, Ruby's Vegas Club associate, Joe Bonds, was convicted of sodomy and sent to a Texas penitentiary to serve an eight-year sentence. In 1959, Jack Ruby became a partner of Joe Slatin in the Sovereign Club in Dallas; however, the two men could not get along and, within a year, Slatin had sold out and Ralph Paul became Ruby's partner. The Sovereign Club later became the Carousel Club.

If the FBI needed a man with a good solid background of strange activities, no one qualified better for the job as "informant" than Jack Ruby.

Ruby was arrested several times in Dallas for carrying a concealed weapon, but no charges were ever filed against him and he was usually released the same day. Despite his background, he was always able to obtain licenses from the Texas Liquor Control Board. Sybil Leek can personally testify that this is no mean feat, since she once operated a private nightclub in Houston and had to go through a very stringent investigation. "I was very happy to know that officially I had nothing against me that would impede getting the license, although it was fully explained to me that licenses were granted only to those with impeccably *clean records.*"

Policemen frequented Ruby's nightclub on a friendly basis and were never charged for their entertainment. The Commission emphasized that the policemen only took coffee and soft drinks, which contradicts the remembrances of so many Dallas policemen that they got "anything they wanted"—booze and broads. Although the Commission did not find any evidence that Ruby was a gambler, a woman named Alice Nichols stated that the reason she never seriously considered marrying Ruby was because he refused to give up gambling. They dated for about eleven years. He knew many gamblers; and when Sidney Seidband, a Dallas gambler, was arrested in Oklahoma City, his list of gambling acquaintances included the name of Jack Ruby. Yet the FBI found no evidence that Ruby was a significant link in any organized-crime activities.

As early as December 1963, Jack Ruby wanted to take a polygraph, truth serum, or any other scientific device that would establish his veracity. His attorneys agreed that he should take a polygraph examination to test any conspiratorial connection between him and Oswald. The defense counsel filed the appropriate motions in court, requesting that the FBI administer such an examination to Ruby. In May 1964, Ruby was still requesting a polygraph, and the lawyer wrote numerous letters to the Commission on behalf of Ruby, again and again requesting such an examination. At the end of the proceedings, Ruby said, "All I want to do is to tell the truth, and the only way you can know it is by the polygraph, and that is the only way you can know it." Finally, the Commission initiated arrangements for the FBI to conduct a polygraph, and the date was set for July 16, 1964. A few days before the test was due to take place, Eva Grant and Ruby's counsel, Joe H. Tonahill, opposed the taking of the test on the grounds that psychiatric examinations showed his mental state was such that it would be meaningless. On July 18th, Assistant Counsel Arlen Specter, representing the Commission, stated that his colleagues were not interested in the test.

Jack Ruby continued to insist that he wanted to take the test. Chief Defense Counsel Fowler opposed the taking of the test and then set down certain ground rules that had to be observed. Finally, the test was administered by Special Agent Bell P. Herndon, polygraph operator of the FBI. The result was as follows:

> Q: Did you know Oswald before November 22, 1963?
> RUBY: No.
> Q: Did you assist Oswald in the assassination?
> RUBY: No.
> Q: Did you shoot Oswald in order to silence him?
> RUBY: No.

In some forty questions, Ruby's replies came as expected. Ordinarily during a polygraph examination, only the examiner and the examinee are present. However, it is the practice of the FBI to have a second agent present to take notes. In Ruby's case, there were representatives of the Warren Commission, the Dallas district attorney, two defense counsels, two FBI agents, the chief jailer, a psychiatrist, and a court reporter. If Ruby was under mental stress, the presence of so many people was guaranteed to make him even more nervous. Special Agent Herndon expressed the opinion that Ruby was not adversely affected by the number of people in the room. Dr. W. R. Beavers, a court-appointed psychiatrist, testified that Ruby was a psychotic depressive and, based on this assumption, Herndon testified: "There would be no validity to the polygraph examination and no significance should be placed upon the polygraph charts."

Hoover later commented on the polygraph test: "In view of the serious question raised by Ruby's mental condition, no significance should be placed on the polygraph examination and it should be considered non-conclusive as the charts cannot be relied upon."

The Commission did not rely on the results of this examination in reaching its conclusion that Ruby and

Oswald did not know each other and were not part of a conspiracy. It had little option in coming up with this conclusion since Ruby's mental condition was a major part of his trial. If Oswald was to be the lone assassin, Jack Ruby had to be mentally incompetent in the cover-up story. This way, anything else he said could be taken with a grain of salt. Such things as Ruby's determination to be taken to Washington to talk to the FBI and to "get away from here" were put down to the ravings of a man who was psychotic. Lee Harvey Oswald had been more fortunate in his requests to see the FBI in New Orleans.

The scenario of the FBI has more loopholes in it than Swiss cheese and, through the loopholes, the perspective changes so that the FBI comes out *not* as a helpful Government body anxious to get at the truth, but as an institution directed to obscure the essential details that the Warren Commission was created to investigate. Too many documents were mislaid or filed in the wrong place or simply destroyed to make this scenario anything but a blatant travesty of the due process of law.

Something was rotten in the state of Texas, and it spread like a cancerous growth to irritate the entire nation. "The Warren [Commission] Report" was like a drug giving remission to the patient but the disease has flared up again.

Was the FBI guilty of just a cover-up—or of something more sinister?

6 | THE COMMUNIST SCENARIO

If you are not prepared to adhere to the lone-assassin findings of the Warren Commission, there is no shortage of alternatives, each with its own scenario. The trouble is that each of the non-Oswald scenarios provides a thread in the tapestry—some with more expressive motifs than others—but the total pattern that emerges is the portrait of a conspiracy.

Webster's Dictionary defines "conspiracy" as: "A secret combination of men for an evil purpose; an agreement or combination to commit some crime in concert; a plot; concerted treason." If the Warren Commission falls apart on the lone-assassin theory, then we are left with the exact elements of this succinct description by Webster. Take any part of this definition, and you can find a scenario to fit it once the lone-assassin theory is rejected.

Communists were in this country in great numbers by the fall of 1963 and, for some reason best known to leading members of the Government, there was the necessity to appease Russia at the time of Kennedy's assassination.

For the first thought in the minds of many a man was that no American would assassinate the President of his country. The obvious culprit was most likely to be a Communist.

Immediately after the assassination, the Russian newspapers published a stern denial that they had anything to do with the assassination, and four days later called on President Johnson to initiate a commission to investigate the matter. Almost on cue, that is exactly what the President did when he created the Warren Commission. It was a political necessity in 1963 to obscure any involvement of Oswald or Jack Ruby with the Communists, and the Warren Commission foundered many times when there were obvious links. But it is in "The Warren Report" that we get the first glimpse of Oswald as a possible agent of the Soviet Union, or even as a double agent, plying the American CIA with tidbits of information, while professing to be enamored of life in Russia. (In fact, the CIA recently admitted it didn't tell the Commission everything it knew about Oswald in Russia!)

There is good reason for the conjecture that Oswald was indeed a Russian agent. He was a Marxist and a defector under unusual circumstances, bartering his American citizenship for a chance to stay in Russia. We also know that when Oswald was in Russia for thirty-two months, he was well looked after, living in a low-rent apartment with a job and a bonus added to his wages by the Russian Red Cross. The Russian Red Cross should *not* be confused with the American Red Cross, a humanitarian organization. The Russian Red Cross is a front for the Soviet secret police, the KGB.

Of all the places where Oswald could have stayed in Russia, he ended up in Minsk, the site of the Communist espionage school. Speculation that this was not a coincidence has gained credence since the Warren Commission concluded its report in 1964. We now can reasonably surmise that a man named Oswald played a role in bringing down the American U-2 spy plane in Russia.

As a result, the pilot, Francis Gary Powers, spent several years in a Russian prison before being traded for Colonel Rudolf Abel, a top Russian spy incarcerated in the United States. Again we come to the arena of absurd coincidence, because some U-2 flights originated from the American base at Atsugi, Japan, where Oswald had been stationed from 1958 to 1959. There he worked as a radar operator assigned to ground control and could certainly have picked up some information the Russians could have found useful.

The U-2 incident in 1960 and the subsequent trial of Powers in Russia were the center of a crisis between this country and the U.S.S.R., but "The Warren Report" omits this. Yet the Commission stated that in its investigation it wanted to put an end once and for all to all types of cloak-and-dagger stories. The Francis Gary Powers story was a near classic, and one would have thought it could not have been ignored. Actually, the truth is that the Warren Commission *did* consider this very special cloak-and-dagger story, but the evidence is now a document in the National Archives bearing a top-secret classification. Bureaucracy is capable of making a slipup even when trying to cover something up and, while the documents themselves may never see the light of day in this century, there is an index file that has surfaced: "Lee Harvey Oswald's Access to Classified Information About the U-2." It is enough to whet the appetite and, through the lack of tangible evidence doomed to lurk in the Archives, we are at liberty to offer our own interpretation. Since there is a card in the index file, someone thought it worthwhile to try to evaluate whatever Oswald might have learned at the Atsugi naval air base.

Another eyebrow-raising index card also gives a clue to yet another top-secret report in the Archives: "Letter from Director FBI 3.6.64 with attached results of an interview with Yuri Ivanovich Nosenko dated 3.4.64."

Yuri Nosenko was a KGB staff officer who defected to the United States on February 4, 1964, three months after the assassination of President Kennedy in Dallas. Again there is no mention of the interview in "The Warren Report," which is hard to understand since the KGB is the Russian police agency whose business it is to interview defectors—such as Oswald. Oswald *was interviewed* by this agency on his arrival in the Soviet Union in October 1959 within a matter of weeks after his discharge from the service. That Nosenko knew Oswald during his sojourn in Russia is evident from an internal memo that managed to appear among papers routinely declassified. ("Internal Memos" are not meant for public reading, and this scrap of paper, among so many others, must have escaped the attention of the people engaged in filing away information. This memo quotes Nosenko as saying, "Oswald was an exceedingly poor shot, and it was necessary for persons who accompanied him on hunts to provide him with game." Yet Lee Harvey Oswald was the main suspect picked up and indicted for an act that demanded both a high degree of precision marksmanship directed toward a moving object and a cool head to calculate just how many shots could be fired from an aged Italian carbine.)

Oswald became obsessed with Marxism during his stay at Atsugi, where part of his duty was to guard the U-2 planes. Here he studied Russian and corresponded with several Communist organizations. A fellow marine, Kerry Thornley, testified that one day Oswald received a visit at the base from a strange civilian. The man asked for Oswald at the gate, but Thornley could not verify his name or nationality. However, he noted that, as a result of this visit, Oswald was excused from guard duty, and the two men talked for several hours. It is unusual for any visitor to a high-security military base not to leave any trace of his identity. There is usually a signature required on entry and the time noted of arrival and departure. This could have been checked by the Warren Commission, but again there is no record of it. The Nosenko "internal memo" becomes more important at this stage when we take into consideration remarks made by Francis Gary Powers in his book, *Operation*

Overflight, in which he indicates that Oswald might have possessed knowledge useful to the Russians. The full report of the interview with Nosenko could clarify this, but it is retained in some dark, secret area of the National Archives and may never be declassified.

When the news broke about the defection of former marine Oswald to Russia, it caused enough consternation for the Marine Corps to make radical changes in procedures relating to radar frequencies. One irate marine officer stated that such changes involved thousands of man-hours of work to bring them into effect, so at least we know the marines took Oswald's presence in the U.S.S.R very seriously. The Warren Commission delicately conceded that Oswald *might* have known something important enough to pass on to the Russians. Oswald had the potential to be a spy, for not only was he interested in Marxism but he was prepared to take the drastic measure of leaving his own country to live in a Communist country, carrying with him at the very least a superficial knowledge of the inner workings of an important American military base. It was enough to make the sensitive nerve ends of the Warren Commission act and interact as the political implications were discreetly, albeit unofficially, acknowledged. Moreover, the fact that Oswald married the niece of a ranking Russian officer at the espionage center in Minsk should have caused some concern.

Revealing Oswald as a possible KGB agent allowed to come back into the United States could have brought us to the edge of World War III.

Earl Warren was certainly aware of the implications. When he talked to President Johnson and finally agreed—with tears in his eyes—to take the job as chairman of the Commission, Warren had previously stated that he was unhappy about the job. He knew how tough it was going to be and had misgivings that it was not the correct job for the Chief Justice of the Supreme Court to undertake. He was quoted as saying, "We have got to squash the rumors," and "We have got to calm the fears of the nation because, if we do not, we are going into a nuclear disaster and forty million people are going to be dead." What rumors? Could they be the ones coming from Dallas that Lee Harvey Oswald was part of the international Communist conspiracy? To establish that Oswald was indeed acting on Communist instructions to kill President Kennedy discredited both the CIA and the FBI, who were counted upon as our bulwark in keeping such Communist activities out of the United States.

If Earl Warren thought there was a possibility that revelations about Oswald's Communist activities could lead us into a nuclear war, then he must have known much more than we give him credit for and certainly much more than "The Warren Report" revealed. Lee Harvey Oswald as the lone assassin is something America could deal with, but Lee Harvey "Oswaldovitch", as his fellow marines called him, was a tougher proposition to deal with. And already too many clues were leading several groups of thinking men to conjecture that Oswald might have been not only a traitor to his country but a formidable double agent, running with the red Russian hounds and playing tag with American Intelligence. Oswald or "Oswaldovitch" was something America did not need to intrude on its delicately balanced international political scene.

On June 10, 1964, Secretary of State Dean Rusk, testified before the Commission: "I have seen no evidence that would indicate to me that the Soviet Union considered it had an interest in the removal of President Kennedy or that it was in any way involved in the removal of President Kennedy." And so Lee Harvey Oswald, a known defector to the U.S.S.R., was now posthumously held to be the lone assassin. "I have not seen or heard of any scrap of evidence indicating that the Soviet Union had any desire to eliminate President Kennedy nor in any way participate in any such event. Now standing back and trying to look at the question objectively despite the ideological differences between our two great systems, I can't see how it could be in the interest of the Soviet Union to make such an effort." This we can take as an apparent truth, although foreign governments making arrangements for the removal of a leader in another country are not likely to advertise the act.

The Commission accepted Secretary Rusk's estimate as reasonable and objective—but wishful thinking can be very persuasive. No government, either our own or that of other countries, is ever anxious to claim unity with any of its spies when they get into trouble. For an ordinary ex-Marine, Oswald was able to wander from America to Russia with a great deal of ease, and it is not often easy for a onetime defector to return to his native land with a foreign-born wife and child and still keep up his Marxist enthusiasm. Oswald's income in Russia would have been enough to make the average man smell a red herring, yet the Commission found no basis for associating Oswald's income with Soviet undercover activities. Oswald also traveled easily within the U.S.S.R., although the few United States nationals living in that country could all testify that permission has to be obtained before traveling from one city to another. One American citizen living in the Soviet Union was fined for not getting permission to go from Odessa to Moscow; and since Oswald was a stateless person, one would have thought it would have been difficult for him to travel as he did.

When the Oswalds returned to the United States, they settled in Forth Worth, Texas, where there is a well-established group of Russian-born or Russian-speaking residents. In times of the Oswalds' marital troubles, members of the group were very kind to the couple. One person who became friendly with Oswald was Peter Paul Gregory, a consulting petroleum engineer and part-time Russian-language instructor at the Fort Worth Public Library. In fact, he became the key person who unlocked the doors for the Oswalds to meet almost fifty other Russian-speaking people in the area. About half this number testified before the Warren Commission and all agreed that Marina Oswald was the main reason for their friendship with the Oswalds. But what could the other twenty-five people have testified if they had been interviewed? It was from the Fort Worth Russian community that Dallas police elicited the aid of an interpreter, Ilya Nanantov, to help them in their questioning of Marina.

Mr. and Mrs. George De Mohrenschildt, of Dallas, a multi-lingual couple, kept up their acquaintance with the Oswalds during their residence in this town. Mrs. De Mohrenschildt backed up Marina's testimony that Oswald kept a rifle. When they gave their testimony to the Commission on April 23, 1964, the De Mohrenschildts were residents of Hawaii. Like Peter Paul Gregory, Mr. De Mohrenschildt was interested in oil exploration and had a master's degree in petroleum geology and engineering. George De Mohrenschildt was born in the Russian Ukraine, and his wife, Jeanne, was born in Harbin, China, of White Russian parents. The lone assassin, Lee Harvey Oswald, seemed to have quite a knack of being able to meet interesting people who had an eccentric life-style that enabled them to move freely in several countries. The Commission found nothing to link the De Mohrenschildts with any subversive groups.

Ruth Paine, who eventually became both landlady and friend of the Oswalds, also spoke Russian well and was introduced to the Oswalds by the De Mohrenschildts. According to the Warren Commission, Ruth Paine emerges as a lady who would merit the "Good Neighbor Award"; she was always there when she was needed. It was Mrs. Paine who discovered a draft of a letter Oswald wrote on November 9, 1963, to the Russian Embassy in Washington, indicating that he had gone to Mexico City to "confer with comrade Kostine in the Embassy of the Soviet Union, Mexico City." She did not report this letter to the FBI until November 23rd. Mrs. Paine was an active worker for the Young Friends Committee of North America. In cooperation with the Department of State, this group organized "pen pals" correspondence between young Russians and Americans. Her husband, Michael, was the son of a man who actively participated in the Trotskyite section of the Communist movement in the United States. Michael Paine had security clearance in his work as a research engineer for the Bell Helicopter Company of Fort Worth. This couple was another example of the type of interesting people Oswald, the nonentity, was able to meet. Mrs. Paine made available to the Commission her datebook and calendar, and her address-and-telephone-notation book, in which she seemed to have been very careful to note down any activities of the Oswalds. Apparently, the Commission found nothing unusual in an ordinary housewife keeping such notes and producing them voluntarily at the propitious time. The Commission also found nothing in the background of the Paines to associate them with the assassination of President Kennedy—except, of course, that they appeared to know the lone assassin very well, indeed, and thought fit to keep a record of his activities. One wonders how many landladies in the United States do this!

The Commission discovered that Oswald subscribed to *The Worker,* a publication of the Communist party. From the party offices, he received numerous pamphlets and publications. Arnold D. Johnson, director of the information and lecture bureau of the party, suggested in a letter dated September 19th that "Oswald should get in touch with the organization in New York and we will find some way of getting in touch with you in Baltimore." Oswald duly reported his changes of residence to Arnold Johnson.

When Oswald went to Mexico City, he produced documentary evidence that he was a member of the Communist party of the United States. This was later denied and the mistake attributed to some inaccurate notation on the papers made by Señora Duran, the Cuban consular employee who dealt with Oswald in Mexico City. The Warren Commission concluded that Oswald was not a bona fide member of the Communist party. This has never been cleared up satisfactorily, although it was known that Oswald did indeed make application to join the party. There is a good chance that he had been accepted, since he had spent two-and-a-half years in Russia. Letters sent by Oswald to the party have not been located.

Oswald also wrote to the Socialist Labor party, requesting literature about the association. Howard Twiford in Texas confirmed that he sent such literature to Oswald on September 11th. The material was sent to Oswald's post-office box number in Dallas. On his way to Mexico City, Oswald tried to contact Twiford at his home in Houston and spoke to Twiford's wife, identifying himself as a member of the Fair Play for Cuba Committee, a Communist Front organization. Arnold Peterson, national secretary for the Socialist Labor party, testified that no letters from Oswald were available, and the Warren Commission concluded that Oswald was not a member of this party.

In New Orleans during the period from the end of April to the end of September 1963, Oswald was actively engaged in activities for the Fair Play for Cuba movement. He applied for membership, which was granted, and he also applied for a charter to start a chapter of the association in New Orleans. Despite a letter from the association stating that he would come under pressure if he formed a chapter in New Orleans, Oswald said that he would go ahead anyway and rented Post Office Box Number 30061. He printed circulars proclaiming "Hands Off Cuba," and distributed handbills on three occasions. For this he was arrested and fined for creating a disturbance with anti-Castro Cuban refugees. He also appeared on local radio programs to discuss his activities, although he had no members in his chapter. Vincent T. Lee, former national director of the Fair Play for Cuba Committee, testified that the association did not authorize the creation of the New Orleans chapter.

All things considered, it seems that it would have

been very easy to discover whether Oswald had been motivated by Communist ideals to assassinate President Kennedy, but the Warren Commission seems to have developed a preconceived notion that it had to prove the lone-assassin theory. Yet here we have a self-avowed Marxist who was capable of leaving his country to live in the U.S.S.R., marry a Russian-born woman, be able to return with his wife and family to the United States, and immediately take up residence in a Russian-speaking community, where he met colorful people leading extraordinary lives with an interest in Russia.

The case for Oswald as "Oswaldovitch" could have been developed with just as much ease and more credibility than the lone-assassin theory except that it would have had very adverse reactions on the international political scene and the CIA withheld vital information. The Warren Commission dismissed far too much evidence of a tangible nature, for reasons best known to itself, but certainly not clear to anyone else studying the same evidence. Much that was hearsay was taken as the ultimate in truth, too much that was tangible was thrown away, and the Commission came out with a firm verdict that all Oswald's peregrinations from the United States to the U.S.S.R. and back again did not amount to anything more sinister than a coincidence. At its best, it was a necessary precaution to maintain the balance of peace in a world that was not yet ready for a third world war. At its worst, it was rank negligence to assess reasonable evidence of a viable link between Oswald and Communism. It was a plausible scenario made impossible by a deliberate attempt to negate facts by substituting fiction. On the basis of far less evidence, other people involved with Marxist indoctrination have been convicted or deported.

Lee Harvey Oswald was a dead man, himself the victim of a lone assassin. Yet the major inferences drawn from the background information on Oswald were that he was in an unusual position to mix freely with Russians and could have been part of a well-organized group of Communist-inspired conspirators.

It was too easy a solution and an uncomfortable scenario that had to be scrapped rather than rewritten, so the background of Oswald's Russian associates was never thoroughly probed. If that had happened, it may well have been that Michael and Ruth Paine would have emerged as more than "an overly friendly couple" interested in the welfare of a nonentity like Lee Harvey Oswald. What they said in evidence damned Oswald as an assassin but successfully guarded him from any association—especially one with Communist conspirators.

Oswald's Russian-born wife, Marina, revealed to the Commission that her husband had something to do with the attempted assassination of right-wing spokesman, Major General Edwin A. Walker in Dallas on April 10, 1963. Walker, an active and controversial figure since his resignation from the U.S. Army in 1961, narrowly escaped death when a rifle bullet fired from outside his home passed near his head as he sat at his desk. But, if Oswald, as a Communist, tried to kill Major General Walker, as Marina indicated in her testimony, why did the alert go out for *two men* after the shooting? A fourteen-year-old boy in the neighborhood claimed that he saw two men in separate cars drive out of the church parking lot adjacent to the Walker home immediately after the shooting. If Oswald was one of the two men, then who was the other one? No one knows to this day. With Oswald dead, it was easier to assume that he was solely responsible for the attack; anything was better than considering that there was still another potential assassin wandering around the streets. The letter in Marina's possession in which her husband wrote her what to do after the death of Walker—without mentioning any confederates—was damning to Oswald, but it was necessary in establishing that Oswald was a lone assassin and not part of a plot.

At another time, in another place, and with a different man, similar evidence would have been enough to show that an avowed Communist with many well-placed friends could have been a link in a Communist plot to assassinate President Kennedy.

Lee Harvey Oswald died at the right time, leaving the way clear for any evidence to be distorted and rearranged to make it convenient for the Warren Commission to state authoritatively that there was nothing to link Oswald with any other Communists interested in procuring the death of the President. This was needed for the lone-assassin theory to work!

Or did the answer really lie in Commission member Hale Boggs's open question to the entire Commission: "Could Castro, the target of at least three assassination attempts, have tried to even the score?" Was this more than just an idle thought? Could Castro have used Oswald for revenge? And did the Warren Commission purposely choose to overlook this vendetta in the name of "peace"? The same peace Earl Warren had assured President Johnson he would preserve when he left the White House, with tears in his eyes, after reconsidering his previous refusal to head such a commission.

7 | THE ANTI-CASTRO CUBAN SCENARIO

The first of the assassination scenarios to have a logical base was that of the anti-Castro group, with bases of activity in New Orleans, Los Angeles, and Miami. It was perhaps the most acceptable scenario to many Americans for, at the time of the Kennedy assassination, the United States was still smarting over the Bay of Pigs incident.

On the morning of April 17, 1961, more than fourteen hundred Cuban refugees, trained and equipped by the CIA, made a D-Day-type landing on the beaches of Las Villas Province on the southern coast of Cuba. Despite all the hopes and rumors that spread as quickly as the insurgents spread over the beach—without the promised air cover—their cause soon became hopeless, as Castro's jets and tanks cut off their supplies and slaughtered those within their ranks, reducing the invasion to a short-lived dream and the insurgent army to prisoners-of-war.

The country had soon become used to groups of Cubans immigrating, officially and unofficially, and they were hailed as heroes against the seemingly diabolic force of Fidel Castro—the epitome of the type of dictatorship that Americans had come to hate. However, no one took time to consider why Oswald, if he was an anti-Castro follower, should assassinate a President who had no sympathies toward Fidel Castro and his regime.

A tangled web of circumstances led to the Bay of Pigs episode. The skein stretches back to the Eisenhower Administration when Vice President Richard Nixon was placed in charge of the Forty-to-Twelve Committee, overseeing the CIA in what was to become known as the Bay of Pigs invasion.

By 1961, the CIA had infiltrated successfully into Cuba, and all was set for an invasion and the murder of Fidel Castro. But Kennedy refused to provide the air cover required for a successful coup. The Bay of Pigs quickly deteriorated into a tragic event, leaving certain CIA operatives with the feeling that they had been betrayed. They had risked men to pave the way for the coup and had also spent time and money preparing guerrilla troops for the invasions—all to no avail.

In charge of one of the training camps, of which there were two in Florida, was Loran Eugene Hall. Here was a man with a bizarre background, a colorful and controversial figure popping in and out of the investigations into the assassination of President Kennedy. In 1959, Hall was an organizer for an anti-Castro group of which David Ferrie, the air pilot and gunrunner, was a part. In 1963, Hall was arrested in Florida, and a load of arms and drugs was confiscated. An FBI report on November 23, 1963, indicates that an informant reported that Loran Hall redeemed a 30.06 rifle from a Los Angeles pawnshop. The FBI concluded that the rifle was *not* used in connection with the assassination of President Kennedy. Of course, a 30.06 rifle had been found in the Book Depository and Lee Harvey Oswald was in custody for questioning. All the FBI needed was *one* rifle . . . but two would have caused confusion and brought Loran Hall into the limelight where questioning would have revealed his CIA activities as well as his work in the anti-Castro group.

Hall's name appears in the testimony of Mrs. Sylvia Odio, who identified Oswald as one of the three men who visited her in Dallas, on September 26th or 27th, to solicit her aid as a Cuban expatriate in anti-Castro activities. A man introduced as "Leopoldo" was later identified from a photograph taken in Mexico City as Loran Eugene Hall and mistakenly labeled as "Lee Harvey Oswald." There is also another photograph in existence showing Hall with a rifle taken at the CIA guerrilla training school at No Name Key in Florida. This photograph shows a burly, thick-set man who fits exactly Mrs. Odio's description of the man she knew as "Leopoldo" and one who was associated with the anti-Castro group in New Orleans.

New Orleans District Attorney Jim Garrison tracked down Hall and tried to obtain his extradition from California to New Orleans in 1968. Hall fought Garrison's efforts to get him to testify but, on May 1st, he agreed to do so. Voluntarily, he went to the district attorney's office in New Orleans, admitting that he was present at meetings in California when the assassination of President Kennedy was discussed.

A short time before "The Warren Report" was released, the FBI located three men who appeared to answer the description given by Sylvia Odio about her visitors. With "The Warren Report" substantiating the lone-assassin theory, there was little danger now of Loran Hall being listened to. Three weeks after the FBI found the three men, Loran Eugene Hall and William Seymour were arrested by the Dallas police on a narcotics charge. Their arrest notation said: "Active in anti-Castro movement. Committee to Free Cuba." At this point, Hall admitted that he, Lawrence Howard, Jr., a Mexican-American from East Los Angeles, and Seymour had visited Sylvia Odio.

The importance of ascertaining exactly who visited Sylvia Odio was crucial. If it *was* Lee Harvey Oswald, whom Mrs. Odio swore was the man introduced to her as "Leopoldo," he could *not* have been in Mexico City when the CIA claimed he was. Even though Hall insisted that Seymour and Howard were with him, Seymour said he was not one of the trio but that he was working in Miami Beach at the time. Paychecks from a Miami Beach firm show that he was working there from September 5 to October 10, 1963. (The visits to Mrs. Odio were on September 26th or 27th.)

That still leaves the identity of the third man a mystery, and it *could* have been Lee Harvey Oswald. The FBI, on further questioning of Hall, accepted his explanation that he could have been mistaken about the presence of Howard, although it must be noted that William Seymour resembled Oswald in appearance. The FBI was content to present evidence to the Warren Commission that Oswald could not have been in Mrs. Odio's apartment and had time to get to Mexico City by bus from Amarillo. It ignored the evidence of Mrs. Horace Twiford of Houston, who stated that Oswald telephoned her husband in late September and commented that "he had only a few hours before flying to Mexico City." By air, Oswald could have been in Mrs. Odio's apartment at the time stated, as an agent of the anti-Castro Cuban faction, with two other men, and *also* in Mexico City.

No one can deny that Oswald had an interest in anti-Castro activities. Literature was found in his rooms after his arrest . . . but he also had the names and addresses of several interesting right-wing persons in his diary. One of these was Carlos Bringuer of the Cuban Student Directorate in New Orleans. He told the Commission that Oswald approached him and offered to train Cuban exiles in marine tactics, but he thought Oswald was a plant and did not go ahead with the suggestion. Three days later this same Bringuer saw Oswald distributing leaflets for the hated Fair Play for Cuba Committee and assaulted him, winding up in jail on a charge of disturbing the peace.

The address 544 Camp Street, New Orleans, Louisiana, was stamped on some of the literature Oswald had in his possession at the time of his arrest for disturbing the peace in New Orleans. Yet "The Warren Report," page 408, was not able to connect Oswald with this address—it was left for Jim Garrison to do this. Camp Street was the nerve center for a paramilitary right-wing group, and Oswald's ostentatious "Fair Play for Cuba" advocacy was nothing more than a facade. Number 544 Camp Street is the side entrance of 531 Lafayette Place, where Guy Bannister had his office. Bannister, a former FBI man, was a member of the Minutemen and head of the Anti-Communism League of the Caribbean, an intermediary between the CIA and insurgent movements in the Caribbean. Bannister died suddenly in the summer of 1964, as did his young investigator, Hugh F. Ward. He had been taught to fly by David Ferrie and crashed to his death in a Piper Aztec plane near Ciudad Victoria, Mexico, on May 23, 1965.

A walk-up staircase at 531 Lafayette or 544 Camp leads to the same second-floor space occupied by the Cuban Democratic Revolutionary Front and W. Guy Bannister and Associates. Bannister was one of the most verbose of anti-Castroites. He had been in charge of the FBI office in Chicago—hometown of Jack Ruby—but retired in 1955 to New Orleans, where he served as deputy superintendent of police for several years. A reliable source close to Bannister stated in a newspaper article of April 25, 1967, that he found up to one hundred boxes marked "Schlumberger" in Bannister's office storeroom early in 1961 before the Bay of Pigs episode. The boxes contained land mines, unique little missiles, and rifle grenades. The name "Schlumberger" links these boxes with the 1961 burglary of the Schlumberger Well Company, a munitions dump near New Orleans. At that time, a man named Gordon Novel was wanted for questioning concerning the burglary. When subpoenaed by a grand jury, Novel fled to McLean, Virginia, conveniently next door to the CIA complex at Langley.

There he took a lie-detector test administered by an intelligence officer. After that, Novel went to Montreal and then Columbus, Ohio, where Governor Rhodes refused to extradite him to Jim Garrison who also wanted to question him. Once cleared by the lie detector, Novel said that the burglary was the "most patriotic one in history" and that the munitions bunker was a CIA storehouse for the CIA's use in the impending Bay of Pigs invasion. He also stated that others connected with him, and with the knowledge of the CIA, were David Ferrie, Sergio Arcacha Smith, the New Orleans delegate to the Cuban Democratic Revolutionary Front—and formerly a member of deposed dictator Batista's diplomatic corps—and several Cubans. According to Novel, the munitions were dropped in his own office, at David Ferrie's home, and in Bannister's storehouse. Everything landed back in suite six at 544 Camp Street where the Cuban-liberation groups congregated.

In 1962, the C.D.R. Front closed down, and Arcacha founded the Crusade to Free Cuba, comprising a group of right-wingers. In March 1963, Arcacha moved to Houston and then to Dallas. Garrison was quick to associate Arcacha, Ferrie, and Novel with his investigations, but he could not persuade Governor Connally of Texas to extradite Arcacha.

Numerous witnesses linked Lee Harvey Oswald with the activities at 544 Camp Street, although the Warren Commission chose to ignore them. One of those witnesses was David Lewis, one of Bannister's investigators. Lewis states that in late 1962, he was having coffee in a restaurant next to 544 Camp Street when Cuban exile Carlos Quiroga came in with a young man whom he introduced as "Leon Oswald." Quiroga was an associate of Arcacha. A few days later, Lewis states positively that he saw Ferrie, Quiroga, and Oswald at 544 Camp Street and, about a week later, he interrupted a meeting of the three in Bannister's office. Lewis disappeared after becoming very upset about the sudden and unexplained deaths of Bannister and Ferrie.

Another Garrison witness, Perry Raymond Russo, identified "Leon Oswald" as Lee Harvey Oswald and also stated that on or about the night of September 16, 1963, Oswald, Ferrie, and Clay Shaw met in Ferrie's apartment to discuss the assassination of President Kennedy. He further stated that they talked about "one man who had to be sacrificed in order that the other two gunmen would have time to escape." The escape route was to be by a plane flown by Ferrie. A possible reason for bringing three such totally different men together was that they all had an involvement with the CIA as well as a link with the anti-Castro group.

In 1963, across the street from 544 Camp, was the Government building that housed the office of the CIA. Just one block away at 640 Magazine Street is the William B. Reily Company, where Oswald was employed from May 10 until July 19, 1963, earning the magnificent sum of $548.41 for 11 weeks' work. The personnel manager says that Oswald would disappear from his work for several hours and never gave a plausible answer for his absence. Could he have been paying a visit to the nearby CIA building? Many lines of investigation led to this conclusion, and it is further bolstered by the story of Donald P. Norton, who was in the CIA in 1957.

In September 1962, Norton was sent from Atlanta to Mexico with $50,000 for an anti-Castro group. He registered at the Yamajei Hotel in Monterrey where he was told he would be contacted by "Harvey Lee." The man arrived, and Norton said he looked like Lee Harvey Oswald, except that his hair seemed to be thicker. Lee took the money and gave Norton a briefcase containing documents, which he then delivered to a contact in an American oil company based in Calgary, Alberta, Canada. In 1958, Norton was on a courier trip to Cuba. He was told to meet his contact at the Eastern Air Lines counter at the Atlanta airport. The contact was David Ferrie. Ferrie gave Norton a phonograph record and in the jacket was $150,000 to be delivered by Norton to a Cuban television performer in Havana. The delivery was successfully accomplished. In 1966, Norton was still working for the CIA and was on an agency assignment to Freeport, Grand Bahamas. He returned to Miami where a contact told him "something was happening in New Orleans and he should take a long, quiet vacation." What was happening in New Orleans was an escalation of the Garrison probe, and Norton began to worry about the death of David Ferrie. So he contacted Garrison himself and was given a lie-detector test, which showed no indications of deception and verified his story as the truth.

The CIA official dossier on Oswald (CD 692) is still classified in the National Archives. Among its five documents are two FBI reports on Oswald, two from the American Embassy in Moscow, and one from the marines that deals with his activities at the Atsugi naval station. Oswald had a cryptogramatic clearance and took two courses in electronics in addition to learning Russian. (Whether it was self-taught or CIA-taught has never been learned.) The Warren Commission played down Oswald's proficiency in this difficult language, mainly on the evidence given by Marina Oswald. Yet his former marine comrade, Kerry Thornley, says that Oswald conversed in Russian every morning with John Rene Heindel while at Atsugi.

In an interview on New Orleans radio station WDSU on August 21, 1963, Oswald was less than articulate in his native language. The tape from the radio station, giving Oswald's views on Russia and the anti-Castro activities, is a lengthy mass of hemming and hawing that was deleted in the Warren Commission transcript. But it indicated that Oswald "was under the protection of the . . . uh, American Government," as he said in an obvious slip.

We find the CIA delivering large sums of money to anti-Castro groups of which Oswald and a number of witnesses were members. And then we find the constant reiteration in "The Warren Report" that Oswald was not only a lone assassin but he was a very lonely man as well. Too many leads point to Oswald meeting with the witnesses, most of them in the anti-Castro group, but many of them also with links to the CIA.

Moreover, for a lowly marine with very few friends, Oswald left much evidence of his intellectual status when his belongings were inventoried. His stereo Realist camera possessed highly complicated optical equipment. There was a Hanza camera, filters, a Wollensak 15 power telescope, Micron 6X binoculars, a great deal of film, and another small German camera.

In his address book, the word "microdots" appears on the same page as the address and telephone number of the Jaggars-Chiles-Stovall Company. German intelligence developed microdots during World War II, and they are still used as a means of communication. A document can be photographed and the negative reduced to a size that will fit on a pinhead . . . or a period. Such a microdot can be inserted in any written material . . . even a library book. FBI agents confiscated every book Oswald ever took out of the New Orleans library, which he hadn't returned and, in turn, they didn't return.

It is extremely difficult to believe that Oswald's political interests were limited to the anti-Castro group. His friendship with the bizarre Dave Ferrie is very significant, too. Ferrie trained pilots in Guatemala for the Bay of Pigs invasion, flew planes at extreme altitudes in clandestine flights, and may have been a pilot of one of the U-2 planes, with which Oswald was familiar during his sojourn at the marine base. In addition, Ferrie was Oswald's instructor in the civilian air patrol, a fact attested to by a picture hanging in Marguerita Oswald's living room.

Apart from the address on Camp Street, the Freedom for Cuba party had a house in Dallas at 32128 Harlendale, an area patrolled by Officer Tippit. Deputy Buddy Walthers, who looked through Oswald's belongings in the Paines' house, found leaflets in a barrel that were issued by the Freedom for Cuba group. On November 23,

1963, Walthers advised Dallas Secret Service Chief Forrest Sorrels about the house at 32128 Harlendale and the fact that some Cubans met there on the weekends and were possibly connected with the Freedom for Cuba party, of which Oswald was a member. The Secret Service took no immediate action to contact members of the group and, seven days after the President was shot, the Cubans moved out of the house. Walthers developed information that Oswald was a visitor to the house.

One of the strangest stories that has bobbed up from the caldron of rumors, red herrings, and testimonies from people who knew Oswald but who were never called upon to testify about his activities is that of Richard Case Nagell. Again, we find a link with the CIA, the anti-Castroites, and Oswald. Richard Nagell was a captain in the Korean War, who subsequently became a CIA agent. In 1957, he was injured in a plane crash in Cambodia. (It is important to remember that he was given his CIA training after the plane crash.) In the United States and three foreign countries, Nagell used the aliases of "Joseph Kramer" and "Robert Nolan." On September 20, 1963, Nagell walked into a bank in El Paso, Texas, fired a gun into the air, and then sat down, waiting to be arrested. He stated that he wanted to be arrested in order to have an alibi when "an assassination took place." He believed that "an assassination would take place about September 26th in Washington, D.C." He sent a registered letter to J. Edgar Hoover warning him of this, but never received an answer. On December 19, 1963, Nagell had a short . . . in fact, a remarkably short . . . interview with the FBI and made this statement according to the FBI: "For the record, he would like to say that his association with Oswald (meaning Lee Harvey Oswald) was purely social and that he had met him in Mexico City and in Texas."

Apparently, he was also in court on January 24, 1964, and, as he was being led away, he made wild comments to newsmen, accusing the FBI of not attempting to prevent the assassination of President Kennedy. He was a first offender, accused of discharging a firearm on Government-protected property. But in court he found that the Government literally threw the book at him, and he was sent to Leavenworth Prison. Nagell definitely states that Kennedy was assassinated because the anti-Castro group felt he had betrayed them.

The anti-Castro groups in New Orleans and Mexico City had a code name—"Bravo Club." Kennedy was to be given a "Christmas present" to be delivered on September 26, 1963. In New Orleans two members of the Bravo Club approached Lee Harvey Oswald at the Reily Company, where he was employed at the time, to enlist his aid. The idea appealed to Oswald and, in some way, Nagell thought it satisfied his ego. The site for the assassination was then moved from Washington, D.C., and at a later date arranged in Dallas. The "Bravo Club" sought the aid of the Dallas anti-Castroites, who worked under the code name of the "Delta Club." Nagell says that he was one of the CIA agents sent in to find out more about the plans and, that while the basic idea of the assassination was engendered by the anti-Castroites, there were also a number of right-wingers involved in the plot. Nagell got cold feet and decided he wanted out of the entire thing, so he set himself up to be arrested in order to have an alibi. In a self-prepared petition for habeas corpus, he stated, "I would rather be arrested than commit murder and treason." He also stated that the files of the FBI and CIA contained information on Oswald and that they knew he was using the aliases of Albert Hidell and Aleksei Hidel. Nagell charged the FBI with seizing private documents that he could have used in his defense after the arrest. One of the documents was a private notebook containing the names of CIA associates and the receipt for the registered letter sent to Hoover advising him of the assassination attempt.

A news report shortly after Nagell was sentenced to prison states that he was taken to the Federal medical center at Springfield, Missouri. This is a mental institution, and the implication was that Nagell suffered severe mental damage after the plane crash in Cambodia. But it was *after* this crash that he was trained in intelligence work. Either this indicates that the CIA was not very particular about the type of men it enlisted or that it was deemed advisable to represent him to the public as another deluded creature, in the same genre as Jack Ruby.

There is a third alternative that we must face today in the light of other disquieting evidence surfacing about the activities of the CIA when agents become a nuisance. While in prison, Nagell could have been fed LSD and by now could indeed be a gibbering idiot. Whatever the reason, Nagell is not in a position to make any more statements. If he had a fertile imagination, then he managed to ally it very closely to something resembling the truth. Hoover seems to have been the recipient of more than one letter advising him that assassination plots abounded. And Nagell's letter would not have been the first to be destroyed.

In reviewing the unofficial evidence of people connected with anti-Castro groups, we cannot eliminate the fact that this group could have been responsible for setting Oswald up as a patsy in order for more important members of the group to remain free. Perhaps Oswald should have been shot "while trying to make an escape." It would have saved many people in the anti-Castro group, the FBI, and the CIA a lot of trouble. But Oswald got away. When he was arrested, the shock of reality must have hit him. It is on record that he called out to newsmen: "I didn't kill anybody; I'm just a patsy." The possibility of a denouncement while in the Dallas jail presented a problem that was adequately solved by Jack Ruby and his well-placed bullet.

Jack Ruby favored sixty-six people with permanent passes to the Carousel Club, many of them local businessmen. One was given to Sue Blake, who lived at 10746 D Lake Gardens. She moved out of her apartment, and the next tenant was Sergio Arcacha Smith, formerly of 544 Camp Street, New Orleans. Another co-incidence? Perhaps.

The affinity of Jack Ruby with Cuba and Cuban immigrants is well documented. In January 1959, he made inquiries about buying some Jeeps to sell to Cuba and was concerned about releasing some Cuban prisoners. He also knew Houston resident Robert Ray McKeown, well-known throughout Texas as a friend of Castro. Ruby offered him $25,000 to use his influence to obtain the release of three Americans being held in Havana and gain a letter of introduction to Castro, stating that the money would "come from Las Vegas." On January 6, 1961, there was a news report that three Americans had escaped from the Havana jail and had made their way back to the United States. Ruby's old childhood friend, J. Matthews, visited him after a long absence, but was described in "The Warren [Commission] Report" as a "passing acquaintance of the Dallas nightclub owner." A few months later, Matthews was back in Havana where he spent a year in residence. On October 3, 1963, Ruby telephoned Matthews's ex-wife, who was living in Shreveport, Louisiana. Since he called from the Carousel Club, it was easy enough to trace this call, but Mrs. Matthews denied receiving it; and *that* apparently satisfied the Commission.

Thirty years ago, Matthews ran around with a crowd involved in shady dealings in the Dallas area, including Benny Binion, founder of the Horseshoe Club. Matthews may have been the most likely backer for the Jeep deal that Ruby tried to set up. Ruby went to Havana in September 1959, with Louis J. McWillie, and the Commission accepted Ruby's statement that it was purely for pleasure and that he got bored and left within a week. This is contrary to the statements made, though not to the Warren Commission, that, on his return from Havana, Ruby boasted that he was "in well with both sides" and knew Rolando Masferrer, a former Batista-regime senator who headed the dreaded private army of the dictator, "The Tigers." Masferrer was murdered in Florida in late 1975.

In the spring of 1962, Ruby again visited Havana, saying he wanted to "pick up an act for his nightclub." Somehow, he and many others found it easy enough to get around the travel restrictions on Americans visiting Cuba. Ruby returned without the act, and his employees remember that he was not inclined to talk about the trip.

Narcotics pass into the United States, many of them via Miami, Mexico City, and Havana. Ruby's association with narcotics goes back to more than a decade before the assassination. In 1956, a woman named Eileen Curry told the FBI that her lover, James Breen, went away with Ruby to an unnamed location, "where he had been shown movies of various border guards, both Mexican and American." She was worried that Breen was intrigued by the idea of making quick money and, when Breen failed to return after a trip to Mexico, she went to the FBI and told her story, which she also repeated after the assassination.

Nancy Rich Perrin told the Commission that she and her late husband went to a meeting in Dallas in 1962. There plans were discussed to smuggle guns into Cuba, and she stated that other people at the meeting were Jack Ruby, an army colonel, and a heavyset man who might have been a Cuban or a Mexican. She concluded that Ruby was the "bagman" who handled the funds and that the guns were to be obtained through a Mexican associate.

By 1962, Cuba had arranged a barter agreement with Red China in which Cuban sugar was exchanged for narcotics. Castro was not interested in keeping narcotics in his country, but needed to turn them into cash and did so through selling them to men who could give him American dollars. It was exactly the right type of merchandising for organized-crime elements with whom Ruby had been affiliated since his youthful days in Chicago. Guns were also just as useful as dollars, and Ruby must have known this; whatever the deal was, there was money to be made through it—and *that* was Ruby's "bag!" Since the CIA had infiltrated Cuba so successfully, there was not much in the way of intrigues of which they were not aware.

After the assassination of President Kennedy, a weapons expert, Gary Underhill, told friends that a semi-autonomous CIA group running a profitable business in guns and narcotics was also implicated in the assassination. Within a few months he was found dead with a bullet wound in his head. The official verdict was suicide, although the circumstances would seem to have warranted more investigation, like so many of the sudden deaths that occurred to people who said too much about the assassination.

The decision by the Commission that Oswald and Ruby did not know each other is a remarkable bit of juxtaposition of tangible evidence. They knew too many of the same people and moved too closely in the same circles. At least a dozen newsmen who were in the basement when Ruby shot Oswald will swear that they saw a flicker of recognition in the moment of confrontation.

Even if we tend to consider this as a myth, there is still too much tangible evidence that links the two together. In Oswald's address book was the telephone number of a Fort Worth television station—PE 8-1951. In June 1963, Ruby called this number. On September 24th, David Ferrie's telephone account indicated he was charged for a call to Chicago, number WH 4-4870. This number was called from Kansas City by Ruby's boyhood friend, Lawrence Meyers. Dallas number FR 5-5591 is twice noted in Oswald's address book. The number belongs to Kenneth Cody who is an uncle to Dallas Police Officer Joseph Cody. In the homicide bureau, Cody worked with Detective James R. Leavelle. He was one of the officers escorting Oswald through the basement when Oswald was shot by Ruby. He admitted knowing Jack Ruby and said that he met Ruby several times at Fair Park where Cody enjoyed skating.

Now we come back to Loran Eugene Hall and October 1963, when an amazing number of people just happened to converge on Dallas. Oswald returned from Mexico and checked into the YMCA on North Ervay, not far from the Free Cuban group residing in the Harlendale house. During the two days Oswald stayed at the YMCA, the room next to him was occupied by a Cuban man registered as R. Narvaez, who also stayed for two days. On the night of October 17th, Loran Hall arrived at the same YMCA with Lawrence Howard, and they stayed until October 22nd. A Garrison witness states that at this time Hall was financially embarrassed and asked him to make a substantial donation to the anti-Castro movement. The witness declined but gave Hall $50 and, in exchange for this, Hall gave him a .30-caliber rifle as collateral. A month before the assassination, Hall redeemed the rifle, saying he was going to Dallas to meet with a wealthy oilman. It was this same oilman who posted bail for Hall and Seymour when they were arrested in mid-October. No record now remains of these arrests, and it was not until "The Warren Report" was ready for publication that the FBI managed to locate and interview Seymour. However, Garrison's witness positively states that he was himself questioned about Hall the day *after* the assassination.

Was it a coincidence that Oswald and Ruby shared more than a few telephone numbers together and that a CIA guerrilla trainer, Loran Eugene Hall, and his friends were at the YMCA at the same time as Oswald? Or that both men had strong affiliations with anti-Castro groups?

The more we study the many scenarios connected with the assassination of President Kennedy, the less we believe in coincidence. And, if we do not see coincidence, the alternative is frightening: that two or more men got together as "conspirators" to plan for the dramatic elimination of President Kennedy, the man whom the CIA and the anti-Castroites believed had betrayed them during the Bay of Pigs episode.

For, as one Cuban adventurer stated in the aftermath of November 22nd, many wealthy backers in Miami and New Orleans "would have given money to see Kennedy dead!"

Did they?

8 | THE MILITARY-INDUSTRIAL-COMPLEX SCENARIO

Since 1973, the world, and the United States in particular, has been oil-conscious, almost as if this treacherous substance had only *just* been discovered. For we had only begun to realize that oil was as valuable a commodity as gold and that it could be used as a lethal weapon.

Oil was not only needed during wartime; it could be bartered for guns and ammunition in times of peace. No matter how you looked at oil, it represented big-business complexes that have infiltrated every area of life: gold, oil, and drugs . . . The G.O.D. Machine . . . which we have accepted through the subtle brainwashing of big-business interests to become the deity of modern living.

But, even more than that, big business has become an integral part of the Government and its vast, ever-growing military machine.

During the Civil War, President Abraham Lincoln opposed the Union army generals and Secretary of War Edwin M. Stanton in their plan to occupy the defeated South with a massive punishing arm. Instead, President Lincoln thought that Federal dollars would be better employed in a gigantic reconstruction project. A lone assassin, John Wilkes Booth—albeit aided and abetted by others, but "lone" in the traditional meaning of the word—assassinated President Lincoln. In President McKinley's term of office, the Spanish-American War was fought and won, with Cuba as the prize plum. McKinley did not want military occupation of Cuba, but the United States military establishment wanted Cuba as an American possession. President McKinley was *also* murdered, this time by Leon Czolgosz, another lone assassin.

The precedent for the removal of troublesome Presidents who were not prepared to play the war game was well established by the time President Kennedy was shot. Booth, Czolgosz, and Oswald tore into the annals of history as crazy murderers who *alone* determined to eliminate Chief Executives. Or so it was originally thought.

The post-assassination years of all three assassins brought out theories that in all cases there were enough logical reasons for each of them to have been part of a conspiracy. And behind the conspiracy in every case was an industrial-military complex. If such a complex forced the issue of this nation into a particular path, it is too late now to do or think much about Booth and Czolgosz. But it is different—far different—in the case of Oswald. We are still living in times when millions of people remember President Kennedy, the man and his work, and the trail is still warm enough to follow up clues that seem to escape the distorted vision of the Warren Commission.

Had President Kennedy lived until November 24th, he would have been present at a conference scheduled that day to discuss American involvement in Vietnam. Also present would have been Henry Cabot Lodge, our ambassador to Vietnam, and General Maxwell Taylor, commander-in-chief of the United States forces in Vietnam. Both of these men were in Washington for the meeting, and the big question to be posed was, "Where does America go from here?" No doubt the assassination of

Vietnamese President Nguyn Diem would also have been discussed, since his death had taken place earlier in November 1963. Had Kennedy lived, we would not have gone through another ten years of war before withdrawing our combat troops from Vietnamese soil. Many young Americans would not only be alive today, but billions of dollars would never have been made by the industrial machine that thrives on war. For President Kennedy had begun to express his doubts about continuing to support the effort in Vietnam. He also favored a period of détente with Russia and had engineered the first workable nuclear test-ban treaty. Kennedy had said: "I want American troops home after Christmas," and the year was 1963.

But, most importantly, he had called for an end to the 27.5 percent oil-depletion allowance. These moves, perhaps not singularly but, assuredly in toto, struck at the heart of the industrial-military complex. The cold war without détente was worth eighty billion dollars a year in profit, and men have killed for much less. Thirty pieces of silver was the going price for treachery and conspiracy but, like the cost of living, it has steadily increased!

It is no longer inconceivable to think that the American military machine was involved in a plot to assassinate President Kennedy or that the gigantic industrial complex assisted in the gigantic cover-up. President Kennedy himself did not regard a military take-over as implausible. He had expressed his feelings concerning such a take-over to Paul B. Fay, Jr., on the Kennedy yacht, the *Honey Fitz*, in a discussion about the book *Seven Days in May*.

PRESIDENT KENNEDY: "It is possible. It could happen in this country, but the conditions would have to be just right."

Kennedy went on to outline the conditions to Fay:

1. The country would have to be under the leadership of a young President.
2. There would be a Bay of Pigs episode.

3. Military criticism of the President would inevitably follow.

4. Then, if there were another Bay of Pigs, the military would consider overthrowing the elected establishment.

5. "Yes, if there were a third Bay of Pigs, it could happen."

The President concluded his colloquy with, "But it won't happen on my watch."

Or could it? These were the exact conditions that occurred during the Kennedy Administration. President Kennedy was young, there was a Bay of Pigs episode, and the missile crisis that followed did not result in the expected bombing of Cuba as military advisers had urged. Instead, there was a détente with Russia, and this was followed by the nuclear test-ban treaty. A third Bay of Pigs was vehemently opposed by the Joint Chiefs of Staff.

Just as there is enough evidence for any of the other scenarios, there exists enough evidence to indicate military involvement in the J.F.K. assassination.

It was unusual for Commander James J. Humes, the head of the navy autopsy team, to destroy the original autopsy notes. The autopsy was under the control of an army general who was not trained in forensic medicine and didn't complete the autopsy in an acceptable manner. Then the findings of the autopsy team, minus papers to refer to, were contrary to the findings of the non-military physicians at Parkland Hospital. The pathologists were directed *not* to look at the neck wound of the President, and no X-rays were turned over to the Warren Commission by the military team. Instead of being severely reprimanded for being careless enough to lose autopsy papers, Commander Humes was promoted to the rank of captain.

There are some people who excuse the loss of the autopsy papers by saying they were destroyed at the request of Rose Kennedy, who did not want the world to know that America's first Catholic President had recently

Alleged assassin Lee Harvey Oswald at the moment of his own assassination by Jack Ruby, while police officers J. R. Lavelle (left) and L. C. Graves react.

The famous "fake" Oswald photo. Note the faint line under his lower lip and across his cheek, the best place to superimpose a head shot. Oswald was shown the picture while in police custody and said, "That's my head, but not my body."

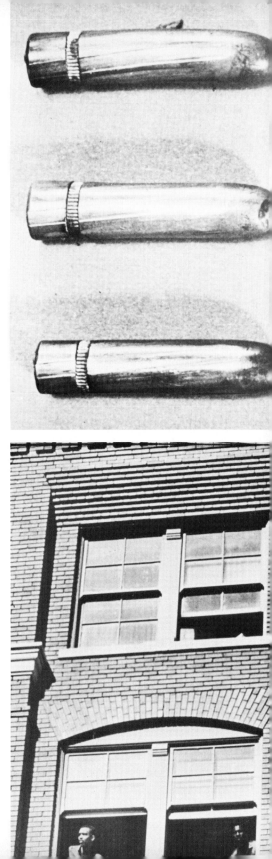

(Top left)   Two pictures of John Kennedy's bloodstained shirt which show that the first (or "magic") bullet struck him lower—much lower than the Warren Commission indicated.

(Top right)   The infamous single bullet (middle) whose magical qualities supposedly enabled it to pass through Kennedy's upper torso, then through Governor John Connally's chest, his right wrist, and thigh, losing only 2 to 2.5 grams in weight.

(Right)   The fifth and sixth floor windows of the Texas School Book Depository Building three seconds after the shooting. The alleged gun perch can be seen in the open sixth floor window. Note the two men, Harold Norman and James Jarman, Jr. at the fifth floor window.

Oswald passing out leaflets for his "Fair Play for Cuba Committee" in New Orleans in the summer of 1963. A rare sample of the handbill.

Photo taken seconds after the shooting of JFK. Note LBJ in third car as Agent Rufus Youngblood starts to push him to floor and Vice-Presidential Secret Service car doors already opened by emerging Secret Service men.

The presidential limousine as it passes in front of the Texas School Book Depository Building at 12:30 P.M., C.S.T., November 22, 1963.

The Dallas motorcade route to the Trade Mart, right from Main Street onto Houston Street and left onto Elm past the Texas School Book Depository Building.

Robert Kennedy flashing the victory sign at Los Angeles' Ambassador Hotel, after winning the California state primary, moments before being shot.

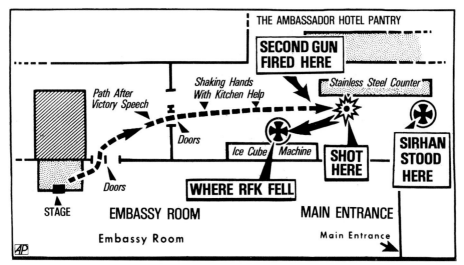

THE AMBASSADOR HOTEL PANTRY

SECOND GUN FIRED HERE

Path After Victory Speech

Shaking Hands With Kitchen Help

Stainless Steel Counter

Doors

Ice Cube Machine

SHOT HERE

SIRHAN STOOD HERE

WHERE RFK FELL

STAGE

EMBASSY ROOM

Embassy Room

MAIN ENTRANCE

Main Entrance

Doors

RFK's path from the stage in the Embassy Room to the Ambassador Hotel kitchen. Note the alleged position of the "second gun."

(Left) The fatally injured Robert Kennedy lies on the floor of the Ambassador Hotel kitchen clutching his rosary beads. (Right) The alleged assassin of RFK, Sirhan Sirhan, being led away from the Ambassador Hotel after the shooting.

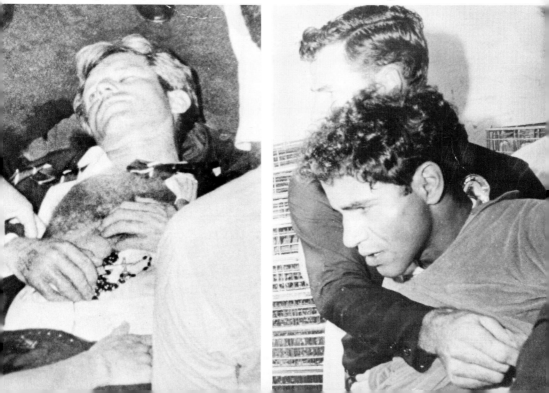

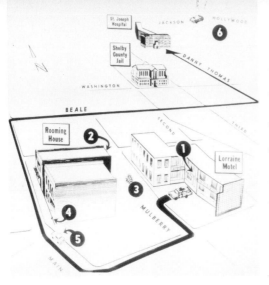

Diagram of Lorraine Motel (1) where Dr. Martin Luther King, Jr. was shot on April 4, 1968; the rooming house (2) from which the fatal shot was allegedly fired; the thicket (3) where witnesses saw a man emerge immediately after the shooting; the spot where the rifle, supposedly used in the assassination, was recovered (4); and the place where a white Mustang was spotted leaving after the shooting (5).

Dr. King on the balcony of the Lorraine Motel flanked by aides Jesse Jackson (left) and Rev. Ralph Abernathy (right).

Seconds after the tragedy: King's aides and the stricken Dr. King on the balcony. Police can be seen coming into the courtyard and drawing their revolvers.

Dr. King's alleged assassin, James Earl Ray, alias Eric Starvo Galt, shown on an FBI "Most Wanted" flyer.

Arthur Bremer, alleged assailant of Governor George Wallace, in Laurel, Maryland, May 16, 1972, wearing a Wallace button and sunglasses.

BREMER

Bremer shoots Wallace at the Laurel shopping center, leaving the stricken Wallace on the ground bleeding.

had a vasectomy. But, if true, we doubt that this was reason enough to warrant destroying invaluable autopsy notes!

Although there has been a lovers' quarrel in recent days between the military and the CIA, at the time of the assassination their interests coincided and they found a mutual enemy in Kennedy. He had undermined both by not providing air cover at the Bay of Pigs. Colonel L. Fletcher Prouty, a director of special operations for the Joint Chiefs of Staff in 1962 and 1963, said that Kennedy issued two directives in 1961 designed to severely limit the power of the CIA. With the military always anxious to maintain a state of war, the motive for the assassination could be viewed as a perverted version of extreme patriotism.

Although America was acutely involved in military activities in Vietnam in 1963, there had never been, and subsequently never was, any *official* declaration of war. The activities were of a covert nature, a terrifying tip of an iceberg that was apparent to the public with the other five-sixths well contained within the consciousness of the military and the insidious CIA. And, over all, lurked the invisible giant of big business, which had so much to gain financially by not only keeping up but actually stepping up the war action.

In May 1963, William Henderson, an official of the Socony Mobil Company, publicly joined those urging President Kennedy to escalate the covert activities in Vietnam. The Socony Company gets its name from the initials of the Standard Oil Company whose trust was officially dissolved in 1911. But, to this day, the Rockefeller family still owns the controlling stock in it. The Socony Company inherited all the major economic interests in Asia when the Standard Oil empire was broken up. Several generations of public-relations experts have led the public to believe that the Rockefellers are really out of the oil business, completely divorced from such a mundane occupation as the continued accumulation of wealth and dedicated only to cultural and humanitarian projects. The family is well known for its liberal and reformist politics in New York, West Virginia, and Arkansas. Against this, the public-relations experts imply that the Standard Oil Companies and their subsidiaries go their own way on a much less elevated plane. But such is *not* the case!

Early in 1963, Socony Mobil gave a party at its research laboratory in Dallas, which Lee Harvey Oswald attended. It was here that Oswald met Ruth Paine, the ministering angel who was to keep an eye on Oswald and his wife until that fateful day, November 22nd. The hosts of the party were Everett Glover and Betty MacDonald, who talked to Oswald and his wife, Marina. At one time, Betty MacDonald worked for nightclub owner Jack Ruby. Later, Betty MacDonald was strangled in jail after providing an alibi for a man accused of shooting Warren Reynolds, the man who witnessed the flight of Officer J. D. Tippit's murderer. Considering Oswald was something of a nonentity, he was able to mix freely with a number of very interesting personalities at the Socony party, many of whom were employees of the company. One such employee was Volkmar Schmidt. At one session of the Warren Commission, lawyer Albert Jenner asked witness Bernard Weissman if Volkmar Schmidt and Larrie Schmidt were brothers. Weissman replied that he had never heard of Volkmar Schmidt, and neither Larrie nor Volkmar were questioned by the Commission. Both had recently arrived in the United States from Germany, and it was Larrie who, on October 26th, staged a demonstration against Adlai Stevenson. He also wrote the black-bordered advertisement asking questions about President Kennedy that appeared in *The Dallas Morning News* on November 22, 1963. It was enough to warrant questioning him, but the Warren Commission thought otherwise. Schmidt also worked with Warren Carroll, described as a "former CIA man." At the time Carroll was writing for the "Life Line" program, a syndicated radio show sponsored by Texas millionaire H. L. Hunt.

The program told listeners of Kennedy's tyranny in 1963 and urged extreme patriotism. On the very morning of the assassination, the program warned listeners that it would soon be too late to stop Kennedy, for they would shortly find "no firearms are permitted to the people, weapons with which to rise up against their oppressors." (The "Life Line" program was sponsored by Hunt Oil, Gulf Oil, Sun Oil, Standard Oil of New Jersey—which owns fifty percent of Socony Mobil—Standard of Indiana, Ohio Oil, and a few non-oil companies.)

Oil power counted in both Texas and national politics then, and continues to do so right until the present day.

Adlai Stevenson did not realize that he was being attacked at all levels by Warren Carroll and Larrie Schmidt, who were fast making Dallas into the "Hate Capital of the World." Stevenson warned Kennedy not to come to Dallas because of dangerous right-wing bigots, but to no avail.

In fact, Kennedy's Dallas trip was occasioned by then Secretary of the Air Force, Eugene Zuckert's suggestion that he visit the new General Dynamics TFX plant in San Antonio—a monument to the strength of the military-industrial complex. His tour—expanded to include Fort Worth and Dallas—culminating in his death, may have become an even bigger monument to the same complex.

When Marina Oswald was called upon to give her evidence she did so in her native language—Russian. Jack Chrichton, an independent oil operator connected with the Army Reserve Intelligence, called Ilya A. Mamatov to act as translator at the Dallas Police Station on November 22nd. Mamatov taught Russian at the Socony Mobil Research Laboratory.

In September 1963, Clifton C. Carter, now deceased, set up an office in Austin, Texas. He was chief adviser to then Vice President Lyndon B. Johnson. A former intelligence agent, he commanded OSS operations in Italy during World War II. His brother was General Marshall

S. Carter, a deputy director of the CIA who later became head of the National Security Agency, engaged in communications intelligence. Clifton Carter was himself manning communications on November 22nd from a car following the one in which Johnson was riding. Behind Carter in the motorcade was Dallas's mayor, Earle Cabell, brother of General Charles Cabell, General Carter's predecessor as deputy director of the CIA.

Cilfton Carter remained close to President Johnson for several days after the assassination and, during the first part of the Johnson Presidency, he visited him every day at the White House, although he was never actually employed there.

Nelson Rockefeller was advising the new CIA director, John McCone, at that time. McCone owned a million dollars' worth of stock in Standard Oil of California. It was Rockefeller who recommended General Marshall S. Carter as the new deputy director of the CIA. As recently as 1971, Nelson Rockefeller was still advising the intelligence community. It must have been a sensitive and important position because, at the time of the Attica prison riot, Rockefeller was in Washington, attending a meeting of the Foreign Intelligence Advisory Board. Since 1936, all covert war activities had to be approved by this little-known "special group" of the White House. This makes a farce of the Rockefeller Commission that was conveniently set up to examine CIA operations in 1974, a group designed to investigate itself and quickly structured to counteract Senator Church's subcommittee. But the public was kept well in the dark about Rockefeller and his powerful position as adviser and even about the "special group."

McGeorge Bundy was Kennedy's liaison officer and continued in that position under Johnson. It was Bundy who first indicated that "there was no conspiracy." This seemingly innocuous remark takes on greater implication when we realize that Bundy was closely connected with the military complex and that his brother, William, was Assistant Secretary of Defense for International Security Affairs in 1963. According to Colonel Fletcher Prouty, who served for nine years as Pentagon liaison officer for all CIA military activities, William Bundy "was used as a conduit by the CIA to get its schemes for Vietnam to and past such men as McNamara and Rusk."

As Director of National Security, McGeorge Bundy was able to direct the CIA and coordinate intelligence from the State and Defense Departments, operating under the National Security Act, passed on July 26, 1947 by Congress.

President Johnson, shortly after becoming the Chief Executive, confided to General Eisenhower that he felt very confident about domestic affairs, but did not know enough about foreign affairs or feel that he had a staff good enough to handle it. Eisenhower suggested that some of his former advisers could help the new President and, until the 1964 election, Johnson concentrated on the "Great Society," leaving foreign affairs almost entirely in the hands of Secretary Rusk and McGeorge Bundy. It did not take long for their power to be felt in the United States.

On Johnson's first day as President, McGeorge Bundy accompanied the President into the Situation Room at the White House, where they met with the director of the Central Intelligence Agency, John McCone, to discuss national security and foreign affairs. The next day at ten A.M., McCone and Bundy went to the President's Spring Valley home in Washington, D.C. to discuss foreign affairs and prepare Johnson for a special meeting that afternoon. The meeting took place with Henry Cabot Lodge and top national-security advisers present, and the topic of discussion was mainly Southeast Asia. Within a few hours of his meeting, the news broke that President Johnson had pledged the United States to continue to give "aid to Vietnam." ·

Each year after the assassination we become more aware of just what "aid to Vietnam" meant in terms of men, munitions, and a vast military machine operating

in that country. And there was now some question
whether President Johnson was following through with
his predecessor's expressed desire to "have all American
troops back home after Christmas." The festive occasion
came and went in 1963, and the nation was still mourning President Kennedy when on March 27, 1964, a
memorandum from the office of the Secretary of Defense
directed: "Previous guidance re Model Plan Projection
for phase-down of U.S. forces and government of South
Vietnam is superseded. Policy is as announced by the
White House 17 March 1964. . . ." It was the coup de
grace to the withdrawal plan, and the United States was
committed to an undeclared war. And soon seven-and-a-
half-ton bombs were falling on the tiny Southeast Asian
country.

A prediction made in 1921 by Senator W. E. Borah
was being fulfilled. At that time, he said: "To promote
their vast designs, these oil magnates are capable of
starting revolutions in Mexico, instigating civil wars in
Asia, or setting fire to Europe and the world. . . ." With
the help of the CIA, the United States war machine, and
the industrial complex, mainly comprising oilmen, this
became true—starting in 1963.

A lot of important people in the military-industrial
complex had much to gain by the death of President
Kennedy and were able to move very quickly after his
death to put their plans into effect.

The military-industrial members did not often conceal
their satisfaction at the death of President Kennedy.
Writer Karl Oglesby remembers: "I was sitting at my
desk as military editor for the military-industrial complex when the assassination took place. And, as soon as
the word spread through the company, everyone made
the assumption that a right-wing conspiracy was behind
it. It had something to do with Kennedy's handling of
the defense budget. I was editor for the Bendix Systems
Division, and that is where I was when I heard. I
remember that . . . everyone remembers where they
were, and I remember how the company reacted. Mostly

glee. Upper management . . . there was a lot of suppressed happiness. You could feel that they were not going to have any more of this Massachusetts nonsense of scaling down the defense budget every year and of cancelling nice fat missile projects. Because Kennedy had just cancelled one, the TFX missile, the Eagle missile. Everyone just sensed Johnson was different, was something else."

The famous "Pentagon Papers" shocked the nation. Their release—in an edited version—in *The New York Times* and *The Washington Post* as well as the trial of the man accused of releasing them, Daniel Ellsberg, and the subsequent burglary of the office of his psychiatrist focused the mind of the nation on the enormous escalation of the war in Vietnam.

Senator Gravel of Alaska did his best to alert the country to the real danger of the war when he produced the unedited version of "The Pentagon Papers," including the following pertinent information:

A formal planning and budgetary process for the phased withdrawal of U. S. forces from Vietnam was begun amid the euphoria and optimism of July 1962, and was ended in the pessimism of March 1964.

The rationale behind the phased-withdrawal policy was by and large internally consistent and sensible.

To put Vietnam in the perspective of other U. S. world interests. Vietnam, at this time, was not the focal point of attention in Washington. . . . Even in terms of Southeast Asia itself, Laos, not Vietnam, was the central concern . . .

To avoid an open-ended Asian mainland land war . . . this was a central tenet of U. S. national-security policy and domestic politics . . .

To treat the insurgency as fundamentally a Vietnamese matter, best solved by the Vietnamese themselves . . .

To increase the pressure on the GVN, Government of South Vietnam, to make the necessary reforms . . .

To put the lid on inevitable bureaucratic and political pressures for increased U. S. involvement and inputs into

Vietnam. It was to be expected and anticipated that those intimately involved in the Vietnam problem would be wanting more U. S. resources to handle the problem.

Pressures for greater effort, it was reasoned, eventually would come into play unless counteracted . . .

To deal with international and domestic criticism and pressures. While Vietnam was not a front-burner item, there were those who already had begun to question and offer non-consensus alternatives . . .

The White House issued a U.S. policy statement on Vietnam on October 2, 1963,

. . . Secretary McNamara and General Taylor reported their judgment that the major part of the U.S. military task can be completed by the end of 1964, although there may be a continuing requirement for a limited number of U.S. training personnel. [Emphasis added.] They reported that by the end of this year, the U.S. program for training Vietnamese should have progressed to the point where one thousand U.S. military personnel assigned to South Vietnam can be withdrawn . . .

Strangely, as a result of the public White House promise in October and the power of the wheels set up in motion, *the U.S. did effect a one thousand man withdrawal in December of 1963.* [Emphasis added.] All the planning for phase-out, however, was either ignored or caught up in the new thinking of January to March 1964, that preceded NSAM, National Security Action Memorandum 288.

"Phased withdrawal was a good policy that was being reasonably well executed. In the way of our Vietnam involvement, it was overtaken by events . . ."

Listed in the Chronology of "Phased Withdrawal of U.S. Forces, 1962–64" is,

"3 Dec. 6 (material missing) Region/ISA, Office of International Security Affairs, The Department of Defense, Memorandum for the ASD/ISA, Assistant Secretary of Defense International Security Affairs, (word missing) nam developments, for a 'fresh new look' at the program, second-echelon leaders outlined a broad interdepartmental 'Review of the South Vietnam Situation.' . . .

"*Before the month of March was over the CPSVN, comprehensive Plan for South Vietnam . . . finally received the coup de grace . . . (it was) formally terminated, for the record, on 27 March (1964) in the OSD, Office of the Secretary of Defense,* [Emphasis added.] message reproduced below: . . . 3. Previous guidance re Model Plan Projection for phase-down of U.S. Forces and GVN forces is superseded . . .*"*

Thus ended *de jure* the policy of phase-out and withdrawal and all the plans and programs oriented to it. Shortly, they would be canceled *de facto*.

American oil interests, the Central Intelligence Agency, and the military machine had achieved all they had set out to do—none of which would have been accomplished had President Kennedy lived to fulfill his term of office. Time neither became a healing factor nor wiped out the memory of the assassination or the horrors that it unleashed. And more then eighty billion dollars' worth of war equipment flowed into Vietnam. The oilmen kept their interests intact, and the CIA had a vast area to operate in . . . gold, oil, and drugs. The New G.O.D. Machine was running smoothly, even though we paid dearly for a war that never could end in victory for the United States.

Even that was never part of the plan. With the vast resources of American war technology, it seemed logical to most Americans that we *had* to win the war over a small group of insurgents backed by a small country. No one could figure out why we weren't "winning"—an American neurosis. The answer was that a continuing war spelled money for those who had no sense of sorrow about the death of a President, so how could they have a conscience about the death of American soldiers? All was right in their world as long as fortunes could be made; and the fortunes were made not only by the businessmen.

The military-industrial complex was merciless in wielding its power through the days of President Johnson and into the administration of Richard Nixon. It did not stop when Nixon went into exile with a pardon for crimes he may have been part of, but for which he was never given the chance to defend himself. And then came the administration of Gerald Ford, a member of the Warren Commission.

We have come full circle to where it all began . . . with the cover-up story officially condoned by the Warren Commission and its verdict that there was "no conspiracy."

If it was not so diabolically serious, we could see this verdict as the biggest hoax ever perpetrated on a nation, but the military-industrial complex was never, and still is not, a joking matter.

For, unlike the actual assassins of Kennedy, Martin Luther King, and Robert Kennedy, the real possibility exists that those involved in this scenario are still at-large and still creating their own moneyed beat for us to march to. Was it the drumbeat of assassination?

9 | THE RIGHT-WING-EXTREMIST SCENARIO

Great men in history always make mistakes, but death has a way of giving most of them a dispensation so that we remember such men for their positive achievements. And sometimes we even imbue them with a more Godlike stature than they deserve. Great men also make as many enemies as friends. President Kennedy was no exception.

Shocked as the nation was at the assassination, there were many people in all walks of life who had little good to say about any of the Kennedys. The Camelot designation and motif for the Kennedy Administration was fostered by press agents delighted for once to have a handsome young man in the White House with a wife who compelled attention and brought an aura of culture to the home of the Chief Executive. Besides, it was necessary to soft-pedal some of the background of the family history of the Kennedys—especially the life of J.F.K.'s father, Joseph Kennedy. Many people still remembered him as a tough man who made his fortune quickly in a quasi-mysterious manner and with little regard for other people. The taint of the Kennedys and their fantastic fortunes were not quite in keeping with the public's idea of a President with a democratic outlook. Most of all, John Kennedy was no fool and, despite his youthfulness, he had inherited much of the tenacity of his mother and the stubbornness of his father.

While the press ground out his virtues, John Kennedy knew he had enemies who were not deluded by Camelot and saw him as a danger to their interests. He was also blunt rather than diplomatic, and once said: "Right-wing extremists are a greater threat than the Communists." And America had plenty of right wingers who surfaced during his administration.

There were the ultra-right-wing fanatics, too—the paramilitarists who had many of the qualities of the Fascists, with dreams of taking over the world. It would be a mistake merely to think of the Minutemen as childish "patriots," content to play with guns and dress up in uniforms. The truth is that they were a new breed of revolutionary in America, a country that had never had the close association with the Fascism most Europeans knew. Once Europe had ignored the youthful Brownshirts of Hitler and jeered at them as "Boy Scouts trying to be military men"; but Europe lived to see the holocaust wrought by the Nazis. Ignoring the rise of Fascism took Europe back into the Middle Ages, and the Continent has barely recovered three decades after the war. Yet, some Americans viewed Fascism as the right and proper course, and praised Hitler's Brownshirts as dedicated men of ultra patriotism who were prepared to bring Germany back into power.

During the Kennedy Administration, some of these same domestic ultra-patriotic groups propagated and propounded identical ideological claptrap, yet they took action as well. Not only did they direct minor offensives toward the Jews of America, but there was also a burning hatred of black people and the newly discovered black power.

From time to time the country has been aware of the Ku Klux Klan, the most prototypically American of all

secret societies. But another group—the Minutemen—
emerged during the 1960s, and was not content to remain silent. They began to show their predilection
toward gaining their political ends through violence and
intrigue. At an early meeting of Minutemen in California, the rhetoric frequently dealt with assassination as
the only way to cleanse the country and make it fit for
patriots to live in. There were death threats to the three
"K's" . . . Kennedy, King, and Kennedy.

It is not easy to associate Lee Harvey Oswald with
the right-wing extremists except as a "patsy," because
Oswald was a self-proclaimed Marxist, the type of Communist the Minutemen were swearing vengeance upon.
Or was he? For we know that Oswald was associated
with all too many extreme groups. According to reports,
Oswald was a chameleon who could change his political
affiliations within twenty-four hours. He used the 544
Camp Street, New Orleans, address on his Fair Play for
Cuba literature, but it was also the headquarters of two
right wingers, Guy Bannister and Jack Martin.

If a conspiracy and cover-up story had been planned,
then by creating the confused issues in the life of the
captured assassin, the plot was likely to succeed. Obvious
and non-obvious clues continually emerged, but not as
satisfying facts because they were never meant to do so.
We have the picture of Oswald as a Marxist, yet he
knew a large number of right wingers. No one wanted
to admit knowing Oswald. He was the classic outcast of
all times. Sometimes we think that many of the organizations protested too much that Oswald had nothing to do
with them. And the Minutemen were no exception. At
first, some members of the neo-Fascist group spoke in
praise of Oswald because he had done something they
had merely talked about doing many times. Then the
limelight was directed too forcibly on the Minutemen
and, after the assassination of Oswald, a warning letter
was sent out to every member of the organization, with
expediency but also with secrecy. One man on the
mailing list was an undercover agent who had infiltrated

the organization. (In fact, at one time so many CIA and FBI agents had infiltrated the Minutemen organization that it seemed there was no room for anyone else.)

The letter, addressed to its members, read:

Dear Patriot,

The Minutemen organization is now the object of intensive investigation. Apparently, this is part of the announced plan of the Warren Commission to investigate 'possible connections' between the radical right and the assassination of President Kennedy. All real patriots will recognize that such an implication is without foundation. If Robert Kennedy had spent as much time investigating the Communist-Socialist movement as he did worrying about the pro-American movement, then his brother would probably still be alive.

This will not prevent the 'conspiracy' through the use of the controlled news media from trying to give the impression that the right wing is somehow to blame for John Kennedy's death.

This is an extremely serious situation.

Most of our members will already be familiar with the fact that Earl Warren has voted to favor the Communists in almost every case involving this nation's internal security that has come before the Supreme Court since he has been a member of that body. Most, too, will be aware that when Earl Warren first heard of Kennedy's death, he immediately issued a statement blaming the assassination on 'right wing' fanatics. In fact, this investigating committee was set up just three days after the Communist newspaper, *The Worker*, made a suggestion to that effect. *The Worker* also suggested that Earl Warren be made head of a committee exactly as has occurred. Nicholas Katzenbach, who was in charge of the Federal marshals at Oxford, Mississippi, has been named as chief investigator for the Warren Commission.

J. Lee Rankin, general counsel for the Warren Commission, in a recent letter to Congressman Henry B. Gonzales (of Texas) stated: 'I assure you that any relationship between the Minutemen and the assassination of President Kennedy will be carefully explored.'

Many (perhaps all) major FBI offices have received identical memos from Washington to investigate Minutemen activities in their areas. Treasury agents are making a special effort to determine the existence of any automatic weapons that might be owned by members of this organization. From several cities, we have received reports of postal employees being assigned the special task of listing names and addresses of persons who receive mail from the John Birch Society and other anti-Communist organizations.

There is considerable evidence to indicate that a nation-wide propaganda campaign to blame President Kennedy's death on the right wing had been organized before the assassination. If it had not been for the very good fortune that Oswald was quickly captured and identified as being a Communist, it is probable that hundreds of American patriots would be behind bars today.

We are now witnessing the gradual take-over of our government by hidden Communists to such an extent that loyal Americans are being subjected to 'investigation' harassment and economic persecution.

THE TIME IS PAST WHEN THE COMMUNIST-SOCIALIST MOVEMENT CAN BE SUCCESSFULLY OPPOSED BY ORGANIZATIONS THAT OPERATE IN THE OPEN. SUCCESSFUL OPPOSITION TO THE COMMUNIST-SOCIAL-IST MOVEMENT NOW REQUIRES THE SECRET METHODS OF A PA-TRIOTIC RESISTANCE MOVEMENT.

We realize that many patriots will not give up the hope of winning by political means, but we must remind our members again that there are many people willing to work politically and only a few who will now begin to build the final line of defense.

Although most individual agents of the FBI are loyal Americans of the highest type, we must constantly keep in mind that any information they obtain about us will be sitting in their files when the Communists take over and will certainly be used against us.

If you are questioned as to whether or not you are a member of this organization, we advise you to deny it absolutely. Keep your mind on the fact that they cannot prove you are a member. Such information will NEVER be given out by the National Regional Headquarters. Our files are kept in such a manner that they cannot be seen under any circumstances. If you are confronted with evidence indicating membership of the Minutemen, say that you did inquire, have received literature from us, and possibly even subscribed to our newsletter simply because you are an open-minded person who likes to see both sides of every question, but you did not join. In making con-tact with our members, we are faced with increasing costs due to the necessity of sending all mail first class and from many different post offices. We need the continued financial support of every member if we are to operate in a secure and efficient manner. Enclosed is a special sheet of practical suggestions regarding security measures, which we recommend all members to follow.

Now is the time for each of us to determine whether or not

we have the strength and courage of our forefathers. Are we
made of the same mold as those Americans who pledged their
lives, their fortunes, and their sacred honor to the cause of
freedom?

The existence of such a letter indicated that the
Minutemen were nervous about the rumored association between Oswald and their organization. But the remarkably quick capture and demise of Oswald helped to
put an end to rumors. Against this, however, was the
constant reiteration through the media, which played
down the possibility that Oswald was a Communist—although there was plenty of evidence to indicate he was.

If the right-wing organizations did know anything
about the assassination, then they chose a very inappropriate city for the murder to take place—inappropriate
for them.

Dallas was known as the City of Hate, strong in its
right-wing attitudes; so it was logical to conclude that
right wingers did, indeed, have something to do with the
assassination—as was the initial report. It was preferable
at the time not to upset Russia by dwelling on the
known association of Oswald with Communists. It is
doubtful if the Warren Commission ever gave serious
consideration to the idea that Oswald was a right
winger. They even ignored the fact that the perfect
front would have been for Oswald to be a right winger
but deliberately set up to look like a Communist. After
all, the right-wing movement knew all about infiltrating
other movements, just as it was itself infiltrated by Government officers. If Oswald had been planted by the
right wing, then it was a subtle move that succeeded in
distracting attention from people like H. L. Hunt. The
letter from the Minutemen organization is important to
consider because it showed the paranoia the organization was experiencing after the assassination. They still
had to live down the famous "Kill the three K's," a
rhetoric that had been spewed out at every meeting of
the Minutemen, especially in their Southern California
stronghold.

Jim Garrison tried to prove that Oswald functioned in the milieu of the right wingers and that his "Fair Play for Cuba" was nothing more than a facade. But most of his information came from Jerry Milton Brooks, a defector from the Minutemen organization. It was Brooks who linked Maurice Brooks Gatlin, Sr. to the CIA, alleging that he was "a bagman" who carried $100,000 of CIA money to a French right-wing group whose ambition it was to assassinate General De Gaulle of France. Maurice Gatlin was legal counsel to the Anti-Communism League of the Caribbean. He was never sought by the Warren Commission for questioning and, in 1964, he fell from the sixth floor of the El Panama Hotel in Panama. He was killed instantly, adding his name to the ever-lengthening list of people who touched the life of Lee Harvey Oswald even remotely.

The Minutemen harbored a natural hatred of President Kennedy. This grew even more intense when, on August 1, 1963, the news broke that a NATO-Warsaw bloc non-aggression pact was imminent. The same day, another story broke about an FBI raid on a house on the north side of Lake Pontchartrain in New Orleans. A ton of dynamite, twenty one-hundred-pound bomb castings, fuses, napal ingredients, and other war materials were seized. The owner of the house, William J. McLaney, said the house had been leased to José Juarez, newly arrived from Cuba. Mr. McLaney was a gambler associated with the Tropicana Hotel of Havana before Castro ousted the casinos and their operators in 1960. The press did not follow up the story, giving the impression that no arrests were made. The truth is that eleven men were arrested quietly and, just as quietly, released. Among them were Acelo Pedro Amores, a one-time former Batista official in Cuba, and Richard Lauchli, Jr., one of the founders of the Minutemen organization. Lauchli had a Federal license to manufacture weapons in his Collinsville, Illinois, machine shop. He was again arrested in 1964 by Department of the Treasury investigators, who posed as buyers of munitions from a South American country.

Also arrested with him were a number of Cuban exiles and American adventurers.

Although Jim Garrison was prepared to consider the possibility that Minutemen were behind the assassination, he also thought that it was more likely a renegade group rather than a plan sanctioned by the official headquarters. Similar assassination plots were known before the Kennedy assassination. There was the case of John Morris, who was given money by Minutemen in Kansas City and asked to arrange a sniper slaying of Senator William Fulbright of Arkansas. Robert Bolivar De Pugh, national leader of the Minutemen, heard of the attempted assassination and aborted it.

Had the Warren Commission really delved into Minutemen activities, they would have come up with the fact that the Minutemen had the propensity to kill—both by rhetorical declaration and the precedent of the attempted assassination of Senator Fulbright.

However, there was dissent even within the ranks of the Minutemen as well as a struggle for power at the top in the feud between De Pugh and the late George Lincoln Rockwell, leader of the American Nazi Party. Although Fascist in concept, the Minutemen preferred to think of themselves as ultra-patriots evolving their own concept of what was right for the country rather than one based on the mistakes made by the old Nazi regime in Germany. After all, that had failed. But within the Minutemen, despite their condemnation of Rockwell and his officially declared Nazi movement, there were all the homogeneous elements that go with Fascism. There was anti-Semitism, anti-Communism, and many members of the Minutemen had a personal interest in overthrowing Castro in order to recoup financial interests they once had held in Cuba.

We ask the question . . . if Oswald was indeed a right winger, why did he attempt to assassinate Major General Edwin Walker of Dallas, himself a well-known right winger? Yet, if we ask this question, we are posed with still another one. Did Oswald actually go out one night, taking his rifle, and head for the residence of Major General Walker with the intention of killing him? To substantiate this supposed act by Oswald, we have only the testimony of Marina Oswald and Ruth Paine, and we are not impressed with the validity of either of these witnesses. Also, the only witness at the time—whose testimony was ignored—says that he saw *two men* running away after the shots were fired and he could not identify Oswald as either of them.

In its most extreme possibility, it could have been part of the over-all facade to lend credence to the idea that Oswald was a Marxist determined to wipe out right winger Walker but, in reality, was himself a right winger determined to distract investigators from his association with the right wing.

When Oswald returned to the United States, a photograph of him was sent to *The Daily Worker,* the Communist party newspaper. In this photograph, Oswald is depicted with a revolver at his hip, a rifle in one hand, and the party organ, *The Militant,* in the other. The photograph is a typical Minuteman stance! Could Oswald have been as confused about his identity as others have been?

When Oswald was arrested, the FBI found his address book and in it were the addresses of Major General Walker and George Lincoln Rockwell. These improbable names only add to the confusion of other addresses such as that of FBI Agent Hosty, whose connection with Oswald has never been cleared up.

It was a member of the Southern California branch of Minutemen, Mrs. Carol Aydelotte, known as the "den mother" of the branch, who gave Garrison a photograph of Eugene Bradley. It was this photograph that flashed onto the television screen on December 22, 1967, at the exact moment when Roger Craig walked into his New Orleans apartment and "recognized" him as the man who identified himself as a Secret Service agent outside the Book Depository on November 22, 1963. A New Orleans court clerk, named Gonzales, also identified Bradley as the man he had seen twice before with David Ferrie at the Lakefront Airport in New Orleans. Both Bradley and Ferrie were linked to right-wing groups. Bradley was also an associate of the Reverend Carl McIntyre, an extreme right winger. A woman who once lived next door to Bradley testified to Jim Garrison that she saw Clay Shaw and Colonel William Gale visit the Bradley home. Shaw was Garrison's prime suspect in the Kennedy assassination; Colonel Gale was identified by the California attorney general as a right-wing paramilitary activist, head of the California Rangers, which had much in common with the ideals of the Minutemen.

But it was never established just "why" Mrs. Aydelotte gave the photo to Garrison. Was it because she wanted to help? Or did she want to personally avenge her slights at the hands of Bradley, who had called her a "whore"? Or was it because she merely wanted to mislead investigators and misdirect them away from the hierarchy of the Minutemen?

Could the right-wing activists have killed President Kennedy? If they did, then did Earl Warren, known for his liberal attitude and who, himself was the subject of a hateful "impeach Warren" campaign, cover up for them and so surrender his political convictions?

But how much sense did it make for the right wingers to kill Kennedy in such an ultra-right city as Dallas? To do so was to attract attention immediately to them and their mecca of hate, Dallas. And yet the strange fact is that it did *not*, despite the fears expressed in the letter sent to members of the Minutemen organization.

The lone-assassin hypothesis had to come out as a reality and, to do that, Oswald's affiliation with Communism, his knowledge of right-wing activities in his own area, and his ability to be a politically motivated chameleon were ignored by the Warren Commission. The FBI and the CIA for once forgot their natural aversion to each other and combined to mislead the Commission by providing only enough evidence to lead to the ultimate conclusion of the Warren Commission that Oswald acted alone and was not part of any conspiracy to kill President Kennedy. Such a conclusion could not upset anyone—either the right or left wing, the CIA or the FBI, the pro- or anti-Castroites, the military-industrial complex, or the members of organized-crime units.

But why was J.F.K. killed in Dallas? Who stood to gain from it? Could it have been the right-wing extremists?

10 | THE CIA SCENARIO

In one of the best selling songs of 1975, "Why Can't We Be Friends," a stanza sung by War went:

> I know you must be in the CIA
> 'Cause they wouldn't have you in the Maf-i-aa . . .

In just a few short years the CIA, with its "dirty deeds" and assassination attempts revealed to a formerly trusting public, had come into total disrepute.

But it wasn't always thus. Before 1963, no one talked much about the Central Intelligence Agency because it seemed that no one really knew anyone associated with it. The organization kept a low profile. We knew they existed, but it was practically the same type of acknowledgment with which a religious devotee accepts the existence of the saints. They did their work presumably for the good of mankind, but they did it unobtrusively. In fact, one could almost say that the CIA, until recent years, was the Ghost Squadron with intangible qualifications that the ordinary man could not visualize.

It was enough to know that we had a group of faceless, nameless men with a subtle mystique woven around them.

Then the assassination of President Kennedy exploded on the world, followed by the assassinations of Martin Luther King and Robert Kennedy, and we became conscious that the Ghost Squadron really consisted of flesh-and-blood men even more dedicated, more fearless, and more adventurous than the FBI, but dedicated more to the CIA than to the U.S.A. Of course, we knew other countries had their own branches of super-secret service men and networks of espionage. England had its MI-5; and Russia had its KGB, which was not quite as romantic and always cast as the villains. But we had the CIA, and were reassured that it was working for the "good of the country."

It is difficult to estimate exactly when the CIA emerged as flesh-and-blood men, although we began to know a lot about them when Watergate cascaded its sewerage on the nation. The rot was in the United States, and it started in 1960 when the CIA took an interest in Cuba. We know that in the early sixties no less than six assassination attempts were directed toward Cuba's dictator, Fidel Castro, only to fail. But who issued the orders for the assassination plots? Was it President Kennedy, who was in office at the time? If so, Castro outsmarted the CIA, the Government body in charge of overseeing the attempts.

Undoubtedly, there were plans to eliminate the Cuban leader before a CIA invasion force landed in Cuba. Remove a charismatic leader, and the rank and file would fall apart, making it easy enough to reassert American influence in Cuba—not for the good of that country but because Cuba was a good place for making money.

To carry out the assassination, the CIA enlisted the help of Johnny Roselli, an underworld figure, big-time enough to be a friend of Robert Matheu, at that time the right-hand man of billionaire Howard Hughes.

Roselli was well-known in Las Vegas and Chicago, early homes of Jack Ruby. The CIA, not to be outdone by the exploits of 007 of MI-5 fame, were able to furnish Roselli with poison capsules, poisoned cigars, and even a poisoned shell, which Castro, a skilled diver, might be interested in picking up. Roselli was to be a liaison in the poison-pellet assassination plan. After searching for a contact with two companions, William Harvey and James O'Connell, he delivered the poison pellets to a Cuban contact at the glamorous Fontainebleau Hotel in Miami Beach on March 13, 1961. The hotel has links with Las Vegas, so it kept everything within the family. Both the murder plot and the invasion failed. And although Castro was reported to be "ill," he recovered in time to repulse the abortive Bay of Pigs invasion on April 17, 1961.

Castro had outfoxed the CIA. The Cuban who managed to get the poison to Castro's chef was never seen again, but the CIA did not give up easily. The second attempt on Castro's life came when a triple dose of the poison was shipped from Miami Beach to Cuba, and again it failed. Roselli made heroic dashes in a power-boat to deliver high-powered rifles, explosives, and two-way radios, as well as instructions, to an assassination team. The drops were made at secret landing spots on the Cuban coast. The assassination team smuggled into Cuba had been trained by the CIA at No Name Key in Florida at a school for assassins. (One of those in attendance was Loran Eugene Hall, a burly Spanish-speaking man, the same Loran Eugene Hall who was one of the men to visit Sylvia Odio's apartment.) The assassination team managed to get within striking distance of Castro in March of 1963, but again the dictator survived.

On the *very* day John F. Kennedy was assassinated, a CIA plot to assassinate Castro was in progress, and the FBI knew about it. For on November 22, 1963, a poison pen device was being given to a highly-placed Cuban official, known by his code name *AM LASH*, by a CIA operator.

It was frustrating, to say the least, that the CIA super-men were being outsmarted at every turn. It is certain that Castro knew the CIA was behind the attempts on his life, and he sent back a message to the United States that any country determined to assassinate him would find that two could play the same game and could ex-pect to have the compliment returned. In fact, when Lyndon Johnson first became President, he was heard by one of his aides to mutter, "I didn't know we were carry-ing on a damned 'Murder, Incorporated' in the Carib-bean."

Although J. Edgar Hoover maintained his own posi-tion and the creditability of his men under the regime of several Presidents, the CIA was never well liked. President Kennedy vowed to "splinter the CIA into a thousand pieces and scatter it to the wind," a threat that did not make for an easy relationship between the Chief Executive and the CIA.

After the Bay of Pigs episode, John Kennedy quietly, but deliberately, gave his brother Robert power over the CIA with instructions to shake it up. Thus, it is ironic—as Lyndon Johnson pointed out—that the several at-tempts made on the life of Castro were done with the knowledge of both Kennedy brothers. For five years af-ter the death of President Kennedy, it is more than likely that Robert lived with the constant sense of guilt that his own work might have contributed to the mur-der of his brother. Although the Warren Commission ig-nored the fact, there is a strong possibility that Fidel Castro may have recruited Lee Harvey Oswald to retali-ate against Kennedy, and again we have reason to be-lieve that this constituted a conspiracy—albeit for differ-ent reasons than in the other scenarios. It is a nagging thought that does not go away and continues to lead many people to believe that if all the evidence had been properly examined by the Commission, it never could have come up with the lone-assassin theory. Even one shred of evidence of an association between Oswald and Castro or Ruby and Castro would have lent credence to two or more men plotting the death of the President in a "conspiracy."

Kennedy did not succeed in his vow of "scattering the CIA to the wind." All he succeeded in doing was to make many personal enemies within the organization. In fact, he was so successful in doing this that it was enough to prevent him from ending the cold war. For, added to the Bay of Pigs fiasco, when Kennedy failed to provide air cover, were his stated intentions of withdrawing from Vietnam, exploring détente with Russia and China, and reducing Pentagon appropriations and influence. Any one of these acts could be viewed as treacherous by the CIA hierarchy—but all of which combined could spell disaster to the CIA and to Kennedy himself. However, Kennedy had reached a time in his life when he realized the leader of this country must have vision and courage if war was to be evaded. He made certain there were no missile gaps between the United States and Russia, and he won acclaim in the West by the way he successfully played showdown nuclear politics in the 1962 Cuban missile crisis. By the summer of 1963, Kennedy had unmistakably signaled the end of the cold war, and that would have been the end of men who thrived on war, including the backbone of the CIA.

We have to ask ourselves if the CIA might not have been the prime agent, rather than Castro, in obtaining a man like Oswald to act as a "patsy" to get rid of a President who was bent on the destruction of the agency? The CIA was sophisticated enough to have Oswald run across the entire gamut of political ideology in the United States in order to place all other ideologies on the defensive as possible suspects. In this way, it could ensure that the nation would be so divided and confused on issues that there would be no coalescence of forces to seek retribution for the killing—and thus evade suspicion.

It is now an accepted fact that after the assassination, key foreign-policy changes were put into effect in an amazingly short period of time. President Kennedy knew that his efforts to end the cold war endangered his life. When he saw Nixon after the Bay of Pigs, Kennedy said: "If I do the right kind of job, I don't know whether I am going to be here four years from now. If someone is going to kill me, they are going to kill me. . . ." He also recognized that the danger to his efforts to end the cold war lay in the power of the CIA, which he knew from the past to be a policy-making body over and above its foreign-intelligence role.

Almost imperceptively to the general public, the power of the CIA had grown during the tenure of Eisenhower as President. At that time the Secretary of State was John Foster Dulles, whose brother Allen was head of the CIA. John Foster relied heavily on reports from his brother for his estimates on the usefulness of ambassadors. In effect, John Foster made brother Allen's CIA a kind of ultra-superior foreign service, and he found nothing incongruous in the fact that in many embassies throughout the world the CIA personnel outnumbered the foreign-service employees.

John Kennedy abruptly fired Allen Dulles after the Bay of Pigs, the same Allen Dulles who became a member of the Warren Commission. How can we have anything but doubts about Dulles . . . the man axed from a powerful position only to sit on the commission named to search out the truth on the assassination of the man who fired him? In reading the full report of the Commission, and not the whitewashed version by Gerald Ford or the paperback edition with a foreword by Harrison Salisbury of *The New York Times* staff, it is possible to see how Dulles cleverly circumvented any attempts by the Commission to get its own investigators. With Dulles keeping his weather eye on the proceedings, the Commission was forced to rely on the file of trivia supplied exclusively by the FBI.

On January 21, 1964, in a secret executive session, the Commission was worried about the problem of dealing with Marina Oswald's evidence that Oswald was a Soviet agent. Senator Russell said: "That will blow the lid if she testifies to that." So, how did the Commission deal with the problem? Isaac Don Levine was at the time helping Marina Oswald prepare a story for *Life* Magazine, and Dulles offered to see Levine, saying: "I can get him in and have a friendly talk. I have known him." The Marina Oswald story was never published, which sounds as if Dulles was capable of influencing evidence, as well as having both book and article suppressed.

Levine is himself an interesting character; he played a central role in the Alger Hiss case in which Richard Nixon also had a major part. Levine had the reputation of a man waging a private war against Communism and, with Marina Oswald "delivered to him," he had the single person in his hands whom the Commission feared might state that her husband was a Soviet agent. Yet Levine, after his interview with Dulles, abandoned his project, and Marina Oswald's testimony on this point was successfully eliminated. Levine, with his background of interests and literary skills devoted to assassination, never wrote one word about the assassination of President Kennedy. Allen Dulles never told anyone how he came to know Isaac Levine, but it must have been through intelligence work.

There is also a strange tie with the CIA through President Kennedy's Assistant for National Security Affairs, McGeorge Bundy, whose brother William Bundy was well situated with the CIA. McGeorge Bundy had followed a hard-line foreign policy and had little use for any idealistic approach such as others, like Adlai Stevenson, followed. At the time of the Bay of Pigs crisis, McGeorge Bundy was one of the planners of the invasion. Allen Dulles was in Puerto Rico, leaving Richard Mervin Bissell as the CIA man in charge of planning. McGeorge Bundy and Bissell were old friends. Bundy had been a student of Bissell's at Yale and worked with him on the Marshall Plan in 1948. Also concerned with the planning of the invasion was General Charles P. Cabell, deputy director of the CIA.

It is again interesting to note that his brother, Earle Cabell, was mayor of Dallas at the time of the assassination. Remember, too, that the mayor of any city always knows the route a motorcade takes in his own town. The route of the Kennedy motorcade was changed. No one has yet pinpointed exactly who it was that gave the orders or who received them. And *no one* questioned if the mayor of Dallas knew of the changed plans.

In the Kennedy Administration and later in that of his successor, Lyndon Johnson, McGeorge Bundy was a key man in the special group making key intelligence decisions for this country. Arthur Schlesinger, a Kennedy adviser, felt that there was a conflict of interest and that Bundy did not serve Kennedy well in the Bay of Pigs. "Moreover, if worse came to worst and the invaders were beaten on the beaches then," [Dulles and Bissell said], "they could easily melt away into the mountains." But the CIA was less than truthful in implying that the invasion forces could escape so easily. The Escambray Mountains lay eighty miles away from the Bay of Pigs. To get to them, the invasion force would have had to traverse a terrible tangle of swamps and jungles, and the CIA agents in Guatemala—where Carlos Marcello was in exile—said nothing to the Cubans about the terrain across this last resort of flight into the mountains.

We do not see how Bundy can be exonerated from misleading the President. Since the CIA was determined to maintain a war footing that would justify its existence, Bundy was doing his work well for them but at the expense of the President. Yet Kennedy turned to Bundy, along with Dean Rusk, Robert McNamara, and Walter Rostow, in determining the direction of his Vietnam policy. And the policy was thoroughly botched up. On October 2, 1963, President Kennedy was all set to announce the phased withdrawal of United States forces from South Vietnam. His death came at a time that was propitious to those who wanted that arena of war maintained.

When the Presidential party made its flight back to Washington on the afternoon of that fateful day in Dallas, the entourage heard the first announcement of Oswald as the lone assassin. In Washington, the plane landed at five-fifty-nine P.M. on the evening of November 22nd. At that time Dallas District Attorney Henry Wade was saying that "preliminary reports indicated more than one person was involved in the shooting. The electric chair is too good for the killers." Oswald was not charged with assassinating Kennedy until one-thirty A.M., on November 23rd, a remarkably long period after the lone-assassin announcement was made on *Air Force One*. In any case, to make a statement less than six hours after an assassination was surely too soon to know there was *no conspiracy*. Yet the White House Situation Room confirmed the "no conspiracy" statement, and the Situation Room was under the personal-and-direct control of McGeorge Bundy!

From that first statement issued by Bundy, the Federal Government was married to the idea of the lone assassin. The Bundy brothers quickly became locked into the administration of the new President, and it was like the old days of the Dulles brothers being the power behind President Eisenhower. President Kennedy's decision to withdraw troops was quickly reversed. It was McGeorge Bundy who recommended to President Johnson that a steady program of bombing North Vietnam take place, and the war in Vietnam was escalated. The Bundys profited by the death of President Kennedy to become the main architects of the Vietnamese war, ultimately to give up their titular Government positions to become interlocked into two important private foundations. McGeorge Bundy became president of the Ford Foundation and brother William joined the Center for International Studies at M.I.T. David Horowitz, a magazine writer, states: "It should be noted in passing that the congeniality of foundation-dominated scholarship in the CIA reflects the harmony of interest between the upper-class captains of the CIA and the upper-class trustees of the great foundations." The interconnections are too expansive to be recounted here, but the Bundy brothers (William, CIA; McGeorge, Ford) and Chadbourne Gilpatrick (OSS and CIA from 1943–1949, Rockefeller Foundation from 1949 on) can be taken as illustrative. Richard Bissell, brother-in-law of Philip Mosely of Columbia University's Russian Institute, reversed the usual sequence, going from the Ford Foundation to the CIA.

Horowitz also established a link between other foundations and the CIA. For instance, the M.I.T. Advisory Board on Soviet Bloc Studies was made up of Charles Bohlen of the State Department, Allen Dulles of the CIA, Philip Mosely of Columbia's Russian Institute, and Leslie G. Stevens, a retired United States Navy vice admiral. Horowitz goes on to say: "If the M.I.T. Center seemed to carry to their logical conclusion the on-campus extension programs of the State Department and the CIA, that was because it was set up directly with CIA funds under the guiding hand of Professor Walter Rostow, former OSS officer and later director of the State Department's Policy Planning Staff under Kennedy and Johnson. The Center's first director, Max Millikan, was appointed in 1952 after a stint as assistant director of the CIA. Carnegie and Rockefeller joined in the funding that, by now, as in so many other cases, had passed on to Ford."

And it is beyond the realm of coincidence to find that Dr. Daniel Ellsberg, a CIA employee, was also at M.I.T. at the same time—the same Daniel Ellsberg who released "The Pentagon Papers." For, as one of his close friends disclosed; "Here was a man who was married to the daughter of the biggest hawk of all (Louis Marx of toy-company fame), who named his sons after generals (Bedell, et al.) and who was such a 'gung-ho' hawk himself in the first days of the Vietnam conflict. He would not only lecture troops on the perniciousness of the "Gooks" (the North Vietnamese), but he also took up weapons personally and even shot at and, I believe, personally killed some North Vietnamese. This is the man hailed as a hero by the left because he leaked 'The Pentagon Papers.' But why did he do it? If you know Ellsberg as we do, you know he's impressionable and easy to lead. Did the CIA put him up to releasing the documents just to put the Pentagon in its place? It's not inconceivable in the whole context of this mess. For, Daniel Ellsberg was, and still is at heart, a CIA man."

No elitist secret-police organization such as the CIA thrives on peace or democracy. It thrives on chaos. The power of intelligence agencies increases in direct proportion to the degree of sickness of any nation. In a sick Germany in 1939, the Gestapo ruled. In Russia after the sickness of revolution, the KGB was supreme; and America, sick with the sorrow of the war in Vietnam, was a patient ready for the merciless attention of the increasingly powerful CIA. The policy of all elitist police organizations is to remove anything and anyone who gets in their way, and President Kennedy was just such a person. When the country is sick enough, then it is ripe for the type of totalitarianism that the Richard Nixon regime almost succeeded in imposing on this country. In 1963 the super-slick CIA kept the war in Vietnam going, and the main ingredient needed to achieve this was the death of President Kennedy.

After that, the going was easy enough, but everything rested on the lone-assassin theory standing up and being accepted in an official report that the Warren Commission obligingly delivered.

It was even helpful to the CIA to have the FBI deliver reams of evidence to the Committee implicating Lee Harvey Oswald as "The Lone Assassin." But it took a much more sophisticated agency to arrange the lifestyle of Lee Harvey Oswald. Only the CIA could have arranged for Oswald to establish membership or contact with the Communist party, the FBI, the anti-Communist Socialist Labor party, the Soviet Union, the ACLU, the ultra-right wing in Dallas, the Fair Play for Cuba Committee, Major General Edwin Walker, the Socialist

Workers party, the American oil interests, the Cuban government, the United States Marines, the American Friends, and the Soviet secret police. If these affiliations did not set up chaos and confusion in the minds of Americans, then nothing could! Gilding the lily is not a new creative art for the CIA. And, by putting the FBI in the limelight, they also placed this organization in a position to take any blame afterward.

The news leaked out that Oswald was an FBI informer, but it took longer for news to leak out that Oswald also had affiliations with the CIA, where he was given the code name of "Thomas Kane." His use to the CIA was more likely to be in their need for a patsy rather than another intelligence-gathering name on the payroll. That Oswald was a patsy as well as a CIA agent is substantiated by Harry Dean, sometimes known as Dean Fallon, a former CIA agent who is now working as a private detective in Alhambra, California. He claims that Oswald was his partner in the CIA. Suddenly, Harry Dean is not available for interviews, after he was recently interviewed by Tom Snyder for his "Tomorrow" show at NBC headquarters in New York. The show was never aired and, while in New York, Harry Dean's hotel room was burglarized.

Ronald Lee Augustinovitch, a former CIA agent, also claims that Oswald was in the CIA and says that he was assigned to him for training under the name of "Tom Kane." This man surfaced in Jim Garrison's New Orleans investigation, but his testimony was not followed up. Augustinovitch had information about the assassination before it happened. The former CIA agent kept a one-hundred-and-sixty-page report under his mattress until it was stolen; however, much of his testimony, given to Garrison, was witnessed by Calvin Barton Bull and Gary Sanders, also witnesses in the Garrison probe. Augustinovitch said he was working for the CIA at the time of the Kennedy assassination and did some post-assassination investigating, but the results of his investigation "did not jive" with those of "The Warren Report."

Much of Jim Garrison's investigation has to be taken with a grain of salt. While crying "wolf" a dozen times or "Eureka, I have found the assassin," he always maintained that his prime suspect, businessman Clay Shaw, was a ringleader of a CIA cabal. By 1975, this was confirmed by another former CIA man, Victor Marchetti. Garrison got a little smoke from which he manufactured a big fire and, in fanning the fire, was instrumental in erasing some of the very evidence he was looking for.

Just as Hoover denied that Oswald had any affiliation with the FBI, with equally dutiful vehemence, the CIA denied that Oswald was or ever had been their man. There was evidence to pose a question mark over both denials, but the Warren Commission had by then been too misled to delve further into it.

First, there is Oswald's record while in the marines. His main duty station overseas was Atsugi, Japan, one of the largest CIA bases in the world. It has been one of the prime launching pads for covert operations to pay unexpected visits into Red China. It also happened to be a base for the CIA U-2 spy planes. At Atsugi, Oswald, who, on the surface did not appear to be a studious type, was able to work as a radar operator and learn Russian in his spare time, most likely taught to him by the CIA—not bad for a high-school dropout who, the year after he left the ninth grade, joined the marines. In September 1959, Oswald applied for a discharge from the marines on the grounds of hardship, based on the fact that his mother had dropped a box on her foot. Someone forgot to note that this was a minor accident and that Marguerite Oswald was back at work in a matter of days, although Oswald got his discharge in the record time of three days. At a CIA base, only a major CIA agent could have made this possible, as anyone in the marines can testify. Back in the United States, Oswald spent three days with his mother in New Orleans and paid $1,500 for his passage to the Soviet Union which, again, must have been arranged in record time. Moreover, his bank account at the time amounted

to $203. Where did he get the money? From the CIA?
He took a boat to England and then went to Helsinki
by plane. But the entry date stamped on Oswald's passport in London proved there was a discrepancy in the
date of his departure to Helsinki . . . the plane departed
the day before Oswald arrived in London. Another minor discrepancy? Or a CIA cover-up? Still, he did get to
Helsinki, possibly by non-commercial means arranged by
the CIA.

At the time of Oswald's return to the United States,
the CIA was questioning even ordinary tourists about
what they had seen in Russia. On the other hand,
Oswald was met at the airport by Spas T. Raikin, whom
the Warren Commission noted was an official of Trav-
elers Aid. It failed to note that Mr. Raikin was the
former Secretary-General of the American Friends of the
Anti-Bolshevik Bloc of Nations, a group known to have
extensive ties to intelligence agencies—and to the CIA!

When Oswald worked at the Reily Company in New
Orleans, he expressed interest in obtaining a job at the
NASA base at Gentilly, Louisiana, and frequently discussed this with Adrian Alba, owner of the Crescent City
Garage next door to the Reily Company. According to
Alba, the Gentilly base was a CIA set-up for clandestine
operations. And Jim Garrison always held that Oswald
defected to Russia with "top-secret radar data," with no
action taken to prevent him from going to Russia and
no punitive action taken when he returned to the
United States.

Oswald never seemed to be concerned about money or
being fired from a job and if, as it now appears to be
true, he was the recipient of two hundred dollars a
month from the FBI, it is also likely that he had an income from the CIA. So why should he worry? The Warren Commission also did not seem to worry about these
sources of income.

The naïveté of the Warren Commission is astound-
ing, for it also glossed over the fact that Oswald took up
residence in the heavily CIA-infiltrated White-Russian

community in Dallas. When Oswald went to Mexico City, the CIA supplied confirmation that he was there, but in its cable described the man as "six feet tall, athletically built with receding hairline." The only part of this description that applied to Oswald was that he had a receding hairline; it stretches the imagination to describe him as athletically built or even six feet tall. The CIA claimed it was a mistake due to the computers.

However, the mistaken-picture episode might be better explained if we remember that E. Howard Hunt was the CIA man-in-charge of the Mexico City office at the time and that, the CIA did have "voice recordings of Lee Henry [sic] Oswald" in the Cuban Embassy (meaning that they "bugged" the embassy), also that they mistakenly sent back a picture bearing a resemblance to Loran Eugene Hall.

The particularly interesting thing about the Mexico City visit is that Oswald's name appears on a visa application filed with the Soviet Embassy and confirmed by William C. Gaudet. On the records of Mexican travel permits, the name of William C. Gaudet appears after that of Oswald. The gentleman lists his employment as editor of the *Latin-American Traveller,* but the Warren Commission should have also discovered that Mr. Gaudet is a former employee of the CIA. Was he keeping a fatherly eye on Oswald, the designated patsy of the CIA, to make sure he did all he was instructed to do? Any connection of Oswald with either the FBI or CIA intelligence-gathering forces provides a rationale for a cover-up story, and a cover-up story shows that there *may* have been a conspiracy.

It was this "dirty rumor" that terrified Lee Rankin and the Warren Commission and that had to be wiped out in a uniquely clumsy manner. Every member of that Commission was specially chosen for his intelligence and legal ability. But, in the aftermath of evidence suppressed or ignored, the members emerge as a frightened group, terrified of tarnishing their own reputations and content to go along with both the FBI and

CIA. It was advantageous to both intelligence-gathering forces that Oswald should go down in history as a lone assassin, and for many years he was granted this doubtful credit.

A lot of CIA money was available to the Cuban exiles in 1963 and many of the regulars at 544 Camp Street, New Orleans, were low-grade CIA informants, or in some way affiliated with this Government agency. Oswald, Jack Ruby, and David Ferrie were no strangers to the Camp Street hangout with its Cuban exiles, White Russians, and CIA activists. In the beginning of his own investigation, Jim Garrison turned over a great deal of evidence to the FBI and CIA, but it was conveniently ignored, just as the revelations by Waggoner Carr were ignored. Such things as phone calls made by Ruby, Ferrie, and Clay Shaw on the day of the assassination were never checked out. One was to MO 4-3581, a Houston number that apparently did not belong to anyone but was a CIA "information drop."

When Oswald was arrested, Clay Shaw was busy on the telephone calling Dean Andrews to represent Oswald at his trial, even before the man was indicted. Andrews also did legal work for Carlos Marcello, the Mafia chief of New Orleans, and he was the attorney for Marcello on the immigration case in which David Ferrie was involved. Andrews was also a familiar figure around the Guy Bannister Detective Agency, whose headquarters was at 544 Camp Street. And Jack Ruby is also alleged to have kept abreast of gunrunning activities out of this address. So many of the main characters had associations with this address, and still the Warren Commission could not accept the possibility of Jack Ruby knowing Lee Harvey Oswald or of both being involved with the CIA. When the FBI and CIA went through the files of the detective agency, a file on Clay Shaw was missing!

A top ranking CIA contact agent, Robert Morrow, recalls making a gun-running trip to Athens with David Ferrie. One of *his* so-called "contacts" in the episode was none other than Jack Ruby. On another occasion, Morrow served as a "go-between" to pick up a package in Paris sent by Lee Harvey Oswald for his employer, the CIA, or as he calls them, "The Company."

Robert Morrow, the CIA contact man, claims he purchased four Mannlicher rifles and turned them over to the CIA which, in turn, gave them to Avery Shaw in New Orleans just prior to the assassination of J.F.K.

On the day of Kennedy's assassination, David Ferrie was in a New Orleans Federal court with Marcello, awaiting judgment on Marcello's immigration case. When Marcello was deported by Robert Kennedy in 1964, it was Ferrie who illegally flew him back into the United States. Ferrie's activities at 544 Camp Street were numerous; he sometimes functioned as a liaison for the Cosa Nostra, sometimes with Cuban exiles, and often with undercover CIA personnel. Oswald had known Ferrie since 1955, when both joined the Civilian Air Patrol. When he was arrested, Oswald had Ferrie's library card in his possession. Like many other people who could have given evidence to the Warren Commission, Ferrie's death came at a convenient time—after he told friends he knew he was doomed. When his apartment was searched following his death, Jim Garrison found a blue one-hundred-pound practice aerial bomb, three rifles, ammunition, a flare gun, bayonet, two Army Signal Corps field telephones, radio equipment for both transmitting and receiving, an altar, religious robes, and some disguises. Not exactly standard equipment for an ordinary pilot, but friends said that Ferrie was a pack rat who never threw any papers or photographs away— and was not ordinary. Among his eccentric memorabilia, no papers or photographs are known to have been discovered. If Ferrie, who died from a karate-type chop across the head, was murdered, it is possible that his assailants also knew what to take away and what to leave behind.

Although Dick Gregory is known primarily in the United States as a comedian, he is also a dedicated assassination student. When the Rockefeller Commission was set up to investigate the CIA, Gregory produced what he claimed to be new evidence concerning the assassination of John Kennedy. Robert Groden and Ralph Schoenman, assistant investigators with Gregory, submitted an amateur movie and still photos, that they purported showed Watergate conspirators E. Howard Hunt and Frank Sturgis at the scene of the assassination. We have seen these films and must in all honesty say that one photograph that the investigators say shows a rifleman hiding in a clump of trees on the grassy knoll of Dealey Plaza is fuzzy and does nothing to justify this statement. But the still photos of three men taken into custody and referred to as "tramps" are quite different. Two could be Sturgis and Hunt, while the third looks like a dead ringer for an FBI sketch of a man wanted in the slaying of Martin Luther King. Schoenman states that the men identified as Sturgis and Hunt were CIA operatives in disguise. The Warren Commission saw these films and dismissed them as unimportant, a not unusual stance for men who had already decided that Oswald, and Oswald alone, was guilty. The tragic thing is that these three men were taken to the Dallas Police Station only to be released immediately without fingerprinting, just as Braden-Brading was released.

The years can make a great difference to any man, and maybe we should discount the evidence of the photographs. However, we are still left with the amazing fact that after an assassination of a President, four men were released without an adequate probe into their backgrounds and without fingerprinting, both usual procedures in more minor cases.

There is also the remarkable coincidence of E. Howard Hunt being the head of the CIA in Mexico City when Lee Harvey Oswald made his mysterious trip there shortly before the assassination. And we again run into the name of E. Howard Hunt at the time of the attempted assassination of Governor George Wallace. Just one hour after the shooting, Hunt was ordered by Charles Colson (reputedly one of the head CIA men in the White House along with Alexander Butterfield who "told" the Watergate Committee about Nixon's tapes) to examine Arthur Bremer's apartment.

Oregon attorney, Mark Lane, has always been vocal in his attempts to link the CIA with the assassination of President Kennedy and the cover-up that followed. At first, it seemed that he was a lone voice, but today he is still steadfast in his claim that the CIA was linked with all four assassination crimes. After years of rumor building on rumor, long after the Warren Commission members had found their own new niche in their professions, we get involved in the sewage flowing from the Watergate episode. Then it became remarkable that all the old familiar faces cropped up again! In 1963 it seemed utterly impossible that so many Government agencies, and possibly a President, could be linked together in the despicable crimes of assassination and attempted assassination. But Watergate brought into focus a sickness from which the United States may never recover until there is a reopening of the investigation into the death of President Kennedy, for that is the starting point of the cancerous growth of further assassinations. As a nation, we are entitled to know the truth and be able to take it, even if it strips away the mystique of the CIA and its ignoble activities in the name of national security. Until that day comes, we can only say that the CIA scenario indicates that this Government body, more powerful than the FBI or any other, could have been involved in the assassination and the cover-up story and, if not the CIA as an instrument of Government—from the top down—then some of those who were connected with it, either directly or remotely.

We do not believe we shall find one single motive linking the three assassinations and the attempt on the life of George Wallace, but it is more than possible that there was a single source that created the climate for murder and mayhem on a scale impossible to conceive even at the time. Then came Watergate, when we all began to review our attitudes, and what came out was a lack of belief in the integrity of the CIA. Richard Nixon disappeared from the scene, granted a pardon for crimes that were never proved. And the pardon was granted by the new President, Gerald Ford, the man who did a good whitewash job of "The Warren [Commission] Report," and the man who appointed David Belin, his old friend, to manage the Rockefeller Commission's inquiry into CIA activities. In its final report, this commission felt that it could not delve into assassinations, and it was left to Senator Frank Church to establish that the CIA included a group of men licensed to murder.

If the President of the United States is said to be in the dark about the activities of his chief intelligence-gathering group, what hope is there for the rest of us to ever know the truth?

11 | THE MAFIA SCENARIO

America has the Mafia to look to for many of the crimes committed in this country. In the days of Al Capone, all too many horrible crimes could safely be laid on the threshold of the Mafia organization. Since those days, many more sections of the community have been educated by the past history of "The Maf" and new ideas added by the fertile brains of authors and movie script-writers. The Mafia and later the Cosa Nostra, became catchall phrases for the many crimes committed by people of every ethnic group and especially for crimes that were never solved by the police . . . most especially those of murder, muggings, and mayhem.

The assassination of President Kennedy was a crime that seemed ready-made to fit into the techniques of the Mafia, mainly when the surface clues of the killing are followed. Again, we get back to that all-important point in any murder: what was the motive?

Robert Kennedy, brother of the President, had vowed a personal vendetta on organized crime and was set to break the power of the organized crime-oriented unions. By killing the President, it was possible that certain members of organized crime knew they would hit back at Robert and the entire Kennedy clan with drastic methods that were in keeping with the Mafia policy to cut off the head when the body became troublesome. Despite the protestations of New Orleans District Attorney James Garrison that organized crime was cleaned up in his city, his good friend, Carlos Marcello, kingpin of Louisiana, had plenty of muscle in the state and elsewhere.

Early in the 1960s, Robert Kennedy had set into motion plans for striking at organized-crime elements in most of the larger cities of the United States. Chicago Mafia boss Sam Giancana was one of the first to fall, going to jail for contempt of court. Joe Valachi was singing like a canary, telling authorities about the inner workings of the Cosa Nostra while he was himself serving a prison term. Another Kennedy victim was a good friend of Marcello's, Jimmy Hoffa, who went to prison for jury tampering. Marcello did not hide his hatred of Kennedy. In 1962, the Louisiana gang boss met with three associates at his Churchill Farms plantation near New Orleans, where he shouted at his guests, "Don't worry about Little Bobby, son-of-a-bitch. He's going to be taken care of!" Perhaps the best way of taking care of the Attorney General was by taking care of his brother. Ed Reid, one of the foremost literary authorities on the Mafia, wrote in his book *The Grim Reapers*: "Any killer of the Attorney General would be hunted down by his brother. But the death of the President would seal the fate of the Attorney General." He also wrote that Marcello had decided to use a "nut" to do the job.

Did the Mafia boss go ahead with the idea that month after month became an obsession with him: to get at Robert Kennedy through his brother, the President?

If so, we have another motive to link organized-crime figures with the assassination. Had James Braden been fully investigated when he was picked up in Dallas, it might have been discovered that despite his protestation that he was not familiar with Dallas, a fact he was still adhering to some eleven years later, he was indeed very well known there for criminal activities. In 1960 Braden married the wealthy widow of a Teamsters Union official from Chicago. The lady became a widow when her husband accidentally shot himself twice in the stomach with a .45 revolver—a very painful and unusual way to commit suicide, but effective in this case. Braden's association with the Teamsters Union had been strong the past fifteen years and his career was a colorful one, to say the least, and a suspicious one . . . certainly enough to justify a thorough examination by authorities interested in seeking motives of underworld characters likely to be linked to the assassination of President Kennedy.

Carlos Marcello's territory, or "turf," ran from New Orleans to Dallas and then to Los Angeles, and the loot from organized crime in this area made Marcello worth more than Rockefeller when it came to counting millions; that is, if the prestigious *Wall Street Journal* is accurate in its assessment of his wealth. Marcello was literally "abducted" to Guatemala by then Attorney General Robert Kennedy, handcuffed and sent to the country he claimed to be his birthplace, for illegal entry into the United States. There he swore vengeance on the Kennedys . . . a Sicilian pact he had more than enough time, energy, and power to carry out. He then returned mysteriously to the United States and was indicted—the date of the trial in New Orleans being set for November 22, 1963—the day President Kennedy was murdered. If this was a Mafia murder, then the timing was planned to get the message through to Robert Kennedy that if he persisted in his intent to bring the Mafia leaders to trial and prison, he might want to think twice about further action.

Within minutes of the assassination, Deputy C. L. "Lummie" Lewis arrested a man and took him to the police station in Dallas, where he gave his name as Jim Braden. It is still a mystery why Lewis was suspicious of

Braden, one of many people outside the Dallas Book Depository Building. The suspicions, whatever they were, did not warrant Braden having his fingerprints taken during his short sojourn in the police station. It would have been the most natural thing to do. The crime of the century has been committed, a man picked up, and no one fingerprints him! Had he only been fingerprinted, the FBI's fingerprint department would have sent back the finding within hours that the prints were those of Eugene Hale Brading, a notorious ex-convict who was well-known in Dallas for his hoodlum activities that had made newspaper headlines years ago. But Braden swore he had never been in Dallas before, and his word was accepted. In the ensuing years, Al Chapman of Dallas collected photographs of the crowd in the vicinity of the assassination. One man, wearing a hat and topcoat, eyes covered with dark glasses, appeared in a photograph that was shown to Lewis. He identified it as a photograph of the man he took into custody . . . the so-called oilman, Jim Braden of California. The Warren Commission seemed to skirt delicately around the testimony of Deputy Lewis and that of Deputy Roger Craig who, with Lewis, was one of the first officers to reach the doorway of the Book Depository after the assassination. In fact, the Warren Commission definitely ruled that Craig was not a reliable witness and said it could not "accept important elements in his testimony."

The credibility of Craig's entire testimony was shattered when he said he told a Secret Service official what he had seen, namely Oswald getting into a light-colored Rambler station wagon. But no Secret Service agent came forward to substantiate Craig's testimony and apparently he did not ask the man for identification. Or perhaps he did and it was later found out to be a fake. Obviously, had Craig's testimony been accepted, the entire premise of Oswald as a "lone assassin" would have been destroyed, because Jack Ruby owned a light-colored Rambler station wagon! Subsequent evidence not presented or ignored by the Warren Commission definitely linked Jack Ruby with elements of organized crime in several cities in America over a long period of time. Craig, now dead, becomes more and more important in adding up the pros and cons of the assassination of President Kennedy to its links with organized crime.

On December 22, 1967, a picture of another man, Eugene Bradley, of North Hollywood, California, was flashed on the television screen during a news bulletin just as Craig entered his apartment. Craig turned to his wife and shouted, "That's the man who identified himself as a Secret Service agent. I have had a picture of that face in my mind all these years. I can remember his smooth complexion and the cleft in his chin. I can remember every word said that day." Craig swore out an affidavit that the man on the screen was the man who had impersonated the Secret Service officer. Jim Garrison asked Governor Reagan of California to extradite Bradley but to no avail. Then Max Gonzales, a New Orleans court official, testified that he had twice seen Bradley in the company of David Ferrie, a pilot with Mafia connections, who was ready to run drugs and arms anywhere in the world if the price was right. Bradley swore that he was in El Paso and Anthony, Texas, on the day of the assassination. This created enough doubt for Governor Reagan to deny the extradition request from Louisiana.

Details of both Gene Bradley and a Gene Brading were in computer files at the Los Angeles Police Department, and a faulty computer service literally threw out the information to Garrison who erroneously put the two images together to make one man. Both images had a strong facial similarity.

Edgar Hale Brading *was* in Dallas at the time of the assassination and was registered at the Cabana Motel, one of the many business enterprises financed by the Teamsters Union Pension Fund, under the leadership of Robert Kennedy's avowed enemy, Jimmy Hoffa. A witness, Dennis Mower, testified to Garrison that Brading-Braden offered him ten thousand dollars to kill John

F. Kennedy in 1960 when he was a Senator from Massachusetts and was campaigning for the Presidency. This testimony has to be taken with a grain of salt for, in 1960, Dennis Mower could not have been more than fourteen years old, hardly the age to receive a murder contract! So, although there were red herrings thrown into the trail of other red herrings, there is plenty of tangible evidence to link Brading-Braden with organized crime. And, for those who want a Mafia Scenario, there is enough meat to provide more than mere food for thought—it could be a feast.

The Warren Commission had enough evidence to present a strong case for a Mafia-style assassination, but they either overlooked the obvious or chose not to pursue it. You can make your own evaluation of their investigation—or lack of it.

Their target could well have been Kennedy's brother, Robert. The Attorney General had prosecuted more Mafia mobsters than any other Federal prosecutor in the legal annals of America.

The Mafia also had a stake in the Cuban invasion that John Kennedy aborted when he failed to supply the promised air power at the Bay of Pigs. Always interested in the chance to make money—if Castro had been overthrown—organized-crime elements in the U.S.A. would have reopened the gambling establishment that Castro had closed down. It was like showing a child all the presents on a Christmas tree and then not letting him have one. Besides, a lot of hard groundwork had been put into "opening up" Cuba by Meyer Lansky. But President Kennedy vanquished the dream of another Las Vegas.

Gene Brading-Jim Braden was also well aware of the Midas touch in gambling in the days when he was a courier, siphoning mobsters' money from the tender but grasping hands of Uncle Sam to the more sensitive hands of the gnomes of Zurich and Amsterdam. A good, reliable bagman is literally worth his own weight in gold. If he was in Dallas on Mafia business, you can bet your last dollar that plans had been made well in advance to protect him—and that meant there had to be a sound, reliable, strong contact in the law-enforcement offices. The oversight of not taking his prints indicates that someone knew enough to make him forget the basic rules when taking in a suspect. Perhaps this was the best cover of all ... for, while he was there, the heat was transferred to someone else. As the lone assassin, Oswald, was being sought, Brading-Braden lurked in the most obvious place—Dallas Police Headquarters.

Brading-Braden was an ex-convict on parole with a criminal record dating back to the mid-thirties. He was a well-known associate of a Denver-based Mafia family, and of Jimmy (The Weasel) Frattiano, known on the West Coast as a "hit man" in several incidents of gangland violence. The FBI report on Brading-Braden stated, "Braden has no information concerning the assassination, and both Lee Harvey Oswald and Jack Ruby are unknown to him." His word was taken as the gospel truth, so there was no need to take his fingerprints, which would have told a different story ... at the wrong time. He was free to return to California and mix with his friends at fashionable La Costa Country Club, which was built by Jimmy Hoffa's Teamster Pension Fund moneys and a place where mobster and entertainer alike hung out.

We do not believe for one moment that Brading-Braden fired any bullets at President Kennedy, but this does not absolve him from being a small cog in the conspiracy wheel. Any small-time crook taken into custody for investigation of a less serious crime than murder would have been carefully interrogated and fingerprinted. If he had any record, there was always a likelihood that he would be associated with whatever crime had been perpetrated. And if it was later found that he had associations with any group of organized crime, the chances would be slim that he would escape. Brading-Braden was a very fortunate man because he had friends in the right places. He was fortunate that his real identity did not emerge until 1968, after the assassination of Robert Kennedy in Los Angeles. Again Brading-Braden was questioned with a variation on the story he had told at the Dallas Police Station. He said he was reporting to the Dallas Federal parole board, a condition of his being allowed to make the trip to Dallas from North Hollywood. He said he watched the procession from a window in the Federal building. A Dallas Federal parole officer denied this and said, "Our office was closed at that time so that employees could witness the parade." Brading-Braden said that he did not give his real name to the Dallas sheriff's office because no one asked him. No one asked him?

When Lee Harvey Oswald was struck by a bullet fired by Dallas nightclub owner Jack Ruby, it seemed to many people that there might be a God who was concerned with retribution and His own methods of meting out justice. To others, it was an enigma how a man could get into a closely guarded area full of police and reporters, walk up to a prisoner, and shoot him in the guts. Added to the lone-assassin theory was another lone assassin who, in a fit of nationalistic outrage, instantaneously made up his mind to kill the suspect and save both the country and the widowed first lady the torture of a lengthy and expensive trial in the courts of law. Who was this man, Jack Ruby, whom the Warren Commission decided had no part in any conspiracy and who ended his days in a prison hospital dead of cancer at the age of fifty-five?

Jack Ruby had come a long way from the ghettos of Chicago. He arrived in Dallas where he became the owner of the Carousel Club, which he once described as a "f—— classy joint." That was a matter of opinion. The Carousel Club made no pretense of being glamorous, situated in the 1300 block of Commerce next to Abe Weinstein's Colony Club. It was part of Dallas's downtown nightclub life, officially innocent enough, with plenty of girls and drinks available. Dallas cops frequented the place, but no one remembers them paying for their entertainment and drinks.

Jack Ruby had the reputation of being foul-mouthed, hypocritical about sex, and rarely inclined to demonstrate any neighborly instincts toward Abe Weinstein. He was not averse to saying that neighbor Abe cheated on his Internal Revenue Service returns. Yet it was Ruby whom reporter Hugh Aynsworth of *The Dallas Times Herald* says the FBI tried to recruit to work for them at least eight times. It seems likely that they succeeded, but how much information he passed on we shall never know.

What we do know is that he employed Jada, a dancer from New Orleans, Oswald's hometown, where she was known as Janet Adams Conforto.

On the day of the assassination, Ruby had had one of his regular quarrels with Jada, which presumably added fuel to his already-burning indignation against the accused assassin of President Kennedy. When Ruby fired at Lee Harvey Oswald, the act was seen by millions of television viewers, including Ruby's off-and-on girl friend, Jada. She was in the Purple Orchid and, turning to the bartender, remarked: "Well, Jack's finally gonna get recognized."

The Warren Commission studied the actions of Jack Ruby for the few months before the assassination. The Commission received assistance from the Department of State, the CIA, and the FBI. Some information furnished by these agencies was of a highly confidential nature and has still not been publicly revealed. Why not? Either Jack Ruby was an innocuous owner of a nightclub who had a sudden rush of adrenalin and committed murder in the heat of temper or he was something else. We ought to know about the possibility of his being something else. Perhaps if the Government agencies had delved further into the background of Jack Ruby, we might have a different view of this rather sordid little character seeking recognition.

For, back in Chicago, Jack Ruby was known as "Jack

Rubenstein," a cocky little union plenipotentiary. But Jack Rubenstein was also overly friendly with members of the old Al Capone gang.

In 1939, Leon Cooke was murdered. He was the founder and secretary-general of the Chicago Waste Handlers Union. At the time of his death, the secretary of the union was Jack Ruby, who confided to his close friend, Mitch Wolcoff, that he would like to take over the entire union himself. But this was not to be. The new head of the union was Paul Dorfman. He was the father of Allen Dorfman, a regular visitor to La Costa Country Club, situated twenty miles from San Clemente in California. Robert Kennedy noted that in 1949, James Hoffa needed a powerful ally in Chicago and found one in Paul Dorfman. His son Allen had been cited as the link between organized crime and the Teamsters Union Central States Pension Fund with millions of dollars at its disposal. Following Jack Ruby's arrest, the FBI interviewed Paul Dorfman on December 18, 1963. He said Ruby was not a successful organizer and voluntarily left the union in 1940.

In 1947, Ruby moved to Dallas and started two nightclubs, the Carousel and Vegas clubs. When he was arrested, Ruby's financial affairs were not in good shape: there was something like forty-four thousand dollars owed to the Internal Revenue Service and further debts to his brother, Earl Ruby, and to his friend, Ralph Paul. No one was exerting pressure on Jack Ruby, and it is difficult to understand why the Internal Revenue Service was not doing much about retrieving the outstanding taxes. It is even more surprising that when he was arrested, Jack Ruby had three thousand dollars on him, and more cash was found in his automobile.

"The Warren [Commission] Report" gave a great many details about Ruby's life, including the fact that he took his dachshund, Sheba, out on the Sunday morning before he killed Lee Harvey Oswald. They found nothing to link Ruby to organized crime and, while various phone calls were reported to the Commission, a few unusual ones were not commented upon. For instance, Irwin Weiner talked to Ruby for twelve minutes on October 26, 1963. Weiner was later acquitted with Allen Dorfman when both were charged with fraud in connection with the Teamsters pension-fund case, a case that came to light in April 1975. At the time of the 1963 phone call, Weiner was a Chicago bail bondsman with alleged ties to organized crime. Shortly after the phone call from Weiner, Ruby began to telephone Barney Baker, another Chicago resident, who was known as an enforcer in the underworld and was often used by the Teamsters Union. In June 1963, Baker was released from the state penitentiary. On the night before the assassination, Baker called the Miami representative of the Chicago mob. (Ruby's sister, Mrs. Eva Grant, testified to the Warren Commission that her brother knew the Yaras brothers in their Chicago days, admitting that they were tough characters but indicating that, because of this, they had little to do with them. Yet Ruby was in touch with Baker who was in contact with the Yaras.)

It should have been enough to alert those on the Commission that Ruby *did* indeed possess a dubious background and that there was a strong possibility that he had maintained contact with mobsters right up to the time of the assassination.

It was also established that Ruby called Al Gruber, a boyhood friend, at his home in Los Angeles. Although Gruber stated that he had had contact with Ruby only once in the past ten years, it is stretching credibility to understand why Ruby would call him only twenty minutes after the news of the assassination was out. It is also a coincidence that Gruber saw Ruby in Dallas early in November 1963. He said that he was traveling from Joplin and, since Dallas was only a hundred miles away, he thought he would look up his old friend, Jack Ruby. Joplin, Missouri, however, is not one hundred miles from Dallas but four hundred miles, a considerable distance to go out of his way to see a friend he had presumably ignored for more than ten years. Gruber has a

rap sheet listing numerous arrests, including grand lar-
ceny; and he often used a number of aliases, which puts
him right into the same class as so many of Ruby's other
friends. Gruber was a scrap-metal dealer in Los Angeles
and a friend of Frank Matula. Again there exists a link
with the Teamsters Union. Jimmy Hoffa named Matula
as a trustee of the International Teamsters Union when
he was released after serving 114 days in jail for perjury.
Matula was very active as an enforcer in the garbage in-
dustry in Southern California.

How much more the Warren Commission would have
needed before it linked Ruby with organized-crime elements is difficult to imagine. It seems as if the Commission fell over backward to pad out all reports on Ruby
with a load of totally irrelevant details when the main
ones were ignored. We are convinced that members of
the Commission had a good reason for deliberately playing down any evidence that would disrupt the preconceived idea of the lone assassin. Lee Harvey Oswald
had his mouth closed and could not defend himself, and
it was almost too easy to disguise relevant facts among
the numerous pages that ended up as "The Warren
[Commission] Report." So many threads led to connections with the Teamsters Union and Jimmy Hoffa,
the thorn in the flesh of the President's brother, Robert
Kennedy. Hoffa called both Bobby and Jack "creeps."

In the years since the lone assassin was killed by the
lone assassin, there have been a remarkable number of
Mafia-type killings of people who had connections with
Jack Ruby. One or two such killings might be accepted
as coincidences. But, when the total goes to more than
twenty, it is time to eliminate any thought of coincidence and assume that these people were killed because they knew too much. Every death is a story of its
own. All together they add a sinister note to the Mafia
scenario.

Reporters Bill Hunter of *The Long Beach Press Telegram* and Jim Koethe of *The Dallas Times-Herald* went
to Ruby's apartment on November 24, 1963, a few hours

after Ruby killed Oswald. These were the only two reporters known to have paid a visit to the apartment and gotten inside it. They went there with Attorneys Jim Martin and C. A. Droby, who had acted as legal advisers to probe into some of Ruby's affairs in the past. Tom Howard, another attorney, also went along and later was to be one of the lawyers acting in defense of Ruby. The newsmen met with the lawyers in a bar a block away from Dallas Police Headquarters, and they were invited by the lawyers to accompany them to the apartment. There they met with Ruby's room-mate, George Senator. Ten months later Koethe, Hunter, and Howard were all dead. Hunter was shot on April 21, 1964, as he sat at his desk in the pressroom of the police department in Long Beach, California. A policeman's gun was accidentally fired, and Hunter fell dead at his desk. On September 21, 1964, Koethe was found dead in his East Dallas apartment, felled and killed by a karate chop to his throat. Two months later, criminal lawyer Howard succumbed to a heart attack, although he had no previous history of heart trouble. Attorneys Martin and Droby believed that astute Tom Howard had a trick up his sleeve that could have saved Ruby from the death sentence and obtained a short prison sentence for him. We shall never know if Koethe and Hunter had an inkling of what Attorney Hunter's "trick" was. It is possible that it was discussed and the reporters were biding their time to pull off a journalistic scoop. Their lips were efficiently sealed when they died in such unusual circumstances.

Five women employees of Jack Ruby met with violent deaths soon after the assassination. There was Karen Bennett Carlin, known as Little Lynn, the girl Jack Ruby always took a very personal interest in. The star stripper of the Carousel Club was found shot to death in her Houston hotel. Another stripper, Marilyn Magyar, who worked under the name of Marilyn Moon, died two years after the assassination, shot seven times in her Omaha, Nebraska, home. Rose Cherami was thrown out of a car in southern Louisiana on November 20, 1963, and was taken to the hospital, where she told friends: "Better watch out; there is going to be a big disaster in Dallas. They are going to kill the President." She was still in the hospital when the assassination took place and was asked if Oswald knew Ruby. She replied: "Did Ruby know Oswald? Shit, they were bedmates." Rose Cherami worked for Ruby as a stripper. A few months later she was struck by a car in Big Sandy, Texas, and this time the accident was fatal. Also associated with Ruby were Nancy Rich and Betty MacDonald. . . . Both died violently.

Thomas (Hank) Killam was married to a woman who worked for Ruby and his best friend roomed in the same apartment house as the nightclub owner. Killam was found dead in Pensacola, Florida, in the early-morning hours of March 17, 1964. Police concluded that he had been careless enough to walk through a plate-glass window and died from a cut throat. A witness to the shooting of Patrolman Tippit, Harold Russell, was pistol-whipped to death by a policeman on July 23, 1965, in Sulphur, Oklahoma. Taxi driver William Wahley, whose small moment of fame came when his testimony before the Warren Commission was preferred to that of Roger Craig, added another unique moment of fame when he became the first Dallas cabdriver in forty years to die in an automobile accident in that city. Earlene Roberts, owner of the house Oswald roomed in and who had known Jack Ruby through her sister died on January 10, 1966.

oh come on already!

The Warren Commission concluded that Jack Ruby and Oswald did not know each other, but there are many witnesses who could have testified differently. The Warren Commission appeared to put Jack Ruby under a microscope, but what they saw was a distorted vision with the main facts out of focus. Probably not the least of the main facts overlooked was Ruby's longtime association with organized-crime persons and the fact that he knew Lee Harvey Oswald. One witness, Dallas District

Attorney Henry Wade, could have been called and
would have testified that Oswald often took a cab that
deposited him outside the Carousel Club. Wade was following up on the theory that Oswald and Ruby were
part of a conspiracy and would have produced such evidence in Ruby's second trial. Then in December 1966,
doctors diagnosed Ruby as suffering from terminal
cancer, and there never was a second trial.

When Sybil Leek lived in Las Vegas, Mrs. Lewis
McWillie, Cuban-born wife of Lewis Joseph McWillie,
whom Dallas police described as "a gambler and murderer," told her that she was upset about the death of
Jack Ruby whom she knew. She feared "someone had
done away with poor Jack." In "The Warren Report,"
McWillie is described as a gambler ... one wonders why
the Dallas police added "murderer" to his description.
He worked in Havana before Fidel Castro flushed out
the underworld types who were controlling vice under
the favored eye of former Cuban dictator Fulgencio
Batista. After Castro came to power, McWillie and his
wife moved to Las Vegas, where he worked at the Thunderbird Casino.

On the evening of November 21st, "The Warren Report" states that Ruby met with some Chicago friends in
the Bon Vivant Club of the Cabana Hotel. Was it another coincidence that this was the same hotel where
Brading-Braden was staying with a friend from California, ex-convict Morgan H. Brown? They occupied a
suite on the third floor facing the Stemmons Freeway.
Another coincidence is that Ruby met with Jean Aase,
who had recently received a telephone call from Dave
Ferrie in New Orleans. It surely stretches the credibility
that Brading-Braden, Ruby, and Ferrie did not know
one another—or that all three didn't know Lee Harvey
Oswald. Earlier in the day Brading-Braden is now
known to have visited the offices of oilman Lamar Hunt
and a number of oil speculators. Brading-Braden denied
that he went to the office but, if he did, it is very likely
he would have been there at the same time as Jack

Ruby. That's because Ruby drove Connie Trammell to an interview for a job with Bunker Hunt, Lamar's brother. Ruby left without Miss Trammell, which was either an ungallant thing to do or might have been because he had other business to attend to. Coincidences continue to pile upon coincidences, adding up to the possibility that Brading-Braden, Hunt, Ferrie, Ruby, and Oswald all knew—or should have known—one another and also knew of Brading-Braden's and Ruby's involvement with certain Mafia figures.

The conclusion of the Warren Commission was that the investigation produced no grounds for believing Ruby's killing of Oswald was part of a conspiracy. Ignorance was a blissful dismissal of any involvement with the Mafia, and all of Jack Ruby's strange friends emerge as whiter than white. Just as there was a strong case for Oswald being part of a Communist plot to assassinate the President, so there is a stronger case for believing that Jack Ruby was part of a Mafia-inspired cover-up to the assassination. Too many people were prepared to look to their own instincts for survival. Had the Commission come up with involvement with the Mafia in the assassination, again the lone-assassin theory would never have survived as the final conclusion of "The Warren [Commission] Report."

But the main ingredient missing was any hint of a Godfather, without whom not a single Mafia killing could ever have been instigated.

Of course, the irony of the possibility that the Mafia was in any way even remotely involved in J.F.K.'s assassination is that John Kennedy, unknowingly, had worked for the Mafia at one time. The time: during one of Kennedy's summer vacations from study at Harvard. At the time his father, Joseph Kennedy, had built an empire based on the importation of whiskeys into the United States. His associates were somewhat less than the savory businessmen whom you might suspect inhabit the corporate towers of New York and, for that summer, John Kennedy was unwittingly lent to them to run er-

rands as a "gopher" (as in go-fer coffee, go-fer the paper, etc.) . Now the link had come full circle!

In fact, the link between J.F.K. and the Mafia persisted for several years. Some years after the assassination
Miss Leek was invited to lunch at the Carlyle Hotel in
New York. Her hostess and companion was the niece of
onetime Mafia kingpin Joe "Bananas." As she recalls the
incident: "My companion looked around the lovely din-
ing room and saw men at another table whom she recognized. We saluted them through the cascading center-
piece of flowers, and she told me that they were Johnny
Roselli and his friend Sam Giancana from Chicago. I
had quite a conversation going with our waiter, whom I
remembered seeing in a hotel in Paris, and we were
reminiscing about the good old days in Paris. Noticing
our salutation to the two men, he told us that they often
came to the hotel but generally brought a lady with
them, a Mrs. Judith Campbell. 'She always visited
President Kennedy when he came here,' said the waiter.
'Sometimes she came with one of the men, sometimes
with both, but they always waited for her when she went
to see the President alone.' At the time I put it down to
just another rumor that the late President Kennedy was
a ladies' man.

"Today I see those meetings as much more meaningful than any clandestine romantic interlude could be.
The lady's choice of companions was unusual, and I
remembered that Robert Kennedy often had to suggest
to the President that he should be careful not to be seen
at the parties given by entertainers with Mafia connections."

This conversation took place not too long after the
Warren Commission came into being to seek out the
truth of the assassination of President Kennedy. The
Mafia scenario was part of that truth, but it got lost in
the wealth of trivia that was unearthed about Jack
Ruby. And, somewhere in the world, the missing Godfather must have laughed a lot. It was another triumph
for the Mafia but one that was never paraded before the

public. There is one thing about "The Warren [Commission] Report"—you can pay your money and take your choice of any number of scenarios.

Yet was the Mafiia part of it . . . alone or in concert with someone else?

12 | APRIL 4, 1968

As 1968 passed into history, it was to become known as one of the most turbulent and tragic years in the annals of the United States. The rest of the world was jolted all too often by news of tragedies and upheavals. Violence was increasing in the undeclared war in Vietnam, in the Middle East conflict, and the revolts on American college campuses. Scenes of seemingly endless war and terror were brought home to every American family through television and newspapers. Most disturbing of all was the sudden realization that the assassination of President Kennedy was not an isolated event but one that changed the path of American history. If there were any redeeming features in this year, it was the return of the crew of the U.S.S. *Pueblo* and the fantastic journey of Apollo 8 to the moon.

Overshadowing everything was the fact that 1968 was the year of two assassinations—the Rev. Dr. Martin Luther King, Jr., was murdered on April 4th, followed by Attorney General Robert Kennedy on June 5th. While black people mourned the death of their leader, Dr.

King, white people began to talk about the curse of the Kennedy family being fulfilled.

The big mistake was to think that the murder of Martin Luther King, Jr. was a symbol or symptom of the racial unrest in America. True, he went to the grumbling town of Memphis to deal with a minor labor dispute, the two-month-old strike of 1,300 predominantly black garbage collectors. The white mayor of Memphis, Henry Loeb, refused to meet the demands of the sanitation workers for an increase in wages. Dr. King, the conqueror of disputes in Montgomery, Birmingham, and Selma, was naturally attracted to the situation.

Threats on his life were nothing new to Dr. King and, when his Eastern Air Lines jet was delayed for fifteen minutes at takeoff because of a bomb scare, it could have been taken as an omen of worse things to come. Although an anonymous caller phoned to say there was a bomb in the baggage area, airline searchers found nothing. The plane took off to enable Dr. King to keep his appointment with a destiny not planned by an avenging God but by powerful men who resented Dr. King and all he stood for.

King arrived in Memphis to meet a challenge. Newspaper articles attacked King who, as the prophet of the poor and downtrodden, had stayed in luxury twenty-nine-dollar-a-day hotels when he went on his visits to campaign for the poor. In an effort to counteract these damaging and personally infuriating references, Dr. King checked into the black-owned Lorraine Motel, just about as nondescript as any two-story cinder-block building could be. For thirteen-dollars a night, King and his entourage would live in drab-walled, rust-spotted rooms. The Lorraine was on Mulberry Street, and on a slight rise across the road was a nameless rooming house with a metal awning of wilting green-and-yellow stripes for a nameless clientele. Actually the rooming house consisted of two buildings, one for whites, the other for Negroes. Connecting the two buildings was a dark passageway. About the time Dr. King checked into the Lorraine, a young dark-haired white man in a nondescript business suit checked into the opposite building. He registered as "John Willard" and he asked for room number five. There was nothing remarkable about this room except that it had the only clear view of the Lorraine. The manager of the rooming house, Mrs. Bessie Brewer remembered that a "John Willard" paid her eight dollars and fifty cents for the week and gave her a crisp twenty-dollar bill, a bill not usually seen at the downtrodden rooming house. It was the twenty-dollar bill that stuck in the memory of Mrs. Brewer, as well as the inane smile on the face of the man. At the time there was no reason to think any more about the man; he had paid in advance and looked pleasant about it, and that was enough for a not-too-prosperous rooming-house manager.

In the Lorraine, Dr. King and his aides settled down to a day of strategic planning for the march that Dr. King was going to lead in defiance of a Federal court injunction forbidding it. Later, his aides were to remember that King talked about death threats, probably brought into focus by the latest bomb scare they had experienced before the Eastern plane took off for Memphis. "Maybe I have the advantage over most people," said King. "I have conquered the fear of death."

After the strategy meeting, Dr. King washed and dressed for dinner. Then he walked out of room 306 onto the second-floor balcony to get some air. As he leaned casually on the green iron railing, he talked to workers attending to his Cadillac sedan in the courtyard below him. He then called out to soul singer Ben Branch, who had accompanied him to perform at the rally later on in the evening. "I want you to sing that song 'Precious Lord' for me ... sing it real pretty." He was never to hear the song again for, at that moment, a single rifle shot hit him. The heavy-caliber bullet smashed through Dr. King's neck, exploding against his lower-right jaw and severing his spinal cord. The impact of the bullet sent him reeling against the wall as his two aides, Jesse Jackson and Ralph Abernathy, automatically fell to the floor of the balcony. They had nothing to fear; the single bullet meant for Dr. King had reached its target. Memphis police, who had kept King under surveillance from "peek holes" in the fence, quickly converged on the motel. Some thirty of them milled around so much that they missed any chance to get the assailant, although someone saw a man run from the passageway of the rooming house to the street. An ambulance came and took the mortal remains of Dr. King to nearby St. Joseph's Hospital. In the emergency ward, Martin Luther King, Jr., age thirty-nine, was pronounced dead within one hour of the shooting.

Beside the front door of the rooming house, police found a scope-sighted 30.06 Remington pump rifle neatly packed up in its original box, as well as binoculars and a suitcase . A spent cartridge case was found in the lavatory, a tiny room so cramped that it would have been difficult for any man but a contortionist to use a long-barreled rifle and aim with such accuracy for one bullet to kill a man. Yet, because of the casing, it was concluded that this was the place from which the rifle was fired.

On the day of the funeral, one hundred and twenty million Americans tuned into the scene through the miracle of television. Nothing so dramatic and tragic had happened since the death of President John F. Kennedy. The funeral march lasted three hours, twice as long as that for the President. Coretta King, widow of the murdered man, brought an unexpected and macabre touch to the church service. She requested that a tape of her husband's last sermon be played. The rich voice intoned: "If any of you are around when I have to meet my day, I don't want a long funeral. Tell them not to mention I have a Nobel Peace Prize. That isn't important. I'd like to mention that Martin Luther King, Jr., tried to love somebody, that I did *try* to feed the hungry, that I did *try* in my life to clothe those who were naked, that I tried to love and serve humanity."

From the church in Atlanta, there was a four-mile march to the campus of Morehouse College. In death, the humility of Martin Luther King, Jr., was more apparent; and those who accused him of staying in posh hotels at great expense while his brethren went homeless and hungry could find no cause for criticism in this last journey. The simple coffin was put on a sharecroppers cart, drawn by a brace of mules called Ada and Agnes. The funeral route passed the gun-armed police of Governor Lester Maddox at the Georgia statehouse. The governor refused to close the schools for the funeral and protested the flags that fluttered at half-mast.

In the quadrangle of Morehouse College, where King had graduated at the age of nineteen, the aging president emeritus, Benjamin Mays, fulfilled his promise made long ago to Martin Luther King, Jr. Each had agreed that the survivor would deliver the eulogy for the other in the event of death. One might think that it was inevitable that Martin Luther King, Jr., only half the age of Ben Mays, would have survived; but there is no logic in assassination, which takes no notice of age. For it is the young who are the most dangerous to men seeking power and to those who are willing to force issues through assassination. "Too bad, you say, Martin Luther King, Jr., died so young," preached Mays. "Jesus died at thirty-three, Joan of Arc at nineteen, Byron and Burns at thirty-six. And Martin Luther King, Jr., at thirty-nine. It is not how long you live but how well."

In this he made a mistake. To men seeking power and making their own rules to obtain it, it is also a case of what one does to thwart such power that also matters. Dr. King had done a great deal, and he paid for it by becoming a symbolic warning to others who would deign to upset the plans of the faceless group of men determined to gain power through the White House.

Long before the remains of Dr. King were cold in his coffin, America began to have second thoughts about the assassination of President Kennedy. Few were really satisfied with "The Warren [Commission] Report." Another group of people hated the word conspiracy; it savored too much of a contrived undercurrent of diabolic acts with an end product in view, and no one likes to think that the Constitution of the country can ever be undermined. As the rumor mills spewed forth speculation and fear that somewhere there might be a conspiracy existing in the U.S.A., the FBI was discovering clues as to the identity of Martin Luther King, Jr.'s assassin. Fingerprints left on the rifle when the killer fled led to a man called "Eric Starvo Galt," which proved to be an alias for James Earl Ray. He had escaped from prison and had a record for four major crimes, including armed robbery, burglary, forgery of United States money orders, and car theft. It took the FBI thirteen days to check its bank of fingerprints.

Since it does not take a genius to perpetuate the crimes for which James Earl Ray had been convicted, the manner of his escape would indicate a clever piece of maneuvering if James Earl Ray did, indeed, think it out for himself. He left the Missouri State Penitentiary in April 1967, hiding in a large wooden bread box. Twice before he had tried to escape. Once he placed a dummy in his bed and hid in a ventilator shaft. Then he used a makeshift ladder to scale a wall. These were not exactly acts guaranteed to gain him freedom. The third attempt was successful.

After his escape from Missouri, James Earl Ray showed up as "Eric Starvo Galt" in Los Angeles, where he never seemed to be short of money and was frequently seen drinking screwdrivers at the Rabbit's Foot Club. It takes money to travel, and we now know in retrospect that James Earl Ray was able to travel from Memphis to Canada. In Canada he obtained a Canadian passport and used it to go to Lisbon, always a major city in which espionage agents are able to meet and move around freely. Ray then took British European Airways Flight 75 from Lisbon to Heathrow Airport in London, using the Canadian passport issued in the name of Ramon George Sneyd. Perhaps the London immigration

officers were smarter than those in Lisbon, who never
queried his passport. Or perhaps the London immigration office had been tipped off to intercept a man carrying a Canadian passport in the name of Sneyd. Anyway,
Sneyd was invited into a private room by the immigration officials to answer "routine" questions. What
could possibly have been the reason for intercepting just
one of the ninety-six passengers aboard the Lisbon-Lon-
don plane? There was nothing spectacular about Sneyd,
a quiet, unassuming, thickset man wearing glasses. The
interrogation proved to be far from routine. Sneyd was
found to be carrying a loaded pistol in his back pocket.
Moreover, he had not only one Canadian passport but
another in his suitcase. A top detective from Scotland
Yard, Tom Burns, took over the investigation of Ray,
alias Sneyd. Fingerprints proved that the man was
indeed Illinois-born James Earl Ray, alias Eric Starvo
Galt, an escaped convict wanted for questioning about
possible involvement in the assassination of Martin Luther King, Jr. in Memphis. The worldwide manhunt
was over. The lone assassin had been caught. But had
the *real* assassin been captured?

The assassination of Dr. Martin Luther King, Jr. was
a symbolic act, designed to pass a message onto Robert
Kennedy that "they" meant business.

Men existed in the system who needed power more
than anything else and, to get it, they had to look to the
future when their man, their chosen favorite, could
move into the White House. A man like Martin Luther
King, Jr. was not truly in their way, but Robert Kennedy was. As Dr. King was selected to play his part as
the sacrificial lamb slaughtered to promote political
causes and greed, so James Earl Ray was selected to play
the role of the proverbial "fall guy"; to be held up and
displayed to the American public as a man brought to
justice at a time when an increasing number of Americans were beginning to feel uneasy about law enforcement itself. But the scenario specially contrived for
this fall guy had many badly written passages in it, and

it was going to take a lot of legal and political manipulation to hold it together and present it to the public as another "lone assassin" brought to justice.

In the month between the murder of Martin Luther King, Jr., and the time when James Earl Ray arrived in London the first time, the world had witnessed a massive manhunt. Since Ray had been put on the wanted list of criminals, Canadian authorities were already alerted. The Mounties have a reputation for "always getting their man," but somehow Ray evaded them. And this was the man who had failed on two prison-escape attempts and had been imprisoned for offenses that put him in the minor league of criminals. Scotland Yard and Interpol were also alerted. Yet Ray still managed to move around freely, first to Canada from the United States, then to London and Lisbon and then back to London again. As a result of the well-publicized manhunt, people were led to believe that everything was being done to find the assassin of Martin Luther King, Jr.

The manhunt also managed to keep the rumor mills quiet; however, the FBI has a long history of extending its activities from seeking criminals to actually using them to sustain its own ends, and of manipulating the law to suit itself when necessary. It was well manipulated in the case of James Earl Ray. This could explain why Ray was able to travel extensively at a time when airfares were of considerable importance to the pocketbook of any normal workingman. When a man is chosen as a patsy, at least he is sure of being looked after financially until he becomes expendable. Of course, no one tells the patsy he is to play this role. He is led into thinking that he is part of a big operation. It is his chance to make the big time, to be *someone*. A man already under a prison sentence, carefully studied before an offer is made to him, is a "natural." Given the choice of languishing in jail or working for the FBI, even in a lowly position, must surely appeal to a prisoner who has been carefully and subtly assessed. Although he does not need to have superior intelligence, he does need to be trained in obedience and then to be programmed for a specific series of carefully planned actions. First comes the carrot and the ready supplies of money. The big stick is kept well hidden, but it is there ready to use at the right time. And now it was poised in position to beat James Earl Ray.

In London, Ray attempted to plead that having two Canadian passports was just a natural mistake. He said he noticed the name Ramon George Sneyd (a Toronto policeman's name he just "happened" to pick out of a phone book) was misspelled and he went to the embassy in Lisbon to have it changed. He was issued a new passport on May 16th, but the normal procedure of mutilating the old passport on the spot was somehow overlooked. How did Ray get his Canadian passport in the first place? Suppose he was indeed smart enough to set himself up with a Canadian passport; how smart would he have to be to get two? Also, while it is not unknown for criminals on the run to get false passports, it is a hard fact of life that such things cost money. The going price for forged passports in Miami, where there is a big traffic in such papers, is $2,500 and up. Is it likely that Ray got this passport on his own and paid for it with his own money? It would be easy enough for a Government office to supply him with false papers as it has frequently done for espionage agents. The Canadian passport is not as easy to explain. It has been said that Canadian passport laws "are lax." However, in Canada the applicant for a passport not only must swear that he is a Canadian but he also must produce his birth certificate to prove his identity. The story that circulated is that Canadian passport officials literally issue this vital document to anyone. But James Earl Ray was not smart enough to get away with forging United States money orders. (One of his fellow inmates at the Missouri State Penitentiary said, "He couldn't hold up a candy store without getting caught.") So the idea that he, and he alone, managed to obtain a Canadian passport—let alone two—is patently absurd.

If Ray had been picked up in Memphis, a great deal of publicity mileage would have been denied the FBI. Although the worldwide manhunt was a good bit of strategic planning, the giveaway was the pickup in London. For Scotland Yard's strong suit is its effectiveness in pursuing bulletins, and they are best known for "following information received." When Sybil Leek was a journalist in England, she followed many criminal cases and got to know many detectives. "Most of them had regular informants on the local scene who were paid small sums of money for their information. But, on the international scene, it was easy enough to pass on information through the American Embassy to a nameless resident in England and then get him to pass on the 'tip' to pull Ray off his plane and hold him for questioning." When the time came to extradite Ray to his native country, the added impetus to his being a legitimately caught criminal was reinforced by the great reputation of the Scotland Yard officials themselves. By picking up James Earl Ray in London, there was no danger of an assassin getting to him as Jack Ruby got to Lee Harvey Oswald. This time the patsy had to be delivered intact and stand the "due process of law."

No valuable work of art could have been better packaged than Ray when Scotland Yard sent him back to the United States. He was sent to Shelby County, Tennessee, to await arraignment for the murder of Martin Luther King, Jr. At the same time, no one begrudged the accolades that poured into Scotland Yard for its commendable capture of a wanted American criminal. When Ray arrived at Shelby County Jail, he emerged from an armored truck wearing a bulletproof vest over his plaid shirt and armored leggings over his pants. To complete the picture of a dangerous criminal, he wore handcuffs and had a bodyguard of a score or more deputies armed with riot guns. James Earl Ray had come home, and everyone knew it. The number of hours spent by the FBI were recorded in newspaper columns and the manhunt paid off in terms of publicity—publicity that enhanced the wilting image of the FBI. Ray was put in a cell on the third floor of the jail, and the windows of the cell were blocked out with heavy steel shutters. Normally, prison trustees ran the elevators but, on Ray's arrival, these men were replaced by crews of specially selected men from the sheriff's office. Closed-circuit television monitored all movements inside and outside his cell. This time the "lone-assassin" theory had to stand up. James Earl Ray would have his day in court, and all Americans would see the due process of law working. Above all, the idea of the lone assassin had to be sustained. This time, the theory had to stand up, not through the decision of a commission, but through days in court with Ray's defense lawyer facing the prosecuting lawyers in exciting daily sequences, as a catharsis for Americans who wanted "justice."

Ray was in custody for eight months before his trial, during which time his mail was opened, photostated, and delivered to the prosecutor. His first attorney was Arthur Hanes and, in order to get funds for the defense, Hanes persuaded Ray to let author William Bradford Huie write his life story. Huie's first piece, "The Story of Ray and the Conspiracy to Kill King," was published in *Look* Magazine in November 1968. Then Huie changed his ideas in midstream and began to write about the "lone nut," thus substituting the lone-assassin story that the prosecution was intent on proving. James Earl Ray fired Arthur Hanes in an effort to get rid of author Huie as well. His brothers, Jerry and John Ray, contacted Percy Foreman, one of Texas's most famous criminal lawyers. Among the first things Foreman—known as "the Texas tiger"—did was to look at the book contract signed by Hanes, Huie, and Ray and announce that it would be easy to break. John Ray recalled Foreman's first discussion of the case: "Foreman mentioned how he and Ramsey Clark [United States Attorney General at the time] were good friends. He said there was no evi-

dence against Jimmy and that he would get hold of TV
films of King, of cities burning, of rioting, and would
show them to the jury. After two weeks the jury would
want to shoot King themselves. He said he was an attorney who played with the emotions of the jury."

After this hopeful start, it came as a shock at the next
meeting with the Ray family for Foreman—who was
once the attorney for Jack Ruby—to say he wanted
James to plead guilty. They brought a letter from Ray
that listed ten reasons why he was not guilty. Two days
before the guilty plea was entered, John Ray visited his
brother, who was distraught because he did not want to
plead guilty. By this time Foreman had gotten all the
money from the sixty percent of the royalties he had
contracted for on the book on Ray's life, having negoti-
ated himself into the book contract with Huie, eliminat-
ing Ray completely. Huie had even changed the title of
his book from *They Slew the Dreamer* to a now-consist-
ent *He Slew the Dreamer*.

When Jerry Ray saw his brother in prison, he said:
"You don't have an attorney representing you; he's representing a book writer." Ray dismissed Foreman and,
with him, Huie. (In a later evidentiary hearing to determine whether Ray had received "effective assistance of
counsel" at the time he pleaded guilty, his new attorney
said that the contract involving Foreman and Huie constituted a "blatant conflict of interest." Furthermore, he
said that Foreman had begun negotiations for a guilty
plea before undertaking even a cursory investigation of
the evidence, coercing Ray into the guilty plea to
preserve the economic value of the book.)

Had Foreman pursued the evidence with as much
ardor as he did the book contract, he would have seen
the flimsiest of all cases. There were no reliable
witnesses to prove that James Earl Ray was even the
man who had checked into the rooming house at 422½
South Main, opposite the Lorraine Motel. The manager
had described a thin man, weighing about one hundred
and twenty-five pounds but, when he was picked up in

London, Ray was bulky in stature. The State's star witness was labeled by his wife as "drunk and saw nothing." Another described merely "a man" hurrying through the passageway into the street immediately after the fatal shot was fired.

Moreover, because time is of the utmost importance to any criminal, he has to "split" from the scene of the crime quickly. However, the rifle, binoculars, and Ray's other belongings were found neatly and carefully packed in their original wrappings, covered with Ray's fingerprints. They were not found inside the rooming house, but beside the door of Kniep's Amusement Store next door.

Then, there were the clothes found in Ray's abandoned Mustang, which were many sizes too small to fit Ray, yet which would have fit a one-hundred-and-twenty-five-pound man. (Such a man was tentatively identified as the "Mr. Willard" who rented the room and is too close to the description of one of the "tramps" picked up in the railroad yard behind Dealey Plaza after the assassination of John Kennedy to be dismissed lightly.)

For another thing, King's chauffeur, Solomon Jones, and Harold "Cornbread" Carter, a rooming-house inhabitant, claim to have seen a man in the bushes, below the rooming house and directly below the Lorraine Motel balcony where King was shot. And two police detectives, spying on King from a concealed position in the nearby firehouse, felt that the shot came from the bushes below and "not from any window twenty feet above." It had been presumed that the assassin fired from the tiny cramped bathroom where there was scant room to hold and sight a rifle properly. But the bushes atop a wall and bordering a vacant lot that stands between the rooming house and the Lorraine are dense and very thick, a far more desirable place for a gunman to secrete himself away than even Dallas's grassy knoll. The first thing that impresses anyone who has ever paid a visit to the Lorraine is that the distance between the bathroom where the assassin was supposed to have fired the deadly weapon and the second-floor balcony of the Lorraine is about eighty to one hundred yards. However, the bushes were closer—much closer. The most obvious place for finding the location of the assassin had been ignored. Yet the police immediately rushed up the stairs of the rooming house, almost as if they knew which room held the spent shell casing that had been conveniently left behind, a familiar replay of the Texas School Book Depository scenario.

And, finally, the ballistic tests failed to link Ray with the "murder weapon," but were suppressed by the prosecutor.

Ray states that he met a mysterious French Canadian named "Raoul," a husky, swarthy, underworld character enmeshed in a lucrative gun-smuggling and narcotics operation. It was Raoul who brought Ray to Memphis in 1968 to meet an international gunrunner to run guns to South America. Or so Ray thought. Raoul said it would be a get-rich-quick operation. Ray ran errands for Raoul in Memphis, but he did not rent the room at the motel, even though he said he did at his trial. He did this in order to protect Raoul. The rooming-house manager, Bessie Brewer, could not identify Ray as the man who actually rented the room.

Ray was certainly in and out of the rooming house, including one time on April 4, 1968, to deliver a gun to Raoul. Then Raoul gave him two hundred dollars and told him to "get lost" for a while, since he wanted to see the big-time gunrunner alone so that he would speak more freely. Raoul also instructed Ray to leave his white Mustang parked at the curb just a few feet from the stairwell. He suggested that his out-of-town visitor might want to use it later that evening.

A five-twenty P.M., when Ray left the rooming house, he noticed that the Mustang had a low tire and decided to take it to a local garage for air and then return it to the curb. He drove the Mustang three blocks to a service station. He expressed annoyance that he had to wait for

Ray's version

service because the attendants were very busy. While a black attendant, Willie Green, was putting air in the low tire, Ray saw an ambulance go by and looked at his watch and saw that the time was six-oh-five P.M. He drove the Mustang back to the rooming house only to find the entire block sealed off, with police swarming all over. A policeman standing in the middle of the road yelled, "Get away from here." He asked the policeman if he could make a U-turn, which was illegal under the traffic ordinance, so that he could proceed along South Main Street. "I don't care what you do—just get away from here," said the policeman. Ray made the U-turn and drove south out of Memphis toward Mississippi. About a hundred miles from Memphis, near the town of Grenada, Ray turned on the car radio and learned of the assassination of King at the Lorraine and of the address of the adjacent rooming house.

It is reasonable to ask why Ray traveled away from Memphis. His answer is equally reasonable. Twice during the day in Memphis he had felt uneasy about a man who seemed to be watching him—once in a bar and then in a cafe downstairs in the rooming house. Knowing he was in Memphis for something illegal—that is, to meet with a gunrunner—and being an escapee from prison, he thought the man might be an FBI agent. When he returned to the rooming house from the garage, his first impression was that the FBI had caught up with his friend Raoul and that he had been arrested, which would account for the confusion around the place. Not wanting to do anything that would shorten his freedom, he did what was natural for him—he fled.

Mysteriously, within minutes of the assassination, the Memphis police radio network was penetrated—just as Dallas's police network had been on November 22, 1963—by a bulletin of non-traceable origin, broadcasting that the police were chasing a white Mustang, when, in fact, they were not.

To this day it is not clear how many people were in the rooming house on the day King was killed. We know

of at least one man who was there but was never interviewed by the FBI; and, if one person managed not to
be interviewed, it is likely that others did as well.

Jack Walter Youngblood is an adventurer who has
supplemented his income from time to time by picking
up fees for services rendered to the CIA, the FBI, and
anyone else who needs his "special services." He is a
thin man, with nothing outstanding about his appearance, and unlikely to stand out in a crowd. Youngblood
is known to have a steady hand and a gun for hire.
Writer Wayne Chastain has positive proof that
Youngblood can be identified as a man who was in the
rooming house. But someone forgot to interview him,
probably a convenient form of forgetfulness. Who knows
what might have come out if Youngblood had been
available for a thorough examination by Ray's lawyer?
With James Earl Ray safely delivered to jail and awaiting trial—even though he was identifiable only through
his fingerprints and nothing else—it was enough to
gamble that the lone-assassin theory would again pay off.
Any investigation of too many people in the rooming
house, included Youngblood, would have shortened the
odds against success.

An investigation could also have brought out the fact
that after King had booked his rooms at the motel, the
clerk was approached by a man who specifically asked
that Martin Luther King be given a central room on the
second floor facing the swimming pool. A check with associates of Martin Luther King revealed that they had
no advance man with the authority to do this. Who then
was this mystery man whom the desk clerk describes as
"a white guy with stuff on his face to make him look
like a light black man?" Surely, the routine inquiries
could have been expected. Yet none were ever made.

Ray had no history of hating blacks—despite reports
to the contrary—and his psychiatric report brought out
no deep obsession that could have motivated him to
murder. He was a man caught up in a web of deceit woven by people in need of a character to play the part of

a lone assassin. A man with a criminal record would have little chance of sympathy from the public. He was in the right place allocated for him but at the wrong time for his own welfare. Like Lee Harvey Oswald, James Earl Ray kept a diary; it is amazing how important these diaries become when they are introduced as evidence, and the same rules were applied to James Earl Ray's diary. A more intensive investigation of Oswald's diary led to the finding of the telephone number of FBI agent Hosty. In Ray's diary there was a phone number and, when a Canadian reporter called it, he was surprised to find it was the office of a highway state patrol in Mississippi. On an impulse, he asked for "Raoul." The voice said, "I am sorry, 'Raoul' is not here at the moment." The elasticity of coincidence is indeed stretched, but there are many reasons for believing that Raoul was not a figment of Ray's imagination.

(Remember the three "tramps" who were arrested in the railroad yard behind Dealey Plaza and released without being questioned after the assassination of President Kennedy? One was very well dressed, and none merited the demeaning title "tramp." The best-dressed "tramp" was nicknamed "Frenchy," and bore a startling resemblance to the descriptions given of Raoul. When the FBI's first flyer of the King-assassination fugitive was issued, the hand-drawn picture was a "ringer" for him. And, as in the case of the three "tramps" who were apprehended and quickly released, so was a man called "Jack Armstrong," who was quietly arrested the morning after King's assassination and just as quietly—and quickly—released.)

Russell X. Thompson is a Memphis attorney who worked with Ray's first lawyer, Arthur Hanes, and who offered his services to Foreman, only to have them refused. Six days after King's murder, Thompson was visited by a six-foot-tall man who wore a pinstripe suit and Panama hat, and identified himself as "Tony Benavides." Opening the door with a handkerchief in his hand, "Benavides" sat down and started talking

another version

about the assassination immediately. "I believe my room-mate killed King. It will be my lousy luck that the police will arrest me and charge me with King's murder. They picked me up last Friday." Thompson thought to himself that this swarthy man who spoke English with a Tex-Mex dialect was really the same "Jack Armstrong" who was picked up by the police the morning after the assassination. And was it the same Benavides who was in the vicinity of Tenth and Patton streets when Officer Tippit was shot in Dallas? And the same Benavides who can also be found as a witness, listed in "The Warren Report" as a friend of Jack Ruby?

"Benavides" gave Thompson a plausible scenario for what really happened on that evening of April 4th in Memphis: "That shot could not have been fired from the bathroom window—the spot where the FBI announced that the fatal shot had been fired. For one thing, the elevation is all wrong." How did he know, thought Thompson, unless he had, of course, been in the rooming house? "Benavides" went on, "The shot came from a clump of bushes on a wall across the street from the motel," referring to the patches of tall grass and clumps of bushes at the edge of the wall *below* the rooming house. "Benavides" then stood up and made a strange motion, as if he were trying to scratch his back; but, instead, when his hand came around to his front again, it contained a small revolver. "It was hidden in the pit of my back," said the visitor. "That trick drives the cops crazy. They never think of frisking a guy there. A guy like me with large shoulder blades, can carefully conceal a small pistol there, leaving no bulges, if he knows how to breathe and dress properly.

"The killer shot from the wall outside the rooming house, then disassembled the .30-caliber Savage while he was still in the bushes and threw away the rifle stock and," here Benavides pointed to his back, "strapped the rifle barrel against his back where it fit close to his skin." Thompson remembered that a private detective had claimed he had found a rifle stock a few days later

in a trash heap. It was of the same description as "Benavides" had given him, and he wondered if the same trick
as "Benavides" performed with his handgun could really
be performed with a rifle as well. "The cops from the
fire station and other lookout points around the motel
were so confused that they came running in every direction," "Benavides" continued. "Most ran toward the
Lorraine, jumping down from the wall in back of the
cafe [that adjoined the rooming house] to the sidewalk
below, and then ran across the street to the Lorraine.
The gunman merely emerged from the bushes as incon-
spicuously as he could and joined in the scramble with
the plainclothesmen and firemen." "Benavides" then
boasted, "He was not suspected because he did not appear to be armed and because he was running *toward*
the scene, not away from it!" Then when the police began shooing away the crowd, he walked through the
rear of the motel grounds to a service station, where he
had a motorbike stashed away, and rode off. "And," concluded "Benavides," "nobody suspected him of being the
getaway gunman." When Thompson checked, he found
that the room-mate "Benavides" spoke of back in Denver was known as "Pete." He happened to answer the
same description as Eugene Brading-Jim Braden, the
syndicate figure who was picked up and released in Dallas after the assassination of President Kennedy.

(From a former CIA friend of Sybil Leek's with
twenty-eight years of service, we learned recently that
"Jack Armstrong" is a CIA code name for any soldier of
fortune who hires himself out to the CIA for special
work of a sinister nature. The idea of using this name
obviously came from an old radio theme of the thirties,
"Jack Armstrong, All-American Boy." This leads us to
believe that Benavides-Armstrong may have still another
alias and turn out to be J. Walter Youngblood, the man
who checked into the rooming house and whom no one
bothered to question on the spot.) It is amazing how the
same characters manage to crop up on the scene after assassinations and no one in authority questions them or

checks their backgrounds. But then, why should they be questioned if they are merely fulfilling their missions with the full knowledge of the FBI or CIA?

After all, J. Edgar Hoover publicly referred to Martin Luther King, Jr., as "the most notorious liar in the United States." And a former FBI agent, Arthur Murtagh, in the Atlanta bureau for twenty years, says that he participated in both the Kennedy and King investigations and personally saw "leads being washed out." One lead that was washed out was evidence that he uncovered in Atlanta directly linking Jack Ruby to right-wing members of the Cuban community. He says the same practice of ignoring leads and washing out evidence occurred again when he was investigating James Earl Ray.

Texas attorney Percy Foreman might have gotten useful information from lawyer Russell Thompson, but Foreman wanted no such help.

And so James Earl Ray, alias Eric Starvo Galt, alias Ramon George Sneyd, identified by no witnesses, linked by no ballistic tests to the murder weapon, and coerced into a plea of guilty by a defense attorney who may have been looking out for his own interests, molders away in solitary confinement in a heavily guarded jail cell, serving a ninety-nine-year sentence as the "lone assassin" of the Rev. Dr. Martin Luther King, Jr.

The only thing that James Earl Ray is guilty of is not that he was a "lone assassin," but that he was a "loner" and a perfect fall guy.

But for whom?

13 | JUNE 5, 1968

When Lyndon B. Johnson stepped into the shoes of a dead President, he walked warily in them until the next election. Winning with an unprecedented landslide of fifteen million votes, he was able to walk more easily through the next four years. It seemed that he would continue to do so for a further term of office. Then, out of the blue, came the surprise announcement that President Johnson would not seek re-election in 1968. Four days after the announcement, Martin Luther King, Jr., was killed by an assassin's bullet. His death was to stay the disenchantment of a country ripped apart by the Vietnam war and turn it into agonized grief. It seemed as if one of the greatest nations in the world could not bear any more national sorrow, but more was in store; for, on June 5th, 1968, Senator Robert F. Kennedy was shot down.

When President Johnson withdrew from running for another term, he tried to insure that his Vice President, Hubert Humphrey, would be the candidate of the

Democratic party. However, out on the hustings, was the charismatic figure of Robert Kennedy, reviving memories of the thousand days of Camelot. Victory followed victory in the primaries, and Kennedy's speech at the Ambassador Hotel in Los Angeles after the California primary seemed to be the final touch to a successful candidacy. With the ringing sounds of jubilation in his ears, he left the podium and took an unusual route from the platform through the kitchen of the hotel. Close by him were his aides and security men. It seemed that nothing could stop Robert Kennedy, and then it happened! As he made his way through the pantry, a tiny Jordanian appeared before him, waving his .22-caliber Ives Johnson gun. In full view of some one hundred spectators, the Jordanian fired his gun. Assistant maître d' Karl Uecker, former football star Roosevelt (Rosie) Grier, and Olympic champion Rafer Johnson immediately threw themselves at the gunman, pinning him down to the steam table. The heavyweight men seemed to entirely cover the tiny body of the Jordanian as they wrenched his gun away from him. But Robert Kennedy, brother of an assassinated President, was lying on the floor, shot in the head, bleeding and dying, arms spread-eagled, his glazing eyes still open in stupified wonder.

A hundred people were in the pantry with him, and no one was sure where the bullets came from or how many bullets were fired. . . . They only knew that another terrible page in American history was being written right in front of them.

The Jordanian proved to be a young man named Sirhan Bishara Sirhan, and he was standing in front of Robert Kennedy when he was flung onto the steam table. Attention was diverted to Sirhan as Kennedy fell to the floor. The Los Angeles County coroner, Thomas T. Noguchi, who performed the autopsy, found that a fatal bullet had entered the skull of the Senator, from the rear, just one inch below the ear, and was lodged in his brain.

Another, passing through his right armpit, had

worked its way up and was lodged at the base of the neck. Still another had passed through his body, ending its route in the high ceiling. This bullet has never been found and, within days of the assassination, the ceiling panels had been removed, never to be seen again.

These bullets were all fired upward, from right to left, back to front. There was a fourth bullet hole in the Senator's left shoulder pad. This bullet seemed to come from a different direction than the other three. The bullet that hit his shoulder pad was found embedded in the wall. Of the one hundred people in the pantry, five spectators were also wounded, and each had a bullet removed. This made a total of nine bullets ... four that had struck Senator Kennedy and one each in five different people. Nine bullets and, according to some witnesses, as many as thirteen. And yet Sirhan Sirhan's gun fired only eight bullets. Where did the extra bullet(s) come from? If, indeed, there were more than eight bullets, there must have been two guns. And two guns spell "conspiracy."

Once again, the lone-assassin idea was presented to the American public. The coroner, however, found deeply embedded powder burns around the head wound, the sort of burns that occur only when the muzzle of a gun is mere inches away from the entrance wound—at point-blank range. But, according to the testimony of Grier and Uecker, the nearest Sirhan Sirhan came to Kennedy was a minimum of two feet and a maximum of seven.

The advocates of the lone-assassin theory suggested that Kennedy had turned slightly to his left to shake hands with Juan Romero, a Puerto Rican busboy; however, this still leaves the question of the powder burns unresolved. At no time was Sirhan Sirhan near enough to hold a gun literally against the head of the Senator. It looked like a replay of Dallas, but no one wanted those types of rumors again. Noguchi's autopsy views were confirmed by DeWayne Wolfer, the acting director of the Los Angeles Pathology Department.

Sirhan Sirhan came to trial as a young Jordanian whose passions were enflamed by Senator Kennedy's support of Israel. Everyone wanted a conviction, which was indeed the verdict, yet still those damning rumor mills continued. The Los Angeles chief of detectives, Robert Houghton, stated that he was not prepared to "make it easy for the clever people who stand by to profit from the cry of conspiracy, to hook their theories to journalistic wagons before the Arlington soil is trampled."

(Sybil Leek had her own experience in being part of American history on the night when Robert Kennedy was killed. "My son Julian and I had been to dinner with friends in Beverly Hills and, on the way home, we decided to drive to the Ambassador Hotel. Julian was new in the States, and I wanted him to see the hotel that I had described to him in letters. We drew up outside the hotel at almost the exact moment the murder took place. Julian, a professional photographer, sensing something newsworthy was happening, grabbed his equipment and disappeared, leaving me in the car. About an hour later, he came back with several reels of film he had taken. In the interim, I had heard what had happened, but it was made more real by the on-the-spot report that my son gave me. The confusion was terrible, though finally we managed to get away, still shocked at yet another assassination. I could not help but remember the time when I had met Robert Kennedy at Kipps Bay in New York and felt a terrible aura of impending tragedy about him. At first, I thought it was connected with the death of his brother; then I knew that Robert Kennedy, too, would die tragically. Perhaps it was some of my intuitive qualities that prompted us to drive to the Ambassador Hotel on that fateful night, because there were certainly many other hotels that would have interested Julian just as much.")

And on the very day when Sirhan Sirhan was transferred to the Los Angeles jail, Sybil was unhappily visiting the son of a friend of hers there. The security precautions for visitors were phenomenal . . . everyone was carefully searched before taking his place in front of the screens separating the incarcerated from their visitors. The prisoners were not supposed to know that Sirhan was in the prison. But they did and, most amazing of all, the person she was visiting told her that all the prisoners in his block knew everything that was going on and were aware that a conspiracy had been responsible for slaying Senator Kennedy. It did not matter what their political convictions were or their crimes; the prisoners had already formed their own opinion. "It was the first time I actually thought of a conspiracy because, like all other United States residents, I was only conscious that R.F.K.'s assassination, following so closely on that of Martin Luther King, Jr., was not likely to enhance the United States in the eyes of the rest of the world.

"Away from the harrowing experience of being a prison visitor," Sybil recalled that she "heard the word 'conspiracy' whispered everywhere I went, for the next few days and for years after I left Los Angeles." As time passed, there seemed to be more substance than ever to the theory that the assassination was not the work of a lone demented Jordanian with a personal hatred toward Kennedy, *but more likely part of a plot that linked the assassinations of President Kennedy and Martin Luther King, Jr., with that of Senator Kennedy.* Since there were no less than one hundred people in the pantry at the time of the assassination, there were a number of witnesses who remembered the occasion very well. Karl Uecker stated that he was leading Kennedy by the hand unknowingly *toward* Sirhan Sirhan. Four witnesses testified that Robert Kennedy was turning to the left in order to shake hands with a waiter. A friend of the Senator, Frank J. Burns, stated that he was standing off Kennedy's right shoulder when the shots were fired and that Kennedy had turned almost ninety degrees; therefore, he could not be facing the muzzle of the gun held by Sirhan. His testimony was backed up by Edward Minasian, Jesus Perez, Vincent Di Pierro, and Martin Petrusky—all employed in the kitchen of the Ambassador

Hotel. At the trial, the prosecution neatly bypassed the dilemma posed by the witnesses who placed Kennedy away from the muzzle of Sirhan's gun. The prosecution argued that the eyewitnesses who testified for the Government must have made a mistake. It was as simple as that.

Then the prosecution fell afoul of its own deduction when David Fitts, the prosecuting attorney, said: "With reference to the circumstances of the shooting, Your Honor, Your Honor has heard Karl Uecker and any number of witnesses who attempted to describe what happened. One witness has put the muzzle of the revolver some three to four feet from the Senator's head; others have it at varying ranges. The only way we can clear up whatever ambiguity there may be there and to show the truth is by the testimony of witness Wolfer who, on the basis of the powder tattooing and the experiments he performed with respect thereto, will testify that the muzzle range with respect to the Senator's head was about one inch." Defense Counsel Grant Cooper agreed.

If the autopsy estimate was correct, then Sirhan could not have fired the shot that killed the Senator. Columnist Pete Hamill stated that Sirhan was seven feet away from Kennedy. The busboy who had just shaken hands with Kennedy, Juan Romero, estimated the distance as three feet. College student Valerie Schulte said that "Sirhan's arm and gun were fifteen feet away from me and something like three feet away from the Senator." Edward Minasian, walking a yard in front of Kennedy, thought the barrel of Sirhan's gun was "approximately" three feet away from Kennedy. The evidence of the autopsy therefore, presents a problem. Neither the prosecution nor the defense counsels seemed inclined to probe deeply into the matter of distance. Sirhan's defense was based more on an insanity plea resting on "diminished capacity" than on raising reasonable doubts about the physical evidence. There would have been no doubts if all the bullets fired in the pantry could be identified as coming from the same gun.

In the grand jury hearings on June 7th, DeWayne Wolfer testified that he had examined the "near-perfect" bullet removed from the neck of the Senator. He said that he established that it was fired from Sirhan's gun because he had test-fired the gun into a water tank, thus enabling the spent bullets to be retrieved unharmed. De-Wayne Wolfer took four of the "test shots" to the grand jury and was able to testify that the microscopic tests comparable with the four bullets agreed with those of the one in Kennedy's neck. Wolfer did not use Sirhan's gun when making the test but a "similar one," a major difference in the evidentiary submission to the grand jury. The serial number on the gun used in the tests by Wolfer was H 18602; the serial number of Sirhan's gun was H 53725. (The Los Angeles Police Department later said that it destroyed the test gun in July 1969.) At the trial, Exhibit Number Fifty-Five was listed as a bullet from IJ .22 gun, presumed to be the murder weapon, serial number H 18602.

And the vitally important spectrographic evidence was also missing a year later.

The use of a test gun has provided confusion and added to the uncertainties. The four test bullets recovered from the water tank were put in an envelope. No one questioned Wolfer's word about these bullets. Either Wolfer made a mistake in identifying the exhibit and wrote the wrong serial number on the envelope or submitted the wrong bullets into evidence. Nonetheless, a major mistake was made.

Sirhan had been in prison a year (although Kennedy staff members hoped he'd be released so that they could kill *him*) when a dedicated film maker, Ted Charach, tracked down ballistic expert William H. Harper. Harper is often employed as a consultant by the Pasadena, California, police. With a partner, Marshall Houts, he had constructed an extraordinarily accurate microscopic testing device called the Ballisab Camera. The main

purpose of this invention was to find minute details
that the spectrographic technique might miss. Harper
pointed out to Charach that many discrepancies existed
in the official ballistics report. What had been surmised
by a few people was not bolstered by facts from an expert. One of the people wounded in the pantry was William Weisel. His bullet was labeled Exhibit Number
Fifty-Four. It did not match up with Exhibit Number
Forty-Seven, the bullet lodged in the neck of Senator
Kennedy. Yet, logically, the two bullets should match
since they were supposed to come from the eight shots
fired by Sirhan. Categorically, Harper states that the two
exhibits represent bullets fired from two different guns.
Obviously, if the professional opinion of this respected
ballistics expert is correct, then the fact of a "second
gun" is established despite the evidence at the trial. In
short, if true, there is now proof of a conspiracy, negat-
ing the idea of a demented assassin working on his own.

Part of the affidavit made by Harper in December
1970, reads: "For the general circumstances of the shooting, the only reasonable assumption is that the bullet removed from victim Weisel was, in fact, fired from the
Sirhan gun. This bullet is in near-perfect condition. I
have therefore chosen it as the "test" bullet from the
Sirhan gun and compared it with the bullet removed
from the Senator's neck. My examination disclosed no
individual characteristic establishing that Exhibit Number Forty-Seven, the bullet from Kennedy's neck, and
Exhibit Number Fifty-Four, the bullet from Weisel, had
been fired by the same gun. In fact, my examination disclosed that bullet Exhibit Number Forty-Seven had a rifling range of approximately fourteen percent greater
than the rifling angle of bullet Exhibit Number Fifty-
Four. It is therefore my opinion that bullets Forty-Seven
and Fifty-Four could *not* have been fired from the same
gun."

This expert opinion of William Harper's was made
public in the spring of 1971, causing an uproar. Acting
on behalf of Harper, an attorney tried to block Wolfer's

appointment as chief forensic chemist in charge of the LAPD Crime Laboratory, charging incompetence. However, Wolfer was appointed anyway. Then District Attorney Joseph P. Busch reacted by stating that since there was concern about the authenticity of certain exhibits in the Sirhan case, the matter was serious enough to justify a grand jury investigation into the handling of such exhibits at that time. The grand jury duly reported that it also had reservations "about the present integrity of the ballistics exhibits." But, in the autumn of 1971, a board of inquiry dismissed all questions raised by William Harper and Ted Charach.

We do not believe that any future ballistic tests will *prove* a second gun, since it is doubtful if Sirhan Sirhan's actual gun will ever surface again to make such a test totally legitimate. Moreover, a recent forensic re-examination of the different bullets was inconclusive. There was nothing to support the conclusion of a second gun. Conversely, there was no conclusive evidence that there was *not* a second gun. (The passing years since the tragedy have eroded the reproductive markings of the bullets, and these insufficient markings have made the re-examination totally inconclusive.) This does not eliminate our conviction that there was indeed a second gun; it confirms our belief that this assassination was as carefully planned as its predecessors. Very little was left to chance, and yet it is chance itself that provides the solution. We must come to grips with the fact that the original medical report indicated there were powder burns on the head, as if a gun had been fired at Senator Kennedy from a point-blank range, not more than a few inches away.

This always puzzled us until Sybil remembered that a relative of hers had worked in a carefully concealed office-workshop beneath the offices of a well-known magazine in New York. After the Second World War, he was engaged in preparing very delicate and very, very secret weapons for use of specially chosen CIA personnel. The hazard of espionage work is that when a spy dies abroad, he rarely knows where the danger will come from, as his death is arranged either by a double agent or by a colleague. Even spies become expendable when they begin to know too much and, in so doing, become jittery, thus representing a hazard to the people they work for. Unusual lethal weapons disguised as fountain pens or rings or other seemingly innocuous everyday objects have been produced for years on one of New York's main thoroughfares.

That random remembrance took on even greater significance for Sybil when she chanced to meet a CIA agent who has been based in Washington for some twenty-eight years as well as another CIA agent who had retired after twenty years of service, mainly in the Middle East, Russia, and Rumania. Both told her the same story. The CIA had developed a superior gun, barely three inches long. It could be held in the palm of the hand, safely hooked to the middle finger, and could be fired close to an unsuspecting victim. All the killer had to do was to raise his hand as if to wave it, then press the trigger, and the deadly deed is done. "The only criterion for success," said both her friends "is that the killer must be very close to the victim. He could even be a security agent or a bodyguard!"

This is how the second gun was used, and would clearly account for such a wound found on the head of Robert Kennedy, complete with the powder burns. The men who planned the assassination had no need to worry about another ballistic test . . . the tiny three-inch gun was not likely to make its appearance again. Even this gun, now said to be unavailable, could prove to be just another red herring. Yet there are those who know that such a gun exists and could easily have been used.

Ted Charach also received a strange statement from newsman Don Schulman. He said that on the occasion of Kennedy's visit to the Ambassador Hotel, the hotel found itself one security guard short. A call was made to the Ace Security Guard Company of Van Nuys, a suburb of Los Angeles, although the hotel had no

record of anyone making such a request. This was reason enough for Charach to go in search of a security
guard who was known to have been near Senator Kennedy. He found the man and, in an angry interview,
gleaned a few more facts. The "security man," Thane
Eugene Cesar, told Charach in no uncertain terms that
he had no use for any of the Kennedy family. Cesar
said: "I voted for Wallace in the [1968] primary because Kennedy wanted to shove them minority groups
down our throats. When somebody does that, you either
vote him out or take things into your own hands."
There had been no need to vote Kennedy "out" because
he had never lived to the final contest for the Presidency
with Richard M. Nixon. Did Cesar take things into his
own hands and, if so, by whose instructions? On that
memorable night at the Ambassador Hotel, Cesar was
standing slightly behind and to the right of the Senator,
as Kennedy made his way through the pantry, and he
admitted that he was indeed the security guard in question. He also told Charach that he once owned a .22,
but he sold it in February 1968 to somebody in the Mid-
west for fifteen dollars. Apparently, the man to whom
he sold the gun reported it lost and, in notifying the police, he also gave them the receipt for the sale. It was for
fifteen dollars, but the date read September 1968—three
months *after* the assassination of Senator Kennedy and
seven months after the date Cesar stated he sold it.

Another piece of evidence damning to the prosecution
of Sirhan comes from Richard Lubic, an independent
television producer. He stated in an interview that he
dropped to the floor when the shooting started and the
Senator fell at his feet. "As I was on the floor, looking to
my left and in back of me, I saw another gun. The gun
was pointed in a downward position and it was held by
a guy in an Ace Guard uniform. I didn't see him shoot."
Who is Thane Cesar, the mysterious security guard
whom no one remembers engaging? We come back to
that country club, La Costa near San Clemente, developed with money from the Teamsters' pension fund.

Sybil has a personal memory of Thane Cesar. For two years she lived in Las Vegas, Nevada, in the dual capacity of being something of a celebrity as well as a reporter. "I was often invited by public-relations people to attend cocktail functions. At the time when the Thunderbird Hotel was changing hands, I went to a cocktail party honoring a dancer who was appearing in the Thunderbird show. Within a few minutes of entering the room, I had the irritating experience of being greeted by a man whose face I knew, but I could not remember his name. He was friendly and got me a drink and some food; then he sat beside me and reminisced about the last time we met. Then he moved on to meet other people, and I got into a conversation with a longtime entertainer in Las Vegas. He seemed amused and asked how long I had known the man who had supplied me with the drink. I confessed I knew him but could not place his name. 'Not surprising,' said my friend. 'He has quite a few names and, anyway, they don't matter. What puzzles me is why he is here . . it's a long way from Florida.' Well, Florida was really my adopted home state, so I concluded I must have met him there. But I was surprised when my entertainer friend went on: 'He is a hit man for a Florida group. I wonder if he is here for business or pleasure.'

"My interest perked up for I could not truly believe I had ever met a known 'hit' man before. So I watched him very carefully. He always seemed to be near a sturdy, well-built and quite interesting-looking man, but they never spoke. So I asked my Las Vegas friend who this other man was. 'He's a professional bodyguard,' he replied; and I remarked that if I was looking for a bodyguard myself, he would fit the bill perfectly. 'You are too late,' said my friend. 'He is owned by Howard Hughes and his name is *Thane Cesar* and he is as tough as they come.'

"Cocktail parties in Las Vegas are never boring, but this one was surpassing itself . . . a hit man from Florida and one of Howard Hughes's bodyguards eyeing each other and never actually speaking. I noticed that Cesar left first but was quickly followed out of the room by my Florida acquaintance.

"In January 1975, *Harper's* Magazine published an article in which the name Thane Cesar again came up, and I remembered this incident, which seemed unimportant at the time." Since that article appeared, no one has seen Cesar again. Perhaps the heat was now too much for him and, if he was associated with Howard Hughes, he probably knew several ways to do a disappearing act—or maybe someone else decided he should vanish.

Another lingering mystery is the disappearance of "the girl in the polka-dot dress." Sandy Serrano, a young campaign worker, saw a girl in a polka-dot dress running from the hotel, shouting: "We shot him. We shot Senator Kennedy." Two other people saw a girl similarly dressed. Hotel waiter Vincent Di Pierro stated he saw a girl and Sirhan smile at each other just before the first shot was fired. Booker Griffin, at that time head of the Los Angeles chapter of the Negro Industrial and Economic Union, recalled seeing Sirhan and a girl in a polka-dot dress in the pressroom. These reports were enough to spark the media into a search for the girl in the polka-dot dress, and the Los Angeles police issued an all-points bulletin on the mysterious girl. The result was that not one but several polka-dot-dress girls emerged over a period of time. On June 8th, a belly dancer, Kathy Fulmer, surrendered to the sheriff's department and claimed she was the "girl in the polka-dot outfit," but she denied knowing Sirhan Sirhan. She also denied wearing a polka-dot *dress*, although Miss Fulmer said she had a polka-dot scarf around her. At the time she was also wearing a blonde wig, which conflicted with the description of a dark-haired girl given by Sandy Serrano and Booker Griffin. As soon as Miss Fulmer was no longer under suspicion, another woman came forward, who was also dismissed by the police. In fact, several other women volunteered that *they* were the original girl in the polka-dot dress but, by this time, the police would not divulge names since they were under a court order not to discuss the case with the press.

So the real identity of "the girl in the polka-dot dress" remains a mystery, but not without some intriguing follow-up stories emerging to further tantalize those pursuing it. Ten months after Senator Kennedy was murdered, Kathy Fulmer was found semi-conscious in a motel room. She had registered under the name of Sandy Rossi. She died in the Los Angeles County–USR Medical Center, officially of an overdose of Seconal, a powerful sedative. On the mirror in her room she scrawled: "Lord, you gave me a mountain. I'd love to climb . . . someday . . . a wooden box will do. . . ." But "the girl in the polka-dot dress" was still missing. Why the police never studied the TV tapes of that night's activity in the ballroom of the Ambassador before Kennedy's speech, is something we will never understand. If they had, they would soon have seen their "girl in the polka-dot dress."

Another theory that surfaced was that Sirhan Sirhan murdered Senator Kennedy while under the influence of a post-hypnotic suggestion. At the time when Sirhan was pinned to the steam table by two heavyweight athletes, the Jordanian's hands were so tightly gripped together that his fingers had to be broken to force the gun from them.

A number of college professors, including Dr. Richard Popkin of Washington University in St. Louis, have expressed the idea that Sirhan Sirhan was hypnotized to the point where he was programmed to kill, a real-life victim of a sinsiter *Manchurian Candidate* type of conspiracy. Dr. Simson-Kallas of Monterey, California, supports this idea, probably with more logic than some of the others. It was Dr. Simson-Kallas who interviewed Sirhan immediately after his arrival at prison in 1968. He insists that Sirhan was neither insane enough nor devious enough to have killed Kennedy on his own. The doctor, who is well known as a top criminal psychologist and a former senior psychologist at San Quentin

Prison, interviewed Sirhan twenty times in all. "Sirhan was hypnotically prepared by someone to draw attention from the real killer," says Dr. Simson-Kallas. "He was programmed to be present at the assassination, to provide the obvious simple explanation, so that people would not ask questions and suspect a larger conspiracy involving many people."

He also firmly states that the notebooks used at the trial to prove Sirhan insane were obvious forgeries. (He should know something about those notebooks, for Dr. Simson-Kallas is also an expert in graphology, the art of analyzing handwriting.) In some courts of law in Europe, the testimony of an expert witness on handwriting is acceptable as legal evidence. The notebooks supposedly written by Sirhan were used to prove that he was insane and planned to murder Robert Kennedy. Dr. Simson-Kallas also says: "The most striking contradiction at the trial was that psychiatrists said Sirhan was a paranoid schizophrenic, and yet not one of the experts informed the court that paranoid schizophrenics do *not* keep diaries."

He sees Sirhan as the ideal scapegoat, a natural fall guy for the real perpetrators of the assassination. "After my interviews with Sirhan, I saw him as an excellent follower, willing to risk his life for an idea and not afraid to die."

An interesting footnote is that Dr. Simson-Kallas says that Sirhan frequently asked him to hypnotize him to find out what really happened. At this stage, any possible hynotic influence was likely to be wearing off, leaving Sirhan confused as to why he was in prison. The doctor was prepared to hypnotize Sirhan when he was suddenly ordered to stop seeing him. Dr. Simson-Kallas is still of the opinion that Sirhan should, indeed, be hypnotized.

As inquiring minds analyze what has already been put forward, new evidence is unearthed to freshen the case. Only recently, former Los Angeles Assistant District Attorney Vincent T. Buliosi, prosecutor of Charles Man-

son and author of *Helter Skelter,* the best-selling book
on the Manson murders, has developed information
that leads him to believe there is more to the Robert
Kennedy assassination than has surfaced. He claims that
the Los Angeles Police Department found Sirhan's fingerprints in a pickup truck driven by Oliver B. Owen.
Owen, a former announcer on television station KCOP
in Los Angeles, recently sued his former employers when
they dismissed him and claimed that: "he was cancelled
because he was a thief; he has burned down several
churches in Arizona; he was involved in the killing of
Robert Kennedy; and he is a criminal." Despite the fact
that one court ruled Owen had been slandered by these
remarks, Bugliosi said he developed information that
would lead him to believe that indeed Owen had more
to do with Sirhan than he admits.

Owen claimed that he did have Sirhan in his truck,
picking him up as a hitchhiker in downtown Los Angeles and dropping him off at the Ambassador Hotel.
However, several witnesses saw Owen shortly before the
assassination with a roll of one-thousand-dollar bills;
and one, William Lee Powers, owner of a stable in Santa
Ana, said that he saw Owen in a car with a man who
bore "a likely resemblance to Sirhan." (This might explain why Sirhan, a seventy-five-dollar-a-week dish-
washer, was paying for his drinks with twenty-dollar
bills on the night of the assassination and asking for no
change.)

But Owen claims that the man identified by Powers as
Sirhan was in fact a young man, Jackie Gray, whose
mixed parentage of half-Indian and half-black gives him
a complexion similar to Sirhan's. Gray himself admitted
it might be him, but also stated that Owen and his own
father introduced him to Sirhan a year before the assassination, thereby contradicting Owen's story that he had
only casually met Sirhan when he picked him up as a
hitchhiker. Gray also remembers that he saw Owen give
Sirhan "money for clothes" and that Sirhan often looked
like he was in a "trance."

A growing suspicion that perhaps Sirhan can no long-er be labeled as the *"lone* assassin" has brought on new demands for a reinvestigation of this puzzling case. The end product may well reveal yet another cover-up designed to protect the real assassins. The body of a naïve young Arab languishing in prison is not enough to satisfy a public now suspicious of the American legal system and of those who are supposed to uphold the law. The idea of one lone assassin killing President Kennedy was difficult enough to believe but, with the encore performances in the deaths of Martin Luther King, Jr., and Robert Kennedy, a pattern seems to be emerging with frightening clarity.

14|MAY 15, 1972

The attempted assassination of Governor George Wallace has never had as much attention from private researchers and the press as it deserves. It is understandable that the high drama of the three assassinations preceeding it was not there because George Wallace *lived*.

Governor Wallace was on what seemed to be a relatively successful Presidential campaign—getting out, meeting the people, and proving that he was not such a bad fellow after all. Certainly, what he was saying made a lot of sense to people longing for a strong man in the White House—a robust, hard-hitting speaker with a populist viewpoint.

It seemed that by May 15, 1972, Wallace was on the threshold of the White House itself. He had won one Presidential primary, placed second in another, and was favored in the upcoming Maryland contest. However, in a shopping plaza in Laurel, Maryland, the Presidential hopeful was struck down by bullets when he stepped from a podium with a transparent bulletproof shield. He was alive, but paralyzed. It was the end of his Presidential campaign in 1972.

A suspect was immediately arrested by the police: Arthur Herman Bremer, twenty-one years old, unemployed, a long way from his home—2433 Michigan Avenue, Milwaukee, Wisconsin. He had fired a .38-caliber, five-shot, snub-nosed revolver and, in altering the course of the 1972 election, he had also reduced the strong man of Alabama to a physical cripple.

When Bremer stepped out of the crowd with his gun, security agents reacted instantly. The assailant's gun arm was hit, causing some of the bullets to fly wildly away from the victim. The gun was taken into custody by the Secret Service, and the Justice Department announced that all five bullets had been fired. Yet the attempted assassination of George Wallace presents still another case where the number of bullets are in doubt. First of all, Wallace was wounded five times—in the right shoulder, right arm, the stomach, left shoulder blade, and the spine. From the five wounds and two operations, only two bullets were removed from his body. One was removed from the stomach, where it had torn ligaments in the small intestine and bruised the large intestine. The second bullet was removed on June 18, 1972, from his spine. Wallace's five wounds were seemingly caused by just two bullets.

Three spectators were also wounded, each suffering one wound: Mrs. Dora Thompson, a campaign worker for Wallace, was wounded in the leg; Nicholas Zorvas, a Secret Service agent standing behind Wallace, had a severe wound in the neck; and Alabama State Police Captain Eldred C. Dothard, personal bodyguard to Wallace, was wounded in the abdomen.

Four people sustained a total of eight wounds, and yet only five bullets were accounted for! Shades of the "magic bullet" theory rise again.

A similar pattern to that of the previous assassinations

became apparent as witnesses came forward at the trial of Arthur Bremer, who was defended by a court-appointed attorney, Benjamin Lipsitz of Baltimore. Pressured by questions from Lipsitz, FBI witnesses conceded that there were no fingerprints or palm prints on the seized gun. Robert Frazier, an FBI firearms expert, stated that he could not prove the bullets came from that particular gun. Witnesses close to the actual firing were not able to identify Bremer as the assailant.

Thus, a familiar modus operandi emerged. More bullets were fired than were located, and Bremer's five-bullet gun could not have fired all eight shots. Was there yet another conspiracy?

Then there are the discrepancies in police communications. Wire services carried the news that there was more than one suspect. Pennsylvania and Maryland state police apparently issued an all-points bulletin for a white male, six feet three inches tall, weighing two hundred and twenty pounds, silver-gray hair, driving a 1971 light blue Cadillac. The bulletin was stopped almost before anyone had time to assimilate it. But a blue Cadillac was found abandoned on the Baltimore-Washington Parkway within a few hours of the shooting. A suspect was stopped and questioned in the vicinity of the Laurel shopping center, although he was not arrested, and there is no report on the questioning. The "phantom" communiqué was similar to the bulletins that penetrated the police network immediately after the J.F.K. and King assassinations!

Wallace's Maryland campaign had been marked by intrigue and danger throughout. According to his personal bodyguard, Captain Dothard, nine days before the attempted assassination, two men with guns were chased from a Wallace rally in Baltimore. One man was arrested but quickly and quietly released. There is no record of the arrest, and nothing is known about his companion. The similarity to the three "tramps" picked up in Dallas is frightening.

The gun in the possession of Arthur Bremer was a

Charter Arms, purchased on January 13th in Milwaukee for eighty dollars. All five bullets in it were spent. Considering that three other people were wounded besides the governor and that witnesses spoke of more than six shots being fired, it is surprising that the search for other bullets was not carried out. However, had such a search been made and more than six bullets found, the conclusion would have to be that there was another gunman . . . and that spells "conspiracy," a nasty word and nasty act.

Bremer's car, a 1968 Rambler, was found at five-fifteen P.M. on May 15th. It was not searched until May 16th when the FBI made a list of everything found in it. The list ran to several pages. On May 19th, police of Prince Georges County, Maryland, conducted a second search and found a fourteen-shot, nine-mm. semi-automatic Browning pistol—not exactly an insignificant article to have been overlooked by FBI agents trained in official search procedures. Either the FBI agents were incompetent or the gun was planted. And guns had been planted before in the other assassinations!

Reporters discovered that Bremer had last worked in Milwaukee on February 15th. After that date, he did a lot of traveling, which included a visit to Ottawa, Canada, a two-night stay at the Waldorf-Astoria in New York, several trips to Michigan, Maryland, and other places. Extensive traveling like this takes money—just as the travels of James Earl Ray had required money.

In his twenty-one years, Bremer had worked as a busboy and janitor. A tax form found in his apartment revealed that in 1971 he had earned $3,016. Apart from the gun taken from him when he was arrested, Bremer also had a tape recorder, a portable radio with police band, binoculars, and other expensive items (similar to the types of articles found in the apartments of Lee Harvey Oswald, James Earl Ray, and David Ferrie). Bremer also had a bank account with the Mitchell Street Savings Bank in Milwaukee. None of those who were supposed to be investigating Bremer's background and motivation seemed concerned about his bank account and made no inquiries.

Bremer's Milwaukee apartment received a lot of attention. Several reporters stated that they saw both left-and-right-wing literature scattered around; yet when the FBI finally made its search, agents found only left-wing pamphlets. Within one hour of receiving news of the assassination attempt, Nixon aide Charles Colson telephoned E. Howard Hunt from the White House and ordered him to fly to Milwaukee to break into and look for evidence in Bremer's apartment. Colson denies this. However, at an executive session of the Senate Watergate Committee on July 25, 1973, E. Howard Hunt testified that he was once again called to Colson's office on the morning of May 16, 1972—that is, one day after the shooting. It is likely that Hunt made a delivery of whatever he found directly to Colson during his visit on May 16th—if he went at all and didn't delegate the responsibility of breaking into Bremer's apartment to another of his trusted aides.

When the FBI left the Bremer apartment, they failed to seal it off. Consequently, many people visited it, and Mrs. Wasche, who ran the apartment house, charged each visitor ten dollars. If the FBI did as poor a job of searching the apartment as they did of searching Bremer's car, who knows what valuable evidence disappeared, appropriated by memorabilia seekers?

Finally, in keeping with the consistent pattern that continues to re-emerge, Arthur Bremer, like Sirhan Sirhan and Lee Harvey Oswald, kept a diary. How many men keep diaries? Especially those that are conveniently found? Where the handwriting of the supposed keeper is suspect?

The FBI on several occasions endeavored to convince Governor Wallace that there was no conspiracy behind the shooting. As with Oswald, it was simply another "lone nut" with a grudge against him. In one news conference, Wallace said, "I have no evidence, but I think my attempted assassination was part of a conspiracy."

On August 4, 1972, Judge Ralph Powers sentenced the "lone nut." Bremer is still in prison and was denied the right to a retrial on August 24, 1972.

Links with previous successful assassinations began to emerge shortly after Governor Wallace was shot. A number of people who might have shed light on the shooting suddenly met strange deaths, under mysterious circumstances. In July 1972, Dennis Salvatore Cossini was found dead in Toronto, Canada. Although he had no history of using drugs, death occurred through the use of a massive dose of heroin. Cossini had met with Bremer at the Lord Elgin Hotel in Ottawa when Richard Nixon was staying there. Members of the Secret Service were there at the same time. Two people, Mae Bussell and Alan Stang, have identified Cossini as a CIA agent. In Cossini's address book there was a phone number belonging to John J. McCleary, who lived in Sacramento, California, and worked at the V & T International Company—a firm that supposedly dealt in exports and imports. Cossini often made telephone calls to this company. John McCleary drowned in the Pacific Ocean in the fall of 1972. His death almost coincided with that of his father, who also drowned in Reno, Nevada.

The list grows longer. Herbert Spenner headed the German-American group in Milwaukee to which Bremer was supposed to have belonged. Spenner died from a gunshot wound.

Earl S. Nunnery was once the manager of the Milwaukee station of the Chesapeake and Ohio Ferry. He was transferred against his wishes to a railway yard in Flint, Michigan. Nunnery told friends he had overheard a conversation between Bremer and an unidentified companion when they were on his ferry early in April. No one knows where Mr. Nunnery can be found today. A friend of Arthur Bremer, Michael McHale, has also slipped from view; and Bremer's friend and mentor, Michael Cullen, was deported to Ireland. He was a master in the art of behavior modification and pyschological programming. His views about Bremer's state of mind would be interesting to know. More interesting still is the idea that Bremer himself might have been programmed or brainwashed.

In all cases of assassination or attempted assassination, there is always someone who has something to gain. *Cui bono*? John Mitchell, in charge of Richard Nixon's committee to re-elect the President, was well aware that Nixon had to combine his own and Wallace's 1968 votes to be sure of victory. A policy known as the Southern Strategy was adopted and, because of this, Nixon favored conservative Southern candidates for Supreme Court nominations, latched onto the anti-busing crusade, and used the "Law-and-Order" platform. Yet before he could fully exploit the "Law and Order," he had to monopolize it and call it his own. And with Wallace in the running, his position was jeopardized.

With Wallace out of the campaign, the chances were good that votes likely to go to one "Law-and-Order" candidate—Wallace—would be directed to the other "Law-and-Order" candidate—Nixon. He may have gained as many as twenty-five million votes that would have gone to Wallace, more than enough to re-elect him. Neither George McGovern nor Edmund Muskie posed any danger to Richard Nixon, but Governor Wallace did. Nixon defeated McGovern by eighteen million votes. If anyone had anything to gain, it was surely the persistently ambitious gentleman from Whittier, California. The assault on Wallace and the assassination of Robert Kennedy was as crucial to the success of Nixon as the assassination of John Kennedy was to the escalation of the war in Vietnam. Doubts continued to nag those close to the Wallace campaign. At first, they believed the attempt was the handiwork of McGovernites; but their thinking changed, and they became convinced that it was, instead, the doing of Nixon's "Dirty Tricks" gang.

[handwritten margin note: and Nixon in the White House was crucial to Rockefeller interests— enter Kissinger]

Among the many White House tapes not released during or after Watergate is one of an emergency meeting on May 15, 1972, a conversation between Richard Nixon and Charles Colson, held minutes after the shooting and preceding Colson's reputed request to E. Howard Hunt to go to Milwaukee. Up to the present date, President Gerald Ford refuses to release these tapes on the grounds that they have nothing to do with the Watergate break-in. But now Mrs. George Wallace is pressing for a reopening of an inquiry into the attempted assassination of her husband. If the tapes have nothing to do with Watergate, what excuses will be given if they are requested as evidence in the new inquiry? Any conspiracy of silence is as bad as conspiracy for assassination. Why won't they release these tapes? Would it be shown that Nixon and Colson had *no* connection with Bremer? Or are they being withheld for a reason?

The other three assassination victims had been shot in the head and killed. Why wasn't Wallace shot in the head? Was the desired effect his removal from the campaign rather than his death? And, if so, wasn't this every bit as much an assassination—the assassination of a campaign for the Presidency instead of a person?

15 | THE ASSASSINA- TION CHAIN

The effect of the death of President Kennedy was not restricted to the United States; it influenced the future course of world events. We should never forget this since it is a vital element in considering why he was assassinated and who may have been responsible for planning two perfect crimes—the murder and its cover-up.

The brutal execution of the Chief Executive was the first link in the assassination chain. But further links had to be added to strengthen it. Those links were to be the assassinations of Martin Luther King, Jr., Robert Kennedy, the attempted assassination of Governor George Wallace and, yes, the character assassination a decade later of President Richard Nixon. In every case, there was the framing of a vulnerable person set up long before as a patsy. Richard Nixon was no exception to this pattern established by Lee Harvey Oswald, Jack Ruby, James Earl Ray, Sirhan Sirhan, and Arthur

Bremer. None of them, including Richard Nixon, expected to be patsies; when they became aware that they had been sold out, it was too late. The silencing of these men was effected in different ways: Oswald and Ruby are dead; Ray, Sirhan Sirhan, and Bremer are in prison with doubts about their sanity; and Richard Nixon is neatly boxed in and condemned to silence through a Presidential pardon surprisingly extended to him by his hand-picked successor—before he was even charged with any crimes for which he could logically be pardoned.

None of these scapegoats were totally innocent of wrongdoing. They were *not* guilty of being the sole perpetrator of murder. But, in some way, all were guilty— some by association, others by prior knowledge, and still others by being *one* of the perpetrators.

There are also degrees in the type of guilt. Oswald and Ruby made the mistake of believing they would be rescued by their associates; Sirhan Sirhan was damned by brainwashing; Ray and Bremer were deluded by the promise of money.

Richard Nixon, a straw man caught up in a mesh of conspiracy by his own greedy ambition for power and wealth, was guilty because he knew more about what was going on than was good for him. He got power, but he paid a price for it. Power corrupts even the already corrupted. And when the tail began to wag the dog, Richard Nixon was deposed.

It is no coincidence that misfortune and tragedy have always followed America's attempts at détente with her main rivals, the Soviet Union and China. Eisenhower had the U-2 incident, Kennedy had Cuba, Nixon had Watergate . . . each one had an effect on American foreign policy and world events.

Prior to Dallas, foreign policy was flexible and moderate, with the possible exception of China, an unknown force. After Dallas, foreign policy became rigid and hard, with the military-industrial complex dominating the body politic of America.

Of all the things that have surprised us, of all the

wealth of theories and facts about the assassinations, and with everyone thinking and talking about a Master Plan, it is most surprising that no one has dared come up with any suggestion about the possible identity of the architect who planned it all.

Was there a Mastermind who created the Master Plan?

Just as all the patsies carried varying degrees of guilt during their lives, so the victims of the assassinations were not without their own share of it. We are apt to see President Kennedy as a glamorous personality, and the tragic circumstances of his death have added a distorted dimension to the life of the man and the politician as well as a martyred aura to his death. His role in history is controversial. His private life must be left for others to judge, but political historians are justified in taking a good look at his political life. The image of liberalism was manufactured by effective public-relations men, although Kennedy was, in fact, a hawkish cold warrior with counter-revolutionary instincts. While speaking of peace, he was a man of war. Cuba, Berlin, and Vietnam were part of his legacy. The mild-mannered, handsome Chief Executive was the toughest cold warrior of them all, and his administration accomplished little. Had he lived, little or no glory would have been added to it.

He came into power at a time when the cold war was at its height, succeeding President Eisenhower who, realizing the dangers of a nuclear confrontation with the Soviets, found his efforts destroyed when an American spy plane was shot down twelve hundred miles inside Soviet territory. A disappointing ending for such a promising beginning. Eisenhower's valedictory was a warning to the country and its politicians that democracy when working hand-in-glove with the military-industrial complex was in danger.

We shall never know if the U-2 incident was a plot to sabotage Eisenhower's attempts at détente, organized by the military. If it was, then Lee Harvey Oswald con-

tributed in no small way to it. The Warren Commission
Document 931, prepared by the CIA and entitled
"Oswald's Access to Information About U-2," will not be
available until the year 2038. It is being held in secrecy
for reasons of national security, but its contents could
probably solve some of those puzzles that are still unanswered.

John Kennedy was elected to office at a time when the
Republicans made repeated charges that he was overly
soft toward the Communists. To counteract this, Kennedy accused Nixon, in the 1960 Presidential campaign,
of jeopardizing national defense by allowing the Soviets
to move ahead in the missile race. It was throwing down
the gauntlet to the old battle horse who had once been
Joseph McCarthy's alter ego.

Once in power, Kennedy was faced with the dilemma
of prosecuting the cold war on one hand while avoiding
a nuclear holocaust on the other. He spoke of this
dilemma in his inaugural address: "Let every nation
know, whether it wishes us well or ill, that we shall pay
any price, bear any burden, meet any hardship, support
any friend, oppose any foe to assure the survival of
liberty. Finally, to those nations who make themselves
our adversaries, we offer not a pledge but a request that
both sides begin anew the quest for peace, before the
dark powers of destruction unleashed by science engulf
all humanity in planned and accidental self-destruc-
tion."

Within eighteen months of his inauguration, Kennedy
knew things were going badly. He committed American
prestige to the CIA-sponsored Bay of Pigs, and it ended
in a fiasco when he failed to give air cover for the invasion. He reacted to criticism by throwing out Allen
Dulles, head of the CIA, as well as his assistant director,
General Pierre Cabell; and he told friends he would like
"to splinter the CIA into a thousand pieces and scatter
it to the winds." When Kennedy turned his attention to
Berlin, the Soviet reaction was to build the infamous
Berlin Wall. And then there was Vietnam, a constant re-

minder that the prestige and honor of the United States might rest on a war in a faraway agrarian country whose population was one-twentieth that of the most powerful country in the world.

Kennedy became a counter-revolutionist when he saw the potential battlefield area changing from Europe to Asia and the underdeveloped countries of the world. By June 1963, Kennedy knew that our foreign policy, which had its roots in 1945, would have to be reversed. In June, he asked the country to re-examine its attitude toward cold-war policies. Total war made no sense in an age when great powers could maintain large nuclear forces and would resort to using those forces.

After the debacle of Cuba came the signing of the Nuclear Test Ban Treaty, which seemed to improve the relationship between the United States and Soviet Russia. The mask of Kennedy as the cold warrior was slipping off and revealing either a man who passionately wanted peace at any price or a man who was afraid of war. Neither image suited the military-industrial complex, where a world without the fear or the reality of war was a world of far fewer opportunities to acquire power, status, and money.

By taking a firm stand for peace in June 1963, Kennedy knew he was jeopardizing his re-election in 1964. His popularity was at a low point in all too many circles, and it was for this reason he had to "mend" his political fences with trips to places like Dallas. The dust of the cold war did not have time to settle on the shadow that had by now distorted his image and popularity. His death precluded his inevitable topple from stature. It is a fact that immediately after he came to power, the 685 military advisers who were in Vietnam in 1961 were quietly increased, reaching 16,772 by 1963. It was enough to frighten a man who understood war as much as he did peace. Despite the advice of military groups, Kennedy could not face seeking a total military solution to the war in Vietnam. In October 1963, the burden of personal guilt was too much, and his last formal executive order was issued to reduce the number of "advisers" in Vietnam.

Warned by both General Douglas MacArthur and General Charles de Gaulle that the United States could not win a conventional ground war in Asia, Kennedy felt boxed in. Since the missile crisis in Cuba, he had tried to follow a policy of détente with the Soviet Union but now China loomed as a threat. A military solution, even if a million troops were poured into Vietnam, would ruin any hopes of progress in Sino-American relations.

He tried to run with the hares and the hounds and was destroyed in the process. J.F.K.'s last planned act was to announce the withdrawal of troops after Christmas. Early in November 1963, the obstinate ruler of South Vietnam was overthrown; Kennedy hoped that the new Minh government would lessen tension and be receptive to his ideas. To the military-industrial complex, this appeared like another sellout . . . even greater than the lack of support for the Cuban invasion.

The assassination of Kennedy cleared the way for the escalation of the war effort in Vietnam. The crucial decisions about Vietnam were made within forty-eight hours of the President's death. Ten weeks after the assassination, Minh was deposed in a bloodless coup by General Khanh, more aggressive than Diem and more open to United States intervention.

If someone masterminded the assassination, he knew exactly what he was doing and could project how much profit could be made by continuing the war. Logically, Vietnam could have been subdued by the sheer weight of American forces—both land and nuclear—but, by March 1971, three million bombs later, America was no nearer a solution than it had been a decade earlier.

Was there a Mastermind?

If there *was* a Mastermind, a strong case could be made that *his* scenario would have taken place in the following manner:

Six seconds in Dallas needed a thousand days of preparation from Los Angeles, Las Vegas, Chicago, Houston, New Orleans, Miami, and Havana. The major ingredients were assembled at No Name Key, Florida. There, death by sudden attack, death by synchronized timing, and death by bullets were taught, practiced, and perfected. The school for assassins was in business under the protective eyes of the CIA. The site was ideal and, if there were any curious glances cast toward it, they came mainly from alligators.

Most humans in civilized countries have a built-in respect for notices warning them to keep out of specific areas, believing that the cautionary signs not to trespass are for their own good. But, in No Name Key, Florida, they served another—far more sinister—purpose. A team of advance men started arriving in the surrounding area weeks before a gun was unloaded. Subtle hints of a secret Government program bringing a touch of prosperity to the area can work wonders in maintaining silence. It worked in Germany when the ominous detention camps were set up. Even when the smoke began to rise in ever-increasing clouds and an unusual stench mixed with the sweet country smells, there were few Germans who wanted or even dared to believe that in the secret government detention camps, millions were dying and that the foul smell came from the rotting bodies flung out from the gas ovens.

So it was in the area surrounding No Name Key.

Slowly, men moved in who were to make death their business. They only knew that they were being prepared for any emergency where the man whose bullet found its mark most accurately would live to fire another shot on another day. In the early training days, no single person was spoken of as being the target. A man has to have the basic instincts to kill before he commits murder—but assassination is one grade up in homicide. Assassination involves far more careful planning than the types of murder we are more accustomed to: the types motivated by passion, greed, vengeance, or a quirk in mental stability. The good assassin must be able to kill under instructions and out of dedication; in addition, he must be able to sublimate normal human qualities. He needs to realize he has something to sell for a price. For some men, it is the promise of easy money beyond what they could normally earn in a lifetime. For others, it is the surge of power that brings thoughts of death; it is the super aphrodisiac, satisfying distorted perverse needs. And for still others, it is the chance to maintain a position of trust as close as possible to the Mastermind creating the plan.

There were plenty of such men to choose from, and many of them gravitated to No Name Key. They were divided into teams, working hard by day in the hot sunshine and spending the evening hours listening to lectures laced with ideology. There were forays into other countries in the thousand days leading to the six seconds in Dallas. Here could be found a mixed bag of nationalities, including Cubans and Italians, but dominated by the figure of one man. There was the constant interchange of languages: the robust Spanish of the Cubans, the clatter of the Italians, and the dialect of the Florida crackers, all responding to the persuasive though totally authoritative voice of that one man. There were men who disappeared as silently as they had arrived, never to be seen again; and there were others who came back.

As time went on, the talk was of a well-planned invasion of Cuba, which the CIA had already penetrated. All that was needed was the air cover promised by President Kennedy. But it never came! So activity was stepped up at No Name Key, and six men were chosen to go to Dallas. Now the activity within the Keys was extending to Washington, New Orleans, Los Angeles, Chicago, and Miami again, key cities in the political lives of several men. The chosen team was briefed on the trend of American history and their role in changing it. It was not the act of assassination that was new to the country; it was the methods and the motives. The men in No Name Key knew their role; however, in New Orleans, a nonentity named Lee Harvey Oswald was chosen. Yet there was another man who was to be known as Lee Harvey Oswald, a ghostly figure who would ultimately appear and make himself known as a Marxist. The real Oswald did as he was told, and his ego was satisfied at the recognition given him by secret Government agents. He began to feel that he had finally become someone and believed that he would be taken care of for the rest of his life. All he had to do was "obey orders."

The night of November 21, 1963, was a busy one. During the day, everyone was in position to take part in the episode known as "six seconds in Dallas." Three confident marksmen pored over their plans at the Cabana Hotel. With their three other companions, they had gone over every inch of the route the motorcade would take. Two men had practiced taking a car into the parking lot behind the grassy knoll; dummy runs had been made by a light-colored Rambler so that they knew exactly how long it took to get from the steps of the Texas School Book Depository Building to an apartment in Oak Cliff. Time was to be the tool for their success. The real Oswald was primed to be waiting on the steps of the Depository, and two other men from No Name Key were to be in the window on the sixth floor. Their job was to fire one shot, then hide the Italian rifle after leaving enough clues near the window to ultimately lead to Oswald. The other Oswald was to go on foot toward East Tenth Street and a car waiting at the intersection. The car would take him to the airfield, where two small private planes were waiting, one to take him to freedom. The second plane would take the other three to Mexico City.

The plans for the infiltration of the police force were complete. While the six trained assassins, now with full knowledge of who the target was to be, were making their final plans, about twenty other men were gathering up their forged Secret Service papers and checking their locations. Others were mingling with Washington personnel, taking their final orders in how to create confusion and a diversion at a given signal.

On November 22nd, the Presidential car slowed down to enter Dealey Plaza, and the first shot was fired from the Book Depository Building—not from the corner window but from the one next to it. There were other shots fired from secure spots in the area. They sounded to some witnesses like firecrackers. It was enough to start immediate confusion and, with split-second timing, the gun barrel fired from the trees fringing the grassy knoll. It only took six seconds, and the assassins had merely to step into a waiting car. A car blocking the entrance to the parking lot moved away in time to let the escape car out.

A light-colored Rambler picked up "Lee Oswald" and took him to the Texas Theatre. His look-alike took a cab to the Oak Street apartment, made a thirty-second token appearance for the myopic, almost-blind landlady, and set off on foot down East Tenth Street. There, Officer Tippit recognized a friend, who was with a small Cuban. Tippit had no time to think because, within a second, Oswald drew a gun and shot Tippit dead. Both men fled in different directions. The waiting car saw the incident, cruised around, picked them up, and took them to the private plane waiting at the airport. Within moments of each other, both planes were airborne . . . one to Los Angeles and the other to Mexico City.

The plan was to have Oswald picked up at the Texas Theatre. It was there that the second mistake occurred: someone misunderstood the pyschology of the man. He had been too well brainwashed into believing that if he followed orders, he would be looked after. So he only put up a token fight at the theatre. The psychologist's report had indicated that he would panic, offer massive resistance to the police officers, and be shot while trying to escape. Oswald placed too much faith in his friends. The dream of a new life in a new country with enough money to last him for the rest of his life was too tempting for him to resist arrest. His faith was his undoing, and he nearly ruined the plan. But the Mastermind was not likely to be without a second string to his bow. Jack Ruby, as egotistical as Oswald, was contacted. Eager to please and already well looked after by frequent financial handouts, he also suffered from a blind faith in his friends. "There is no danger to you," he was told. "We have to get rid of Oswald; otherwise, we are all in danger, and you have as much to lose as anyone else." The nights of November 22nd and 23rd were busy ones for the nightclub owner. They were also busy ones for the men who had to put the final touches to the "six seconds in Dallas." Time, again, was the key to success. Official plans had to be changed; a diversion had to be created in order to allow Ruby to get into the restricted area in the basement of the Dallas Police Building. He was promised immunity, and all he had to do was to rid his friends of the man who by then knew he was the "fall guy" for the Master Plan.

Jack Ruby killed Lee Harvey Oswald and silenced him forever. Oswald fell to the floor alive. Detective Combest knelt down, hoping for a last-minute confession. There was to be no confession. Oswald, in the throes of death, must have had time only to understand that his friend Jack Ruby had wiped him out, or "wasted" him, as Ruby's orders had dictated.

The cover-up story had already been planned by the Mastermind. All he had to do was to rely on his association with the major Government agencies. Ballistic tests and autopsy reports were easy enough to forge or lose, and the plans were already laid to make the new President into a malleable tool who could be useful to fulfill the ultimate purpose of the assassination; that is, to step up military action in Vietnam, making millions of dollars' worth of Government contracts available to the companies controlled by the Mastermind and thus give him more power over the fate of this country.

After the assassination, there had to be a cover-up story, and the Warren Commission unwittingly did this.

Its report became the official version of what happened during "six seconds in Dallas," although it could never be the true story of the thousand days used to plan the assassination. The Warren Commission did its work well—inasmuch as it fitted exactly into what the Mastermind expected. There were moments of near panic when Congressman Boggs and Senator Russell asked the wrong questions, but there was always a high-ranking FBI or CIA agent to cover up. If the minds of the two dissenters were not set at ease, at least they were numbed. Finally, they signed the report. Afterward, there were attacks of conscience that ended only when Russell died and Hale Boggs mysteriously disappeared in a plane off Alaska. Presumably, his plane crashed, but the wreckage has never been found. However, he died at the right time to insure that there would be no chance for him to ever again testify about the role of the Commissioners.

President Kennedy was dead, and President Johnson took over. It was a whole new ball game, this time with a President who was forced to play ball. And when he had an attack of conscience, he announced he would not run again. Waiting in the wings was the man from California, chosen long ago. It was his turn and, unlike Johnson, he was well trained as to what his role was to be. By the time he came to power, the CIA was in control of the White House. It seemed that nothing could go wrong. Although the Vietnam war would peter out after an eighty-billion-dollar profit was made, there were new arenas of war emerging. The Middle East was about to explode, a new lemon to be sucked dry.

Law and order was what the United States needed; and Richard Nixon, the strong right-wing Presidential candidate, offered his version of it. Law and order was for the ordinary people. But organized crime, military maneuvers, and the exchange of gold, oil, and drugs were for the elite. The elite moved into the White House. The Mastermind was in complete control of the Government of the United States, and President Nixon was his man. All he had to do was to toe the line. However, one day the puppet President broke the strings attached to his manipulator and soon thereafter came tumbling down, engulfed in Watergate.

It was his Waterloo. But Presidents are also expendable.

The Mastermind in this scenario was beyond any laws in this land.

Getting Kennedy out of the way served several purposes. The end products were to keep the military-industrial complex in business and to provide the needed power structure for the Mastermind to seek global domination. Death for millions of people in Vietnam and then the Warren Commission investigation were more than sufficient to distract Americans from the real issues at hand. National grief and anger are surefire methods of blinding reason, and the Mastermind was well versed in the psychology of the masses. He could profit from the mistakes made by other seekers of world domination. The twisted genius of his mind would not make the same mistakes that others had made, one of which was to publicly announce his ambition to dominate the world. Although the assassination of President Kennedy was the prologue in a play for power, it was also a gesture containing a warning that, behind the scenes, a series of meaningful actions were going on.

In the chain of assassinations, the death of the Rev. Dr. Martin Luther King, Jr., served two purposes. First, it was a warning to Robert Kennedy, whose vendetta on organized crime had made too many waves. The murder of one of the country's major black leaders was more subtle than the Nazis' destruction of six million Jews. There were riots and confusion again in the country, often incited and always abetted by law-enforcement agencies. The Master Plan was that it should be the law and the order of the instigator himself. not RFK

Robert Kennedy either did not get the message behind the death of Martin Luther King, Jr., or thought that he was above it. Kennedy continued with his usual bullheaded determination and signed his own death warrant by running—and winning—in the Presidential primaries. In Los Angeles, the "City of Angels," Kennedy was assassinated, and the way was clear for the Mastermind to move his "man" into the White House.

Richard Nixon became President, not with a big margin of votes, but with enough industrial muscle to shoulder him into the right place at the right time. He gave the country confidence when he talked about law and order; yet still the gold, oil, and drug traffic rolled on. The G.O.D. Machine could not be stopped. Nixon's first term provided four glorious years for the Mastermind.

And then came the Presidential campaign of 1972 . . . but before this came the publication of "The Pentagon Papers" in June 1971. They must have seemed Godsent to Nixon, enabling him to radically change the basis of American Far East policy, appeasing the liberals and the seemingly powerful peace movement. At the same time, the release of "The Pentagon Papers" gave Nixon a second weapon: it mollified the right wing by claiming that Nixon's China policy was forced onto him by traitors.

Three months after the release of "The Pentagon Papers," Charles Colson called E. Howard Hunt into his office and directed him to discredit John Kennedy by forging a cable suggesting Kennedy had ordered the assassination of Diem. Colson's request was scrupulously followed by Hunt, who carefully examined more than five thousand top-secret State Department cables before producing a classic forgery, in yet another attempt to assassinate John Kennedy. For, although it was almost eight years since J.F.K. had been physically assassinated, his name still endured—and that, too, had to be killed and buried for Nixon to emerge from his shadow.

In 1972, the main threat to Richard Nixon's re-election came from the right in the form of Governor George Wallace. The attempted assassination effectively removed him from the campaign, and the way was clear for Nixon's second four years—except that he forgot he was dependent upon the Mastermind. He thought he was immortal and, for that sin, Nixon suffered Watergate.

If there *was* a Mastermind, the most heinous plan in the annals of American history could have taken place exactly as we have detailed it here. But, again, if there was a Mastermind, it wouldn't have ended there; it would continue and still be continuing today. And its ramifications are just as sinister as the act of assassination itself, if they follow the remainder of our scenario.

There are few men in the United States who can place themselves totally beyond the law. One is Richard Nixon, protected by a pardon conveniently granted by Gerald Ford. This is the same Gerald Ford whose only claim to fame before he became President was that as a Congressman he created his one-and-only literary masterpiece, the inside story of the Warren Commission, titled *Portrait of an Assassin.* It didn't sell well when published in 1965 because, by then, the majority of Americans knew that "The Warren [Commission] Report" was at best a whitewash, suppressing the truth about the assassination. His encore, and just as commendable a whitewash job, was the suppression of evidence that the CIA plotted a number of attempted assassinations and that Kennedy may well have been assassinated as a direct result of these attempts. It brought a familiar odor from the White House, the unmistakable one of yet another cover-up story.

President Ford, under oath, did not tell the truth when he said he hadn't included any material other than what was in the twenty-six volumes of testimony and other exhibits that were made public in his book. The truth is that the very first chapter is a dramatization of the transcript of a secret executive session of the Commission, which was not declassified by the National Archives until eight years after the book came out, and seven months after he lied about it. The occasion was on November 5, 1973, at his confirmatory hearings for the office of Vice President before the Senate Judiciary Committee. He stated in his book that "where doubts were cast on any United States agency, independent experts would be hired and the investigation conducted in such a way as to avoid reliance on a questioned authority." This was *not* true. The Commission relied entirely on evidence supplied by Government agencies, even when the possibility arose that Oswald was an employee of the FBI. There was *no* independent investigation by the Warren Commission.

Since President Johnson's appointment of a credible group of people to form the Warren Commission had worked well, President Ford followed up with the same scheme when he appointed the Rockefeller Commission to suppress information about the CIA. His choice for executive director of this commission? David Belin, his old University of Michigan friend, who was also the chief counsel for the Warren Commission and later chairman of Lawyers for Nixon-Agnew in 1968. (Belin has been accused of suborning Charles Givens, a witness whose original testimony may have cleared Oswald. Givens changed his testimony and, in one FBI document in the National Archives, a Dallas policeman said that Givens proved to be the *only* witness who could provide evidence that Oswald was on the sixth floor immediately before the shooting.)

Today Richard Nixon is safely hidden in his California house, totally discredited, with his reputation as shredded as all too many important Government documents. Like all the other patsies in the assassination chain, he was the ultimate sacrifice. As a man beyond the long arm of the law, life has some compensations for him. . . . The major one is that he is still alive.

And the Mastermind? If he was beyond the law of the land, had he repealed the laws of immortality, too? Or did he forget that he was *not* immortal, that it only seemed that way?

But, if there *was* one man who could have profited most from being the Mastermind, one man who had the motive, the opportunity, and the enormous wealth needed to buy the cooperation of every governmental agency, that one man could well have been Howard Hughes. Or it could have been one of several names that have been bandied about, looming large in any discussion as to who had the most to gain in attempting to sculpt the Government to his own likeness—who, through the swirling mists of time, resembles the Mastermind in deed, if not in visage.

Based upon one startling set of circumstances—that all four assassins had been in Los Angeles at one time or another, a million-to-one coincidence—we decided to pull the one thread that would put the Chain together as if it were the jigsaw puzzle it is and lay it at the door of one man who could qualify in every respect as the Mastermind—Howard Hughes.

For, Los Angeles was not only the "City of Angels"; it was also the original city of his Corporation, the holding company for Hughes's financial kingdom. In fact, Oswald and Ray were "made" entering the sanctum sanctorum of his gigantic computer headquarters there.

In piecing together the crazy jigsaw-puzzle pieces that could irrefutably lead to the conclusion that Hughes assumed more than merely the veil of the Mastermind, but that he *was* indeed the Mastermind, aided by several of his former trusted aides, who supplied us with confidential reports—we came up against the final curtain. For, on April 5, 1976, our leads and investigations came to an abrupt end—caused by the death of the man who may well have been the Mastermind.

He was not immortal; it only seemed that way.

Even if we were able to single out the Mastermind, we would never be able to produce all the proof, which has been so eroded by the passage of time, with the deaths of key witnesses and the disappearance of crucial evidence. Moreover, we would never be able to produce the one piece of evidence that would finally solve The Assassination Chain—a signed confession. This we do not have. But what we do have is a chilling insight into our system and how it could happen.

For, it is an unfortunate reality of our civilization that there is such instant access to worldwide communications and that a neurosis so pervades our society that conspiracies like this could happen again, and again, and again.

It is entirely possible that not only the Mastermind, but several of those responsible for The Assassination Chain are still in our midst, awaiting the opportunity to kill again for their own ends.

This we must guard against, prepared by the complete disclosure of every possible tool and trick at their disposal in initiating another Assassination Chain. For, then, and only then, would we be ready and assured that those responsible can never do their dirty work again—in an Assassination Chain.

Because unless we understand how an Assassination Chain works, we may be doomed to witness a repeat of it.

It happened once before, and it *can* happen again!

THE ASSASSINATION WHO'S WHO

RALPH ABERNATHY
- Aide to Martin Luther King, Jr., in Southern Christian Leadership Council.
- At King's side on balcony of Lorraine Hotel, Memphis, Tennessee, April 4, 1968, when King was assassinated.
- Became head of SNCC after King's death.

DON ABLES
- Jail clerk for Dallas police.
- Appeared as one of three "ringers" with Oswald in police lineup on November 22nd.

JOHN ABT
- New York lawyer.
- Oswald had asked Mrs. Paine to contact him to help with case on November 23rd, and had requested in original interrogation: "Am I permitted to have an attorney? I would like to talk to Mr. Abt, an attorney in New York."
- There are no records to indicate Mr. Abt was ever contacted.

JOHN ADAMCIK
- Dallas police officer.
- One of five officers who searched Paine residence on November 23rd and found photographs of Oswald holding rifle and note purported to have been written by Oswald at time of attempt on Major Gen. Edwin A. Walker.

FRANCIS W. H. ADAMS
- One of several counsel assisting the Warren Commission.

VICTORIA ADAMS
- Employee in Scott, Foresman Publishing Co., on fourth floor of Texas School Book Depository Building.
- Testified she descended stairs from fourth to first floor within one minute of shooting and did not meet Oswald, but saw two other employees, Billy Lovelady and William Shelley, on first floor.

AIB
- The Assassination Information Bureau, headquartered in Cambridge, Massachusetts.
- Dedicated to continuing the investigation of the J.F.K. assassination for a more factual determination of the actual event and those causes leading up to it.

DR. GENE AKIN
- Doctor at Parkland Hospital.
- Testified that J.F.K.'s neck wound was the "entrance wound."

ADRIAN T. ALBA
- Owner of Crescent City Garage, next door to William B. Reily Co., where Oswald worked.
- Testified Oswald spent hours "buried in gun magazines" ("The Warren Report," Vol. 10, p. 226) and was going to get job at Gentilly.

STEPHEN ALEXANDER
- Television cameraman.
- Told FBI that he was in police basement on November 24th and at no time was he asked for identification.

WILLIAM ALEXANDER
- Dallas district attorney, assistant to Henry Wade.

- Held that there was a relationship between Oswald and the FBI.

PIERCE ALLMAN
- Newsman for WFAA-TV (Dallas) who was within several feet of the President when he was shot.
- Was directed to a phone in Texas School Book Depository Building by Oswald, who mistook him for a Secret Service agent.

JAMES W. ALTGENS
- Associated Press photographer.
- Took pictures approximately 3.6 seconds after first shot and approximately 3.2 seconds before last (if 6.8 seconds).
- Took picture of entrance to Texas School Book Depository that showed either Billy Lovelady or Lee Harvey Oswald in doorway.

ACELO PEDRO AMORES
- Batista official in 1960.
- Arrested by FBI in 1963 raid on New Orleans house containing explosives.

MAJ. EUGENE ANDERSON
- U.S. Marine Corps officer.
- Reviewed Oswald's marksmanship record before Warren Commission, pointing out that Oswald's last score—191— was one point above the minimum needed to qualify for the lowest of three ratings.
- Also testified shots from Book Depository were not difficult and that Oswald had capacity to fire them.

DEAN ADAMS ANDREWS, JR.
- New Orleans attorney.
- Testified he had been visited by Oswald several times in 1963 to seek advice on such matters as citizenship status for both his wife and himself and his less-than-honorable discharge from the service, but found no records to corroborate visits.
- Believed he received a telephone call to represent Oswald on November 23rd.

ROBERT SAM ANSON
- Author of *They Killed the President*, 1975.

ARACHA
- Also known as Sergio Aracha Smith.
- New Orleans delegate of Miami-based Cuban Revolutionary Committee.
- CIA group member, according to Gordon Novel.

DON RAY ARCHER
- Dallas police detective.
- Witness to Ruby's state of mind and premeditation to kill Oswald.

ANDREW ARMSTRONG
- Manager-in-fact of the Carousel Club.

GEORGE ARNETT
- Dallas police lieutenant.
- A "good friend" of Jack Ruby's.

(MRS. R. E.) CAROLYN ARNOLD
- A secretary employed in the Book Depository.
- Testified to FBI she had seen Oswald standing in hallway on first floor between double doors and front door a few minutes before twelve-fifteen on November 22nd.

ATSUGI
- Where Oswald was stationed until February 25, 1959, and where Oswald was given Russian proficiency test.
- CIA base.

AUSTIN LEE AUGUSTINOVITCH
- Former CIA operative.
- Presently a private investigator in the Southwest.
- Claims he knew Oswald in CIA as "Tom Kane."

MRS. CAROL AYDELOTTE
- Member of the Southern California branch of Minutemen.
- Identified Eugene Bradley for Garrison.

MRS. DONALD BAKER
- Eyewitness to assassination, standing directly in front of Book Depository.

M. L. BAKER
- Dallas patrolman.
- First person to see Oswald after the assassination.

- Heard shots and went into Texas School Book Depository where he found Truly.
- Saw Oswald on second floor one and a half minutes after.

T. L. BAKER
- Dallas police lieutenant.
- Arresting officer Bentley turned Oswald's identification over to Lt. Baker on November 22nd.

JOSEPH A. BALL
- Warren Commission counsel.

SAMUEL BALLEN
- Member of Dallas's Russian-speaking community.

W. GUY BANNISTER
- Former FBI agent.
- Member of Minutemen and Anti-Communism League of Caribbean.
- Had offices at 544 Camp Street/531 Lafayette.
- Known to Ferrie.
- Died suddenly.

TOMMY BARGAS
- Oswald's employer at the Leslie Welding Co.

GENE BARNES
- NBC cameraman.
- Warren Commission witness who testified to happenings after Oswald was shot.

W. E. BARNES
- Sergeant in Dallas police laboratory.
- Took pictures at scene of Tippit shooting.

W. E. BARNETT
- Policeman.
- Told of shots by Howard Brennan.

DR. FOUAD BASHOUR
- Doctor at Parkland Hospital.

BILLY BASS
- Policeman who, with Officer Wise, took custody of three men turned over to them by Sgt. Harkness.

CHARLES BATCHELOR
- Dallas police chief.

DR. CHARLES BAXTER
- Doctor at Parkland Hospital.
- Held that wound in front of J.F.K.'s neck resembled an entrance wound.

ALVIN BEAUHOEUF
- Traveling companion of David Ferrie.

JACK BEERS
- Staff photographer of *The Dallas Morning News.*
- Nominated for Pulitzer Prize in news photography for photo of Ruby shooting Oswald.

DAVID BELIN
- Staff lawyer for Warren Commission.
- Author of book, *November 22, 1963: You Be the Judge,* published by *The New York Times.*
- Chairman of Lawyers for Nixon-Agnew in 1968.
- Executive director of the Rockefeller Commission.

JACK BELL
- AP wire-service representative in fourth car in cavalcade press "pool" car with Merriman Smith of UPI.

ALAN BELMONT
- Assistant to FBI Director J. Edgar Hoover.
- Gave affidavit to Warren Commission that Oswald was not an FBI agent.

DOMINGO BENAVIDES
- Witness to Tippit shooting.
- Saw policeman on left of police car and man on right of car.
- Heard three shots.
- Used Tippit's car radio to report shooting.

EDDY BENAVIDES
- Brother of eyewitness to Tippit shooting.
- Died mysteriously in February 1964, from gunshot wound in back of head.

GLEN A. BENNETT
- Secret Service agent riding in Presidential follow-up car in Dallas.
- Testified that he "saw shot hit the President about four inches down from right shoulder."

PAUL BENTLEY
- Dallas police detective.
- One of arresting officers of Oswald who first obtained the forged draft card with the name "Hidell" from Oswald's wallet en route to police building.
- Turned evidence over to Lt. Baker.

CLEM BERTRAND
- Name on library card when Oswald was picked up.
- According to Garrison, a "Clay Shaw" alias.

HUGH W. BETZNER
- Eyewitness to J.F.K.'s assassination. He was standing across from Book Depository, taking pictures.
- His pictures of the "Grassy Knoll" hill were taken by Deputy Sheriff Boone, who returned only camera and negatives.

D. L. BLANKENSHIP
- Worked for Lt. J. R. Gilmore.
- Knew "Ruby over the years."

MARY BLEDSOE
- Former landlady of Oswald when Oswald got room under name "A. J. Lee" on Neely Street in Dallas.
- Saw him on the bus with a brown shirt with a hole in it.

JOHN BLOOMER
- Member of the Minutemen.
- Identified as "The Tall Man" by Gary Patrick Hemming in "tramps" photo.

ALBERT GUY BOGARD
- Auto salesman who claimed that on November 9, 1963, Lee Harvey Oswald was a prospective customer in his showroom and took a car on a high-speed test drive.
- Threw card away with Oswald's name on it when he heard Oswald mentioned as assassin.

- Died in February 1966, allegedly by suicide (asphyxiation in a parked car).

HALE BOGGS
- Democratic Congressman from Louisiana who was House whip.
- Member of Warren Commission.
- Disappeared off Alaska in small aircraft and presumed to have perished.

ANATOLE BOGUSLAV
- FBI agent who interviewed Marina Oswald among others.

ABRAHAM W. BOLDEN
- First black Secret Service agent on White House detail.
- Wanted to testify to Warren Commission concerning alleged Chicago plot.
- Was jailed six years on "charges" of counterfeiting.

JAMES BOOKHOUT
- FBI agent who participated in Oswald interrogation on November 22nd.

EUGENE BOONE
- Deputy sheriff who found the rifle in the School Depository along with Deputy Constable Weitzman.
- Took camera from eyewitness Betzner.

GENE BOSTER
- Officer in charge of U.S.S.R. affairs at the State Department at time of Oswald's attempted renunciation of his American citizenship.

DR. J. THORNTON BOSWELL
- Commander, U.S. Navy, retired.
- Present at Kennedy autopsy. Apparently made error in marking back wound too low on autopsy diagram, which corresponds to clothing holes and erroneous eyewitness reports.

ROBERT BOUCK
- Special agent-in-charge of the Secret Service Protective Research Section.

- Was recipient of all autopsy reports and notes turned over by the examining doctors.

GEORGE BOVHE
- Member of Dallas's Russian-speaking community.
- Regarded Oswald as "crazy."

MRS. ROSS BOUVE
- Lived next door to Maj. Gen. Edwin A. Walker.
- Her dog Toby, who usually barked "at anyone or anything in the alley area," got violently sick and was believed to have been drugged in conjunction with shooting incident.

LEE E. BOWERS, JR.
- Railroad towerman.
- Had vantage point from atop railroad tower and testified to the presence of two cars behind fence on grassy knoll for half-hour before assassination, joined a few minutes before shooting by third car. Two of the cars, according to Bowers, bore out-of-state plates and Goldwater stickers. Saw two men at fence.
- Died in a motor-vehicle accident, August 9, 1966.

T. F. BOWLEY
- Came upon scene of Tippit's shooting immediately afterward, claiming it to be one-ten P.M.

BILL BOXLEY
- Name used by William Wood when he worked as Garrison aide in investigation.

ELMER BOYD
- Dallas police officer.
- Saw chicken remnants and soda-pop bottle near cartons on sixth floor of Book Depository.

JIM BRADEN
- See: Eugene Hale Brading.

EUGENE HALE BRADING
- Los Angeles "oil operator."

- At Dallas Texas Building—taken into custody; gave his name as Jim Braden.
- Member of Los Angeles Costa Country Club.
- Long arrest record.

EUGENE BRADLEY
- Mistaken for Brading. Based on identification of Carol Aydelotte.
- Worked for the Rev. Carl McIntyre (right-wing minister).

ARTHUR HERMAN BREMER
- Assailant of George Wallace on May 15, 1972, at Laurel, Maryland.

HOWARD L. BRENNAN
- Warren Commission witness.
- Identified shots as coming from sixth floor, southeast window.
- Construction worker.
- Talked to Officer W. E. Barnett.

E. D. BREWER
- Dallas police officer.
- Testified that "relatively long paper sack" he espied on sixth floor was one in which rifle was wrapped.

JOHNNY CALVIN BREWER
- Shoe salesman.
- Present at Oswald's arrest and, according to one report, supposedly pointed Oswald out in the Texas Theatre.

CARLOS BRINGUER
- Head of Cuban Student Directorate.
- Had fight with Oswald in New Orleans over distribution of pro-Castro leaflets.

JERRY MILTON BROOKS
- Garrison informant.
- Minuteman defector.

ORAN BROWN
- Auto salesman who worked with Albert Guy Bogard.

- Corroborated Bogard's story and claimed he wrote down name "Oswald" after visit, but could not find it upon searching the premises.

JERRY BRUNO
- Advance man for John Kennedy in Dallas, November 22, 1963.

THOMAS BUCHANAN
- Supposed author of *Who Killed Kennedy?* (Secker & Warburg, London, 1964).
- Held by many that the name is an alias for several authors.

ADM. GEORGE G. BURKLEY
- White House physician.

EDWARD BUTLER
- Anti-Communist activist in New Orleans who attempted to gain information on Oswald in the summer of 1963.

GEORGE BUTLER
- Dallas police lieutenant.
- Had "known Jack Ruby for years."

LT. COL. JOEL CABAZA
- Deputy of 112th Military Intelligence Group at Fort Sam Houston (under Col. Maximillian Reich).

EARLE CABELL
- Mayor of Dallas who was in motorcade.
- Brother of deputy head of CIA.

JAMES C. CADAGAN
- FBI agent who worked at the laboratory in Washington, D.C.
- Examined wrapping papers and Oswald's palm print.

TED CALLAWAY
- Witness to Tippit shooting.
- Was with Sam Guinyard.
- Testified he heard five shots.

O. V. CAMPBELL
- Vice president of Book Depository.
- Believed shots came from "grassy area."

KAREN BENNETT CARLIN
- Known as Little Lynn.
- Wired money by Ruby on November 24, 1963.
- Shot to death in her Houston hotel.

CAROUSEL CLUB
- Jack Ruby's club in Dallas.

LIZ CARPENTER
- Member of Presidential party on November 22, 1963.

WAGGONER CARR
- Texas attorney general.
- Headed Texas assassination investigation.

DR. CHARLES J. CARRICO
- Doctor at Parkland Hospital.
- Formed the belief that the front-neck wound was an entrance wound.

BOB CARROLL
- One of three officers who arrested Oswald.

COL. CASTER
- See: Col. Robert Castorr.

WARREN CASTER
- Official of Book Depository.
- Had purchased guns for himself and son two days before assassination and displayed them to workers.

LUIS ANGEL CASTILLO
- Claims to be one of "hit men" in Dealey Plaza (told Dr. Popkin).
- Arrested in Philippines in assassination plot on Marcos.

COL. ROBERT CASTORR
- Retired U.S. Army officer.

- Known as "Col. Caster."
- Close associate of Maj. Gen. Edwin A. Walker.
- Tried to arouse Cubans in Dallas against Kennedy Administration with many speeches prior to assassination.

FIDEL CASTRO
- Cuban dictator.
- Target of several CIA-Mafia attempts on life.
- Focal point of Pro- and Anti-Castroites in New Orleans.

JOSEPH CAVAGNARO
- Front-office manager of Dallas Sheraton-Hilton Hotel.
- Told FBI that Ruby was a close friend of Police Lt. J. R. Gilmore.

THANE EUGENE CESAR
- Security guard at Ambassador Hotel, June 5, 1968.
- Seen by several witnesses removing revolver from holster during shooting.

TOM CHABOT
- Dallas police mechanic.
- Admitted to police basement to check on parking situation an hour-and-one-half before shooting of Oswald.

JAMES CHANEY
- Motorcycle policeman on right rear of President Kennedy's car.
- Testified Presidential limousine had almost come to a complete halt after the first shot.

AL CHAPMAN
- Head of "The Dealey Street Irregulars."

TED CHARACH
- Author of *Second Gun*.

ABRAM CHAYES
- State Department employee.
- Warren Commission witness.
- Testified concerning State Department's seeming "indifference" to Oswald's defection to Russia as well as to Oswald's permission to leave Soviet Union for the U.S.

ROSE CHERAMI
- Stripper friend of Jack Ruby's.
- Said "Oswald and Ruby are bedfellows."
- Killed by hit-and-run car in Big Sandy, Texas.

BILL CHESHER
- Believed to know of a link between Ruby and Oswald.
- Died of a heart attack in March 1964.

JOHN ARTHUR CHISM
- Witness in Dealey Plaza.
- Stood "in front of concrete memorial on Elm Street just east of the triple underpass."
- Of the opinion the shots "came from behind him."

JOE CIVELLO
- Dallas representative at Appalachia Organized Crime meeting in 1957.
- Supposed acquaintance of both Ruby and Carlos Marcello.

BARNARD CLARDY
- Dallas policeman.
- Asked Jack Ruby how he had entered basement of police station on Main Street and was told "by ramp" when Lt. Rio Pierce drove out ramp.
- Didn't report interview with Ruby "until days later."

RICHARD L. CLARK
- Dallas detective.
- One of three Dallas police employees to appear in police lineups with Oswald on Friday, November 22nd.

DR. WILLIAM KEMP CLARK
- Doctor at Parkland Hospital.
- Interviewed on TV after President's death.
- Like other Parkland doctors, failed to note or confirm presence of small, round entry wound in back of head.

MANNING C. CLEMENTS
- FBI agent.
- Allegedly questioned Oswald on Friday, November 22,

1963, in the absence of Capt. Fritz, the FBI, and the Secret Service.
- Examined contents of Oswald's wallet, and found Selective Service card with name "Hidell," which Oswald failed to identify or answer questions about.

MELVIN COFFEY
- Traveling companion of Ferrie to Houston in 1963.

ALWYN COLE
- FBI expert in documents that are questionable.
- Called upon to testify before Warren Commission on the fabrication of the Hidell draft card.

KAY COLEMAN
- See: Kay Coleman Olsen.

WALTER KIRK COLEMAN
- A teen-aged boy who lived next door to Maj. Gen. Edwin A. Walker in Dallas.
- Saw two men leave by car after a shot was fired at Walker's house.
- Not asked to testify before Warren Commission.

WILLIAM T. COLEMAN
- Lawyer on the Warren Commission.

CHARLES COLSON
- Former White House Aide.
- Second man in CIA hierarchy in executive branch 1969-1974.
- Jailed for complicity in Watergate cover-up.

B. H. COMBEST
- Detective who was at Oswald's side when he was shot by Ruby.

JOHN BOWDEN CONNALLY, JR.
- Governor of Texas.
- Sat in jump seat of car in which Kennedy was assassinated on November 22, 1963.
- Hit in ribs, right thigh, and wrist by so-called "single bullet."

MRS. C. L. CONNELL
- Volunteer member of Cuban Catholic Committee which was concerned with welfare and relief of Dallas Cuban refugees.
- Testified to FBI that a Col. Caster, associated with Committee, had tried to arouse feelings of Cubans against J.F.K., in concert with Maj. Gen. Edwin A. Walker.

AUSTIN COOK
- Member of John Birch Society.
- Owner of Austin's Barbecue, where Officer J. D. Tippit worked on weekends to supplement his salary at the time of his death.

GRANT COOPER
- First defense attorney for Sirhan.

JOHN SHERMAN COOPER
- Republican Senator from Kentucky.
- Member of the Warren Commission.

MALCOLM COUCH
- Told Warren Commission that newsman Wes Wise told him he saw Ruby on November 22nd around Texas School Book Depository.

ROLAND COX
- Sergeant on Dallas Police Force.
- In newspaper account of Ruby's entrance into Police Headquarters, reported that Ruby may have "had a camera" to effect his entrance.

ROGER D. CRAIG
- Deputy sheriff of Dallas County.
- Fifteen minutes after assassination, saw man whom he identified as Oswald running down the hill toward light-colored Rambler station wagon.

CURTIS LAVERNE CRAWFORD
- Employee at Carousel Club.
- Oswald look-alike.
- Associate of Ruby's.

- Thought by some to have impersonated Oswald at the auto-sales agency and rifle range.
- Heard Ruby talk about assassination.

W. O. CROSS
- Prison counselor.
- Conducted detailed interviews with Sirhan.

CURTIS CROWDER
- Employee at an Irving, Texas, service station.
- Called upon as witness to verify a reputed sale of a U.S. Army rifle to a mechanic named Taylor at the station by someone supposed to have been Oswald, in lieu of payment for repairs to a car. Did not believe man to be Oswald.

WILLIAM CROWE
- Entertainer at Jack Ruby's Carousel Club in Dallas.
- Used stage name, "Bill DeMar."

KENNETH CROY
- Reserve sergeant on Dallas Police Force.
- Came upon Tippit death scene and talked to eyewitnesses.
- Saw man he believed to be Ruby near railing on Main Street ramp, November 24th (but he may have seen instead Robert Huffaker and mistaken him).

MIGUEL CRUZ
- Picked up in New Orleans fight between Oswald and Carlos Bringuer.

CORDLANDT CUNNINGHAM
- FBI weapons expert.
- Testified before Warren Commission that FBI had originally received only one bullet from J.F.K. assassination, the others residing in the dead files of the Dallas Police Department.

JESSE CURRY
- Dallas police chief and spokesman for Dallas Police Department.

- One of key officials responsible for President Kennedy's safety.

DR. DON TEEL CURTIS
- Doctor at Parkland Hospital.
- Testified that he had neither noted nor seen a small, round entry wound in the back of John Kennedy's head.

WILBUR CUTCHSHAW
- Detective in the Criminal Investigation Division, Juvenile Bureau.
- Knew Ruby well.
- Was in basement when Ruby shot Oswald.
- Testified before Warren Commission.

SOL DANN
- One of Jack Ruby's many lawyers.
- Said of Ruby's death: "Ruby did not want to live. His death was a merciful release."

JIMMY DARNELL
- Cameraman who was on third floor of the Police Building between five and seven-thirty P.M. on Friday, November 22nd, and was told by reporter John Rutledge that he [Rutledge] recognized Jack Ruby, who was there.

BARBARA JEANNETTE DAVIS (AND VIRGINIA DAVIS)
- Sisters.
- Witnesses to Tippit shooting.
- Lived in apartment house on Patton Street.
- Saw man with revolver run across lawn.
- Each picked up one empty shell.

BENJAMIN DAVIS
- Prominent political figure in leftist causes.
- Name on one of four three-by-five-inch file cards found among Oswald's property on November 22nd, along with "G[us] Hall, V[incent] T. Lee and A. J. Hidell."

R. M. DAVIS
- Employee in the office of Dean Andrews, an attorney in New Orleans.

J. C. DAY
- Lieutenant in Dallas's Police Identification Bureau.
- Picked up remains of chicken lunch and empty Dr Pepper bottle found at southeast corner of sixth floor of Texas School Book Depository. Tested bottle for Oswald's fingerprints—which proved negative—but no one else's.
- Took weapon found down to headquarters and examined it; described it in detailed report, not found in Warren Commission's exhibits.

HARRY DEAN
- Private detective in Alhambra, California.
- CIA agent.
- Used name, "Dean Fallon."

PATRICK DEAN
- Dallas police sergeant.
- Testified at first Ruby trial that minutes after killing of Oswald, Ruby confessed he'd planned the murder (to prove premeditation).

WARREN C. DE BRUEYS
- FBI special agent in New Orleans and Dallas.
- According to one Warren Commission witness, Orest Pena, De Brueys first asked him for information on Pro-Castroites and then badgered him.
- Reputed to have been in Pena's bar at approximately "same time as Oswald."

J. E. (BILL) DECKER
- Sheriff in Dallas.

NELSON DELGADO
- Oswald's friend and former fellow marine.
- Testified, by deposition, that FBI intimidated him—particularly when he indicated Oswald was not an expert shot, but was instead a poor marksman.

GEORGE DE MOHRENSCHILDT
- Husband of Jeanne De Mohrenschildt.
- Member of Dallas's Russian-speaking community.
- Acquaintance of the Oswalds.

JEANNE DE MOHRENSCHILDT
- Wife of George De Mohrenschildt.
- Acquaintance of the Oswalds.
- Only person other than Marina Oswald ever to testify that rifle was Oswald's.
- Left Dallas with husband on April 19, 1963, never to see Oswald again.

C. N. DHORITY
- Dallas detective.
- Wrote "description" of rifle that Lt. Carl Day showed him at nine P.M., Friday, November 22nd; omitted, as was Day's description, from record.

TOM DILLARD
- Photographer who took picture of Texas School Book Depository three seconds after shot fired; it shows two black men on fifth floor.

VINCENT DI PIERRO
- Eyewitness to R. F. Kennedy assassination.

DOBBS HOUSE
- Restaurant where Mary Dowling and Mrs. Dolores Harrison worked as waitresses.
- Regularly frequented by both Officer J. D. Tippit and Oswald.

JOHN DONOVAN
- Lieutenant in Marine Corps at time of Oswald's service.
- Testified that upon hearing that former marine Oswald was in Moscow, aircraft call signs, codes, and radio frequencies were changed at Atsugi and that Oswald knew locations of bases, range of radio, codes, and radio frequencies.

JACK DOUGHERTY
- Employee at Book Depository.
- Thought he saw Oswald (only one who saw him enter), but didn't remember him carrying anything in his hands.

KENNETH DOWE
- Announcer on Dallas radio station.

- Testified that Ruby telephoned station on November 23rd, asking when Oswald was being transferred.

MARY DOWLING
- Waitress in Dobbs House, a restaurant allegedly patronized by Ruby and Oswald.
- Told the FBI that she had last seen Oswald on Wednesday, November 20th, at which time Officer Tippit, a regular patron, was also in the restaurant and "shot a glance" at Oswald.

VINCENT E. DRAIN
- FBI agent.
- Received the rifle believed to have been the assassination weapon from Lt. Carl Day at eleven-forty-five P.M., November 22nd.
- Was told by Day that palm print was tentatively identified and Oswald was prime suspect.

DRF
- Frente Revolucionario Democratico, a right-wing group that sought the restoration of a regime like Batista's in Cuba.

WILLIAM MC EWAN DUFF
- Former employee of Maj. Gen. Edwin A. Walker.
- Testified that he believed he saw Ruby visit the Walker residence.

ALLEN DULLES
- Former head of the CIA.
- Member of the Warren Commission.

FRANK DYSON
- Lieutenant on Dallas Police Force.
- Conducted a systematic search of Book Depository Building from twelve-thirty P.M. to two P.M. on November 22nd with Lt. Jack Revill and two other detectives.

A. M. EBERHARDT
- Detective on Dallas Police Force.
- Had known Jack Ruby for five years.
- Testified that he had seen Ruby between six P.M. and

seven P.M. on third floor of Parkland Hospital on November 22nd.

ROBERT EDWARDS
- Warren Commission witness.
- Saw man one minute before assassination from same vantage point as Howard Brennan.

MELVIN ARON EISENBERG
- Warren Commission counsel.

HAROLD ELKINS
- A Dallas sheriff.
- Couldn't remember that there were any other officers with Sgt. D. V. Harkness when he arrested three men in the freight yard.

EDWARD JAY EPSTEIN
- Author of *Inquest,* 1966.

TROY ERWIN
- Manager, A & P store, Irving, Texas.
- Testified that a thirty-three-dollar unemployment check made out to Oswald had been cashed between three P.M., Thursday, October 31, and the close of business, Friday, November 1, 1963.

AMOS L. EUINS
- Witness.
- Age fifteen.
- Alerted police to source of shots at Texas School Book Depository.

J. EVANS
- Listed with "Sgt. Robert Hidell" as a reference on Oswald's application for employment with William B. Reily Co.

JOHN FAIN
- FBI agent.
- Provided affidavit stating that Oswald was not an FBI agent.

DEAN FALLON
- See: Harry Dean

JACK W. FAULKNER
- Member of the sheriff's office.
- Standing on corner of Main and Houston streets when he heard three shots and moved toward Elm Street with the crowd.

JIM FEATHERSTONE
- Reporter on *The Dallas Times-Herald*.
- Told Mrs. Jean Hill that she was wrong in believing she had seen a man running or trying to get away from the slope west of the Book Depository, holding that the shots had come from a window in the Depository.

BOB FENLEY
- Reporter for *The Dallas Times-Herald*.
- Was informed by C. A. Hamblen, night manager of Western Union in Dallas, that Oswald had often come into the Western Union office to collect money orders for small amounts.

DAVID FERRIE
- Worked for Carlos Marcello, Mafia chief in New Orleans, and with Anti-Castro Cubans.
- Alleged suspect in assassination conspiracy.
- "One of the most important individuals of the twentieth century," according to Jim Garrison.
- Died of an apparent suicide, February 22, 1967.

DR. PIERRE A. FINCK
- Lieutenant colonel.
- One of the J.F.K. autopsy surgeons.

RONALD FISCHER
- Witness in Warren Commission who thought he saw man one minute before assassination in window.
- Saw no shots.
- Stood in same place as Howard Brennan.

ALLISON G. FOLSOM
- Lieutenant colonel in U.S. Marine Corps.

- Testified that Oswald's last recorded score of 191 was that of a "rather poor shot."

GERALD R. FORD
- Republican House minority leader.
- Member of the Warren Commission.
- Author of *Life* Magazine article supporting Commission's findings.
- Author of "Piecing Together the Evidence," *Life* Magazine, October 2, 1964.
- Author of *Portrait of the Assassin,* 1965.

KATHERINE FORD
- Close personal friend of Marina Oswald.
- Testified that Marina had told her "Lee had laughed about the attempt to kill Walker."

J. W. FOSTER
- Dallas police officer.
- Under triple underpass.
- Saw sparks as bullet struck manhole cover ar 1 heard fourth shot.

BUELL WESLEY FRAZIER
- Worked at Texas School Book Depository.
- Drove Oswald to work.
- Was standing with Billy Lovelady in entrance to Texas School Book Depository Building at time motorcade passed.

ROBERT A. FRAZIER
- Lab technician in Washington who testified about bullets and rifle.

"FRENCHIE"
- One of "tramps" in photo taken after assassination.
- So-called because of the European cut of his clothing.

WILL FRITZ
- Dallas police captain.
- Interrogated Oswald on night of November 22nd.
- Preceded Oswald out of elevator into basement of Police Building just before Oswald shot by Ruby.

MIGUEL AMADOS FUENTES
- Met with Trapnell to plan killing of R.F.K. in 1963.

JOHN GALLAGHER
- FBI analytical expert who performed spectrographic analysis of bullet fragments and metallic residue in Kennedy's limousine.

DARRELL WAYNE GARNER
- Suspect in attempted killing of Warren Reynolds, a witness to the Tippit shooting.
- Alibi provided by Betty MacDonald (known as Nancy Mooney), who had worked as a stripper at Jack Ruby's club and who later committed suicide.

JIM GARRISON
- New Orleans district attorney.
- Conducted 1967 investigation into "conspiracy" to kill Kennedy and returned indictments against Clay Shaw and others, later acquitted or dismissed.

MAURICE BROOKS GATLIN, SR.
- Legal counsel to Anti-Communism League of Caribbean.
- Associate of W. Guy Bannister.

DR. ADOLPH GIESECKE
- Doctor at Parkland Hospital.

SAM GIANCANA
- Let out "contract" on Castro to Jimmy Roselli.
- Was to testify before Church CIA Committee.
- Killed by a .22-caliber bullet in kitchen of Chicago house.

J. R. GILMORE
- Dallas police lieutenant.
- Longtime friend of Jack Ruby.
- In building during transfer of Oswald.

CHARLES GIVENS
- Witness who originally testified he had seen Oswald on first floor of Texas School Book Depository Building thirty minutes before shooting.
- Under repeated questioning by David Belin, he changed

story to claim he saw him on *sixth* floor (the *only* evidence Oswald was on sixth floor).
- Last known employee to see Oswald in building prior to assassination.
- Worked in southwest section of sixth floor as a member of floor-laying crew.

DAVID GOLDSTEIN
- Assisted FBI in tracing revolver used in Tippit shooting.
- Died of natural causes, 1965.

IRA GOLDSTEIN
- Wounded during R.F.K. assassination.

CLYDE GOODSON
- Dallas police officer.
- Testified that on the afternoon of November 22nd, a man resembling Ruby, but *not* Ruby himself, attempted to enter the Homicide Bureau Office.

HENRY GONZALES
- U.S. Congressman from Texas.
- In motorcade, November 22, 1963.

LEON GOPADZE
- Secret Service agent.
- Interviewed Marina Oswald and Ruth Paine in both English and Russian after assassination.

DAVID GRANT
- Secret Service agent.
- Present at an interrogation of Oswald.

EVA GRANT
- Jack Ruby's sister and business associate in the Carousel Club.

L. C. GRAVES
- Dallas police detective.
- Was at left arm of Oswald as he emerged from an elevator when Ruby, whom he knew, shot Oswald.

CHARLES GREENER
- Owner of Irving, Texas, sports shop.
- Repair tag found in shop indicated Oswald had rifle worked on at his shop.

WILLIAM R. GREER
- Secret Service agent.
- One of four non-medical witnesses present at John Kennedy's autopsy.

DR. CHARLES F. GREGORY
- One of three doctors at Parkland Hospital who attended Governor Connolly.

ROOSEVELT GRIER
- R.F.K. aide who, with Rafer Johnson, wrestled Sirhan to stainless-steel counter and wrested gun from him.

BURT GRIFFIN
- Assistant counsel to the Warren Commission.

J. T. GRIFFIN
- Badge number 279 of the Dallas Traffic Division.
- Found a light-colored zipper jacket identified as possibly belonging to Oswald.

BOB GRODEN
- Film analyst.
- Has made studies of the Zapruder film.
- Co-author of book on J.F.K. assassination with Peter Moedel.

SAM GUINYARD
- Saw man fleeing scene of Tippit shooting.
- Identified jacket as belonging to Oswald.
- One of four witnesses who picked Oswald out of police lineup on night of November 22nd.

STEVE GUTHRIE
- Former sheriff in Dallas.
- Was allegedly offered a bribe in 1946 to permit individuals—including Jack Ruby—to come into Dallas and open a "fabulous" gambling place.

C. RAY HALL
- FBI agent.
- Interviewed Ruby after killing of Oswald.

GUS HALL
- Head of Communist party of America.
- One of four names found on three-by-five-inch cards in Oswald's possession at Paine house on November 23rd.

LORAN EUGENE HALL
- Identified "Bradley" instead of Brading-Braden for Garrison (with Mrs. Aydelotte).
- Trained anti-Castro Cubans for Bay of Pigs (with Ferrie).
- Supposedly visited Mrs. Sylvia Odio.
- May well have been his picture taken going into Cuban Embassy in Mexico City and released by CIA as being Oswald.
- Thought by some to be in car with Oswald from Coast.
- Thought to be picture shown of "Saul" in *Appointment in Dallas*.

CLAUD HALLMARK
- Manager of garage near county jail.
- Overheard Ruby on Saturday, November 23rd, say on telephone. . . . "You know I'll be there. . . ." Believed to be intention of Ruby to be on hand for Oswald's transfer.

C. A. HAMBLEN
- Early-night manager of Dallas Western Union.
- Testified Oswald had received money orders in small amounts.

ART HAMMETT
- Assistant to Dallas Police Chief Jesse Curry.

T. M. HANSEN, JR.
- Dallas police officer.
- Told FBI he had seen Ruby on steps of City Hall between nine A.M. and nine-thirty A.M. on November 22nd, in the company of four or five men.

BILLY HARGIS
- Outside motorcycle policeman on left of Presidential car in motorcade (*and* back).
- Got a face full of blood and brain tissue.

D. V. HARKNESS
- Police sergeant who removed three men from freight train in railroad yard.
- Turned them over to Officers Wise and Bass.

DOLORES HARRISON
- Waitress at Dobbs House with Mary Dowling.

WILLIAM HARVEY
- CIA agent.
- Accompanied Roselli to Miami for recruiting Castro-assassination team.

CLYDE HAYGOOD
- Dallas police officer.
- One of first to find out that James Tague, a bystander at Dealey Plaza, had been struck in the face by fragment of curb caused by bullet.

JOHN RENE HEINDEL
- Supposed to have conversed in Russian every morning with Oswald while at Atsugi.

WALLACE HEITMAN
- FBI agent.
- Interviewed Marina Oswald.

WANDA HELMICK
- Waitress at Ralph Paul's.
- Overheard her boss talking to Ruby on Friday, November 22nd, and saying, "A gun! Are you crazy?"

GARY PATRICK HEMMING
- Loran Hall's Cuban training instructor.

MARGARET HENCHLIFFE
- Nurse at Parkland Hospital.
- Thought hole she observed in front of President's neck

was an entrance wound; had never seen an exit wound that small and not jagged.

BELL HERNDON
- FBI polygraph expert.
- Testified as to a polygraph test Ruby had taken bearing on his whereabouts on the evening of November 22nd, between five P.M. and seven P.M.

MRS. CHARLES HESTER
- Eyewitness to J.F.K.'s assassination.
- Standing near underpass on south side of Elm Street.
- Believed shots came from grassy knoll.

JAMES B. HICKS
- Identified as the mysterious "communications man" who was at Dealey Plaza with headphones and walked in opposite direction from crowd after assassination.
- Now in insane asylum.

A. J. "HIDELL"
- Also Alec James Hidell.
- Also Dr. A. J. Hideel.
- Name on forged draft card that Oswald had on his person when apprehended.
- Name on one of Oswald's four three-by-five-inch cards found at Paines'.

CLINTON C. HILL
- Secret Service agent in Presidential follow-up car.
- Jumped on Presidential limousine immediately after shot hit Kennedy in head.

GERALD L. HILL
- Dallas police sergeant.
- One of the officers to apprehend Oswald at the Texas Theatre and bring him in.

JEAN LOLLIS HILL
- Eyewitness to John Kennedy assassination.
- Claimed she had seen and pursued a man running from the top slope west of the Book Depository.

ALFRED HODGE
- Owner of a bar and grill as well as a gun shop.
- Had known Jack Ruby for fifteen years.
- Testified he met Ruby on an elevator in the Police Building on Friday night, November 22nd.

DR. JOHN HOLBROOK
- Psychiatrist who interviewed Ruby day after he murdered Oswald.

S. M. HOLLAND
- Eyewitness to John Kennedy's assassination.
- Testified he saw a puff of smoke and a muzzle flash about six to eight feet aboveground under a group of trees.

HAROLD HOLLY
- Dallas police reserve officer.
- Told by Officer William J. Newman that Ruby was wearing a press identification card on jacket at time of his shooting of Oswald.

HARRY HOLMES
- Post office inspector and an FBI informant.
- Present at interrogation of Oswald on Sunday morning, November 24th.

J. EDGAR HOOVER
- Head of the Federal Bureau of Investigation from 1924 through 1971.

JAMES P. HOSTY, JR.
- Special FBI agent in Dallas.
- Interviewed Marina Oswald twice before November 22, 1963, and had a file on Oswald.
- Was object of note delivered by Oswald to "leave Marina alone" or "I'll burn building down."
- Destroyed note two days after assassination on orders from someone in FBI.

LAWRENCE HOWARD, JR.
- Mexican-American from East Los Angeles.
- Visited Mrs. Sylvia Odio with Loran Hall and either Oswald or William Seymour.

TOM HOWARD
- Ruby's first defense attorney.
- At Ruby's apartment night of November 24, 1963, with attorneys Jim Martin and C. A. Droby when reporters Hunter and Koethe visited.
- Attorneys agreed he would have gotten Ruby off with prison term and had "trick up sleeve."
- Died in June of 1964.

JOHN J. HOWLETT
- One of six Secret Service agents attached to the Dallas-Fort Worth office.
- Was assigned to the Trade Mart on November 22, 1963.

LEON HUBERT
- Warren Commission counsel.

EMMET HUDSON
- Eyewitness to John Kennedy assassination, standing on steps up to grassy knoll.
- Thought shots came from behind him.

ROBERT J. HUGHES
- Took photo of Book Depository sixth-floor window that showed one silhouette.

DR. J. J. HUMES
- Commander, U.S. Armed Forces.
- Chief autopsy surgeon.

E. HOWARD HUNT
- CIA agent.
- Stationed in Mexico City at time of Oswald's visit.
- Ordered by Charles Colson to visit Bremer's room in Milwaukee two hours after assassination attempt on Wallace.

LAMAR HUNT
- According to building records, was visited by Eugene Brading-Jim Braden on November 21, 1963.

BILL HUNTER
- Newspaper reporter for *The Long Beach Press Telegram*.
- Visited Ruby's apartment November 24, 1963.

- One of only two reporters who got inside (other, Jim Koethe).
- Shot to death April 21, 1964, in pressroom of Police Department in Long Beach, California, when policeman's gun accidentally went off.

LEONARD HUTCHINSON
- Owner of a supermarket in Irving, Texas, where Oswald shopped.
- Testified that Oswald had once tried to cash a personal check made out to him for $189.

HURCHEL JACKS
- Texas State Highway patrolman.
- Served as driver of Vice President Johnson's car in Dallas motorcade.

JESSE JACKSON
- Aide to Martin Luther King in Southern Christian Leadership Council.
- At King's side on balcony of Lorraine Hotel, Memphis, Tennessee, April 4, 1968, when King was assassinated.
- Left SNCC to form Operation PUSH in Chicago.

JAGGARS-CHILES-STOVALL CO.
- Photographic/graphic arts firm in Dallas where Oswald worked upon return from Russia.

JAMES JARMAN, JR.
- Employee on fifth floor of Texas School Book Depository Building.

LEON JAWORSKI
- Counsel to Waggoner Carr's Texas assassination inquiry.
- Watergate prosecutor.

DR. MARTIN T. JENKINS
- Doctor at Parkland Hospital.

ROLAND L. JENKINS
- Radio newsman for KBOX, Dallas.
- Identified man he had seen between five-thirty P.M. and

seven-thirty P.M. on third floor of Police Building as Ruby.

ALBERT E. JENNER, JR.
- Warren Commission counsel.

JOACHIM JOESTEN
- Author of *Oswald: Assassin or Fall-Guy?*, 1964.

MRS. A. C. JOHNSON
- Oswald's landlady, who owned house at 1026 North Beckley Avenue, Dallas.
- Identified him.
- "Did nothing" to keep out visitors.

ARNOLD JOHNSON
- Official of American Communist party.
- Recipient of letter from Oswald mailed November 1, 1963, and delivered four weeks later—one week after Oswald's death.

LYNDON B. JOHNSON
- Succeeded to the Presidency upon death of John F. Kennedy, November 22, 1963.

MARVIN JOHNSON
- Dallas police officer.
- With partner, L. D. Montgomery, found paper sack on sixth floor, folded up twice, which was said to have been sack that gun was carried in.

PRISCILLA JOHNSON
- News correspondent who interviewed Oswald at Hotel Metropole in Moscow in 1959.
- Currently said to be working on book with Marina Oswald.

RAFER JOHNSON
- R.F.K. aide who, with Roosevelt Grier, wrestled Sirhan to stainless-steel counter and wrested gun from him.

DAVID JOHNSTON
- Dallas justice of the peace.

- Issued warrant to search Oswald's room at rooming house on North Beckley.

FRANK WILLIAM JONES
- Counterfeiter who testified against Secret Service agent Abraham Bolden.

PAUL ROLAND JONES
- Chicago teamster racketeer who had sought to bribe the then-sheriff of Dallas to gain a foothold for gambling, to be run by Jack Ruby.

PENN JONES, JR.
- Editor of *The Midlothian (Texas) Mirror*.
- Author *Forgive My Grief*, 1966.
- Chronicler of mysterious deaths of witnesses to J.F.K. case.

DR. RONALD C. JONES
- Doctor at Parkland Hospital.

JOSÉ JUAREZ
- Cuban émigrée.
- Rented home in New Orleans for explosives cache.

JURE
- Junta Revolutionary, a leftist organization dedicated to "Castroism Without Castro."
- Headed by Manolo Ray.

FRANKIE KAISER
- Employee of Book Depository.
- Found clipboard on December 2, 1963, behind book cartons in northwest corner of sixth floor. It had once belonged to him and been appropriated by Oswald when he came to work at Book Depository.

TOM KANE
- Lee Harvey Oswald's supposed CIA code name, according to Ronald Lee Augustinovitch.

SETH KANTOR
- Scripps-Howard reporter.

- Friend of Ruby's.
- Shook hands with him at Parkland Hospital about time President's death announced (one o'clock).

STANLEY KAUFMAN
- Ruby's friend and lawyer.

ROY KELLERMAN
- Secret Service agent.
- In front seat of Presidential limousine.
- Heard "flurry" of shells.

THOMAS J. KELLEY
- Secret Service inspector.
- Called upon to testify regarding nature of President Kennedy's wound.

JACQUELINE KENNEDY
- Wife and widow of assassinated President.
- Present in backseat of Presidential limousine on November 22, 1963.

JOHN FITZGERALD KENNEDY
- Thirty-fifth President of the United States, January 20, 1961–November 22, 1963.
- Assassinated at Dallas, Texas, November 22, 1963.

ROBERT FITZGERALD KENNEDY
- Brother of assassinated President.
- U.S. Attorney General, 1961–1965.
- U.S. Senator from New York, 1967–1968.
- Candidate for Democratic Presidential nomination, 1968.
- Assassinated, Los Angeles, California, June 5, 1968.

MALCOLM KILDUFF
- Press secretary with Kennedy in Dallas, November 22, 1963.

DOROTHY KILGALLEN
- Noted Hearst syndicated columnist.
- Had written many skeptical stories concerning assassination.
- Died of a supposed overdose of barbituates, 1964.

THOMAS "HANK" KILLAM
- Wife worked for Ruby.
- Best friend roomed in same house as Oswald.
- Found dead in Pensacola, Florida, March 17, 1964—accidentally cut throat falling through plate-glass window.

GLEN KING
- Captain, Dallas Police Force.
- Told American Society of Newspaper Editors in April, 1964, that Officer Tippit had been shot three times, a fact then unknown to public and Warren Commission.

JOHN KING
- Name of a Denver oilman, Jim Garrison claims offered him a government post in 1968 if he would abort the Kennedy investigation.

JERRY KIVETT
- Secret Service agent guarding L.B.J. who threw open door in Altgens's photo.

FRANK KLEIN
- First assistant district attorney in New Orleans under Garrison.

KLEIN SPORTING GOODS CO.
- Chicago mail-order house.
- Sold mail-order rifle to "A. J. Hidell" through ad in February 1963, issue of *American Rifleman,* which offered thirty-six-inch Carcano rifle weighing five and one-half pounds, catalogue number C20-7750. (Also offered a 40.2-inch Carcano—catalogue number C20-750—in November 1963, *Field & Stream* ad.)

WILLIAM KLINE
- Chief of U.S. Customs at Laredo, Texas.
- Watched Oswald's movements "at request of Federal agency (in) Washington" checked his entering and leaving Mexico.

JIM KOETHE
- Newspaper reporter for *The Dallas Times-Herald.*
- Visited Ruby's apartment November 24, 1963. One of two to visit apartment (with Bill Hunter, also dead).

- Killed September 21, 1964, by intruder into his apartment with karate chop to throat.

KOMSOMOL
- Communist youth organization.
- Marina Oswald was member but falsely told U.S. Embassy she had never been a member (which would have disqualified her from obtaining visa).

JOSEPH KRAMER
- Name for Richard Case Nagell (also used "Robert Nolan").

PAUL LANDIS, JR.
- Secret Service agent.
- In Dallas motorcade on right rear running board of car behind Presidential limousine.

MARK LANE
- Author of *Rush to Judgment,* 1966.

ROBERT LARKIN
- Former manager of nightclub adjoining Ruby's Vegas club.
- Told FBI Ruby was "particularly friendly" with Officer J. R. Gilmore.

SEBASTIAN F. LATONA
- FBI Identification Bureau, Latent Fingerprint Division.
- Examined rifle received from Dallas police.

RICHARD LAUCHLI, JR.
- One of founders of the Minutemen.
- Had gun shop in Collinsville, Illinois.

WINSTON LAWSON
- Special Secret Service agent in Washington who arranged Dallas trip.
- Liaison contact with head agent Forrest Sorrels in Dallas.

JAMES R. LEAVELLE
- Dallas police detective.
- Handcuffed to Oswald on his right as he was being led from elevator through basement.

"HARVEY LEE"
- Donald Norton's contact man in Mexico.

VINCENT T. LEE
- One of the four names found among Oswald's property on three-by-five-inch file cards in search of rooming house on November 23rd.

———— LEVENS
- First name unknown.
- Operator of the Fort Worth strip joint that employed some of Ruby's strippers.
- Died of natural causes November 5, 1966.

AUBREY LEWIS
- Western Union employee.
- Testified that one of money orders Oswald supposedly cashed was payable to anyone at the YMCA.

DAVID L. LEWIS
- Bannister investigator.
- Witness who identified Oswald at 544 Camp Street.

WESLEY J. LIEBER
- Assistant counsel to Warren Commission.

W. W. LITCHFIELD
- Gave testimony that he had seen Oswald in Ruby's Carousel Club.
- Under pressure, recanted statement.

LITTLE LYNN
- Real name: Karen Bennett Carlin.
- Stripper to whom Ruby sent twenty-five dollars in Fort Worth on November 24, 1963.
- Shot to death in Houston hotel.

LOVE FIELD
- Dallas airport.
- Where Richard Nixon departed November 22, 1963, at approximately eleven A.M.
- Where John Kennedy landed at eleven-thirty-eight A.M., November 22, 1963.

- Where Lyndon Johnson took oath of office in the stateroom of *Air Force One* at one-thirty-five P.M.
- And where, at two-oh-eight P.M., the hearse containing the remains of John F. Kennedy was placed aboard the Presidential plane.

BILLY NOLAN LOVELADY

- According to testimony, mistaken for Oswald in picture taken by Altgens.
- Standing with Frazier and William Shelley in front of Book Depository at time of assassination.

ALLARD K. LOWENSTEIN

- Former New York Congressman.
- Aide to governor of California.
- Advocate of "Second Gun" theory in R.F.K. assassination.

RICHARD LUBIC

- Independent TV producer.
- Witness to R. F. Kennedy assassination at Ambassador Hotel.
- Claims he saw guard raise gun.

K. E. LYON

- Dallas police officer.
- One of those who arrested Oswald at Texas Theatre.
- Failed to mention "Hidell" card in report.

BETTY MACDONALD

- Known as Nancy Mooney.
- Friend of Jack Ruby.
- Provided alibi for man who was accused of shooting a witness to murder of Tippit.
- Committed suicide in jail, February 1964.

MARILYN MAGYAR

- Known as Marilyn Moon.
- Jack Ruby stripper.
- Found dead in Omaha home two years later—shot seven times.

ROBERT MAHEU

- Former member of CIA and aide to Howard Hughes.

- Located Jimmy Roselli as hit man for CIA through Hoffa, Lansky, and Giacana.

WILLIAM MANCHESTER
- Author of *Death of a President,* 1967.

ARTHUR MANDELLA
- Fingerprint expert in New York City Police Department.
- Confirmed right palm print of Oswald.

CARLOS MARCELLO
- Mafioso head of New Orleans and Los Angeles areas.
- Deported by R.F.K., his forceable deportation was overturned on November 22, 1963.

VICTOR MARCHETTI
- Former CIA official.
- Stated that Clay Shaw had been a contact for CIA and CIA wanted to keep those connections quiet.

RAY MARCUS
- Film researcher who discovered two transposed and misnumbered frames in Zapruder film developed by *Life* Magazine.

MRS. HELEN L. MARKHAM
- Waitress.
- Witness to Tippit shooting.
- Identified Oswald.

FRANCIS MARTELLO
- Member of Anti-Subversion Division of New Orleans Police Department.
- Interviewed Oswald in August 1963.
- Testified that Oswald carried a Fair Play for Cuba card in his own name and also a New Orleans chapter card signed "A. J. Hidell, Chapter President."

B. J. MARTIN
- Dallas police motorcyclist.
- Left of Presidential car, closest to car and flanked by Hargis.

- Bloodstains on "left side of helmet" and on "left shoulder of uniform."

———— MARTINEAU
- Secret Service agent-in-charge, Chicago (in Bolden case).

LOGAN MAYO
- Dallas police reserve officer.
- Testified that approximately fifteen minutes after Oswald was shot, a large balding gentlemen with a limp asked to see Ruby and was referred to Lt. Gilmore.

JAMES T. MAYS
- Witness in Garrison investigation.

DR. ROBERT N. MCCLELLAND
- Doctor at Parkland Hospital.
- Assisted in performing tracheotomy on J.F.K.

JOHN J. MCCLOY
- New York attorney
- Member of the Warren Commission.

A. D. MCCURLEY
- Dallas deputy sheriff.
- Eyewitness to assassination.
- When he heard shots, ran to railroad yard and jumped fence, encountering railroad worker who believed smoke came from "vicinity of a stockade fence."

N. M. "NICK" MCDONALD
- Dallas police officer.
- Caught Oswald inside Texas Theatre.
- Photographer Jack Beers originally thought it was him shooting Oswald.

TERENCE MCGARRY
- UPI reporter.
- Told FBI that he was at middle of end of Main Street ramp into basement for five minutes before Oswald shot and no one went past him.

ROBERT RAY MCKEOWN
- Warren Commission witness.
- Testified that Ruby was involved in supplying arms to Cuban underground.

WILLIAM MCKINNEY
- Member of 112th Military Intelligence Unit.
- Revealed unit was told to "stand down" and not come to Dallas.

WILLIAM J. MCLANEY
- Gambler associated with Tropicana Hotel in Havana.
- Ousted by Castro in 1960.
- Knew Ruby.

GARRY MCLEOD
- Secret Service agent with Abraham Bolden who went back to Chicago with him.

THOMAS MCMILLON
- Dallas police officer.
- Testified "days later" that Ruby had told him and three other officers he had gained entry to basement via the Main Street ramp.

JOHN MCVICKAR
- Official at U.S. Embassy in Moscow when Oswald visited and announced "defection."

CECIL J. MCWATTERS
- Bus driver for Dallas Transit Co.
- Picked up Oswald at twelve-thirty-six.
- Issued transfer at St. Paul and Elm streets (seven blocks away) east to Murphy.
- At six-thirty lineup, picked out Oswald.
- Withdrew testimony.

SYLVIA MEAGHER
- Author of *Accessories After the Fact,* 1967.

WILLIAM D. MENTZEL
- Dallas police officer.
- Was officer assigned to the Dallas district (number 109 on

Dallas police radio patrol district map) where Tippit was shot.

JULIA MERCER
- Testified that on her way to work on the morning of November 22, 1963, she had seen man carrying rifle case walk across grass and up grassy knoll.

MICKEY'S BAR
- Where Betty MacDonald and Patsy Moore worked together.

AUSTIN MILLER
- Railroad worker.
- Standing on overpass on November 22, 1963.
- Thought "smoke or steam" came from group of trees north of Elm Street "off railroad tracks."

PETER MOEDEL
- Co-author of book on J.F.K. assassination with Bob Groden.

JOE MOLINA
- Credit manager, Texas School Book Depository.
- Member of "American G.I. Forum," which, according to testimony, "the Dallas police considered possibly subversive."

L. D. MONTGOMERY
- Dallas police officer.
- Discovered paper sack and pieces of chicken on sixth floor of Book Depository.
- Followed Oswald out of elevator into basement just prior to his being shot.

MARILYN MOON
- Marilyn Magyar.

LUKE MOONEY
- Dallas sheriff's department.
- Found bullets.

NANCY MOONEY
- See: Betty MacDonald.

ELMER MOORE
- One of six Secret Service agents in Dallas office.
- Did not file a report on activities of November 22, 1963.

PATSY SWOPE MOORE
- Room-mate of Betty MacDonald.
- Had altercation with MacDonald, after which MacDonald hanged self in jail cell.

T. E. MOORE
- Eyewitness to J.F.K. assassination interviewed by FBI.

MARY MUCHMORE
- Took pictures of motorcade on November 22, 1963.

CHARLES MURRAY
- Sat in attendance at the Warren Commission as observer for the President of the American Bar Association to insure "fairness to the alleged assassin."

LILLIAN MURRETT
- Oswald's aunt in New Orleans.

MARILYN MURRETT
- Daughter of Lillian Murrett and Oswald's cousin.

RICHARD CASE NAGELL
- Former CIA agent.
- Supposedly drew "pension" for his silence.

ROBERT I. NASH
- U.S. marshal.
- Present at Oswald's interrogation.

GLEN NEAL
- Dallas police officer.
- Visitor to Carousel Club and friendly with Ruby.

R. C. NELSON
- Dallas police officer, badge number eighty-seven.
- According to transcript of radio log, was instructed— along with Tippit—to move into the Central Oak Cliff district at twelve-forty-five P.M., November 22, 1963. They

were the only two officers not instructed to proceed to
Book Depository.

WILLIAM E. NEWMAN, JR.
- Eyewitness to J.F.K. assassination.
- Was looking "at him when he was hit in the side of the
  head."
- Standing near west end of concrete standard on Elm
  Street, "thought shot had come from the garden directly
  behind me."

WILLIAM J. NEWMAN
- Dallas police reserve officer.
- "Saw" a man run down ramp after shooting of Oswald
  and a second man "jump over the rail."
- Identified by Policeman Harold Holly as having told
  Holly he either admitted Ruby to basement or observed
  him going in with a press identification card on jacket.

H. LOUIS NICHOLS
- President of Dallas Bar Association.
- Interviewed Oswald and found him not "irrational."

JOSEPH D. NICOL
- FBI firearms expert who testified before Warren Commission.

ORVILLE O. NIX
- Made eight-mm. film of motorcade.
- Sold film to UPI.

RICHARD M. NIXON
- Thirty-sixth Vice President of the United States, 1953–
  1961.
- Unsuccessful candidate for President, 1960.
- Was in Dallas on morning of November 22, 1963, after
  addressing a convention of Pepsi-Cola bottlers.

DR. THOMAS T. NOGUCHI
- Los Angeles County coroner.
- Conducted autopsies on R.F.K. and Marilyn Monroe
  among others.

ROBERT NOLAN
- Name for Richard Case Nagell (also used "Joseph Kramer").

HAROLD NORMAN
- Employee on fifth floor of Book Depository with James Jarman.

DONALD P. NORTON
- Became CIA agent "unwittingly" after threat of exposure as homosexual.

TERESA NORTON
- Dancer employed by Ruby.
- Shot to death in a motel in August 1964.

GORDON NOVEL
- Garrison witness who disappeared. Governor Rhodes refused to extradite him from Ohio.
- Linked to burglary of munitions dump in Louisiana in 1961.
- Worked with Charles Colson.
- CIA contact by own admission.

JAMES O'CONNELL
- CIA agent.
- Accompanied John Roselli to Miami to line up team to assassinate Castro.

ANNIE LAURI ODIO
- Sister of Sylvia Odio.
- Identified Oswald as one of the three men who visited her sister.

SYLVIA ODIO
- Cuban êmigré active in anti-Castro activities and whose father was political prisoner in Cuba.
- Identified Oswald as one of three who visited her September 26th or 27th in Dallas with "Leopoldo" (Loran Eugene Hall), who shows up in picture from Mexico City.

KENNETH O'DONNELL
- Special assistant to President Kennedy.
- Went to Dallas to help Jerry Bruno set up trip.

BARDWELL ODUM
- FBI agent.
- Drove Lt. Day, who found rifle, to police headquarters and radioed in the gun's description to FBI en route.
- Interrogated Bonnie Ray Williams, Mrs. Helen Markham and Sylvia Odio.

DENNIS H. OFSTEIN
- Fellow employee of Oswald at Jaggars.
- Testified to Garrison concerning Oswald's receiving classified mail and government contracts.

DR. ALFRED OLIVIER
- Army ballistics expert on wounds.
- Testified before Warren Commission.

HARRY OLSEN
- Dallas policeman.
- Acquaintance of Ruby and casual visitor to Carousel Club.
- Boyfriend of stripper Kay Coleman (later Kay Coleman Olsen).
- Off-duty on day of assassination.

KAY COLEMAN OLSEN
- Stripper at Carousel Club.
- Girl friend (and later wife) of Dallas policeman Harry Olsen.

FRANCIS X. O'NEILL
- FBI agent.
- Made report with agent James Sibert on the conduct of the J.F.K. autopsy and the findings of the surgeons.

LEE HARVEY OSWALD
- Alleged assassin of John F. Kennedy and J. D. Tippit on November 22, 1963.

MARGUERITE OSWALD
- Mother of Lee Harvey Oswald.

MARINA OSWALD
- Married Lee Harvey Oswald in April 1961.

- Maiden name: Marina Nikolaevna Prusakova.
- Friend and tenant of Ruth Paine.

ROBERT LEE OSWALD
- Brother of Lee Harvey Oswald.

OLIVER B. "JERRY" OWEN
- Picked up Sirhan hitchhiking and dropped him off at Ambassador Hotel.

J. L. OXFORD
- Dallas deputy sheriff.
- Told by witness to assassination that witness had seen smoke "up in the corner of the fence."

MICHAEL PAINE
- Husband of Ruth Paine.
- Owned house in Irving where Marina Oswald and two children lived.
- Reputedly the rifle had been secreted in a blanket in his garage until the morning of November 22, 1963.

RUTH PAINE
- Michael Paine's wife.
- Oswald's landlady in Irving.
- Met Oswald at Socony-Mobile party and got job for Oswald at Book Depository.

PARKLAND HOSPITAL
- Hospital where motorcade took mortally wounded President and Governor Connally.

P. M. PARKS
- Dallas police detective.
- Put together list of Book Depository employees with Detective Westphal. First name on list was "Harvey Lee Oswald . . . 605 Elsbeth"—an address that wasn't Oswald's.

WILLIAM PATTERSON
- One of six Secret Service agents in the Dallas office.
- Assigned to Love Field on November 22, 1963.

RALPH PAUL
- Ruby's "backer."
- Overheard on the telephone talking to Ruby by Wanda Helmick, a waitress.

OREST PENA
- Owner of Habana Bar in New Orleans.
- Anti-Castro activist.
- Testified that Oswald had once entered his establishment with two companions and had lemonade.
- Also testified that he was threatened by FBI Special Agent Warren De Brueys.

DR. MALCOLM PERRY
- Doctor at Parkland Hospital.

JOSEPH SAM PERRY
- Federal judge in Bolden case.

W. E. PERRY
- Dallas police employee.
- One of three men in police lineup with Oswald on Friday night, November 22nd.

DR. PAUL C. PETERS
- Doctor at Parkland Hospital.

HUGH PHARRIS (OR FERRIS)
- Supposed aliases used by Ferrie.

RIO SAM PIERCE
- Lieutenant on Dallas Police Force.
- Was driving a police car that was to have been Oswald's escort from Municipal Building on November 24th and left one or two minutes before shooting.

C. S. B. PIKE
- U.S. commissioner who sat on Bolden case.

EDDIE PIPER
- Employee of Book Depository.
- Testified he saw and spoke to Oswald "down on the first floor, at twelve o'clock."

ELINORA PITTS
- Cleaning woman at Carousel Club.
- Testified that she telephoned Ruby at eight A.M. on Sunday, November 24th, and he asked, "Do you need some money?", one hour before he was called for money by former employee in Fort Worth.

FRANK PIZZO
- Assistant sales manager at auto showroom visited by Oswald.
- Corroborated Albert Bogard's testimony regarding Oswald's test drive of auto.

J. M. POE
- Dallas policeman who arrived at scene of Tippit shooting.
- Was given description of assailant by Mrs. Helen Markham.

DR. RICHARD H. POPKIN
- Professor of philosophy at Washington University in St. Louis.
- Author of *Second Oswald*.
- Proponent of "Manchurian Candidate" theory for Sirhan.

JULIA POSTAL
- Cashier at Texas Theatre where Oswald was captured.

WALTER POTTS
- Dallas detective.
- Testified he was instructed by Captain Fritz to go to "Oswald's or Hidell's room" at Mrs. Johnson's.

NANCY POWELL
- An entertainer at Ruby's Club.

J. C. PRICE
- Eyewitness to assassination in Dallas.
- Testified he saw a "man run toward the passenger cars on the railroad siding after the volley of shots."

ORAN PUGH
- U.S. Customs official.

- Testified Oswald had been checked by U.S. Immigration officials upon entering and leaving Mexico.

JOHN QUIGLEY
- FBI agent in New Orleans.
- Interviewed Oswald after his arrest for breach of peace.
- Saw card with name "Hidell" signed in Marina's handwriting.

CARLOS QUIROGA
- Associate of Aracha.

MRS. LINNIE MAE RANDLE
- Buell Frazier's sister.
- Testified that Oswald came to pick up her brother and that there was a package containing "curtain rods."

J. LEE RANKIN
- General counsel for the Warren Commission.

JAMES EARL RAY
- Convicted assassin of Martin Luther King, Jr.
- Alias Eric Starvo Galt and Ramon George Sneyd.

NORMAN REDLICH
- Warren Commission counsel.

COL. MAXIMILLIAN REICH
- In charge of 112th Military Intelligence Group at Fourth Army Headquarters, Fort Sam Houston.

MRS. R. A. REID
- Clerical supervisor for Book Depository.
- Eyewitness to assassination on sidewalk in front of building with Roy Truly and O. V. Campbell.
- Saw Oswald with Coke dressed in a T-shirt.

FRANK REILLY
- Eyewitness to J.F.K. assassination.
- Testified shots "had come out of the trees."

WILLIAM B. REILY CO.
- Coffee firm in New Orleans where Oswald worked from May 10 to July 19, 1963, earning $548.41.
- Block away from 544 Camp and CIA Headquarters.

JACK REVILL
- Dallas police lieutenant, Criminal Intelligence Section.
- One of three detectives to make systematic search of Book Depository.
- Encountered Charles Givens, who was known to the police on narcotics charges.
- Was told by FBI Special Agent Hosty that Oswald was known to FBI.

WARREN REYNOLDS
- Witnessed the escape of Tippit's killer.
- Shot in head in January 1964; later recovered.

NANCY PERRIN RICH
- Worked at Carousel Club as barmaid.
- Left and tried to file charges against Ruby but dissuaded by Dallas police.
- Testified she and husband were offered gunrunning job and Ruby was "bagman."
- Met violent death.

JAMES L. RITCHIE
- Attorney in the U.S. Passport Office.
- Testified he had received a CIA telegram informing office of Oswald's visit to the Soviet Embassy in Mexico City a month before assassination.

EARLENE ROBERTS
- Oswald's landlady.
- Through her sister, she knew Jack Ruby.
- Testified that after assassination a police car drove up, honked twice, and drove off while Oswald was in room.
- Died January 10, 1966, of natural causes.

VICTOR ROBERTSON, JR.
- Radio and TV reporter, WFAA, Dallas.
- Saw Ruby on third floor of Police Building between five and seven P.M., November 22, 1963.

MARVIN C. ROBINSON
- Confirmed Deputy Sheriff Roger Craig's story that he saw man run down embankment and get into car after J.F.K. assassination.

EVARISTO RODRIGUEZ
- Bartender at Habana Bar, New Orleans.
- Thought he observed Oswald in Pena's bar.

ERIC ROGERS
- Neighbor of Oswalds in New Orleans.
- Contradicted testimony of Marina Oswald and Ruth Paine concerning departure from New Orleans.

CHUCK ROLLAND
- Proprietor of Winterland Skating Rink in Houston.
- Figured in investigation of Ferrie by Garrison.

GUY ROSE
- Dallas police officer.
- Interviewed Oswald and was told by prisoner his name was "Hidell" and saw card with "Hidell" on it.

JOHN ROSELLI
- Mafia "hit man."
- Associate of Giancana.
- CIA selected him to carry out Castro assassination.

ARNOLD ROWLAND
- Eyewitness to Dallas assassination.
- Testified he saw a man in southwest corner window on the sixth floor with a rifle and an elderly Negro in the southwest corner—fifteen minutes before shooting.
- His testimony was disparaged by the Warren Commission.

JAMES J. ROWLEY
- Secret Service chief in Washington.
- Told Martineau about Chicago plot.

JACK RUBY
- Former teamster official in Chicago.
- Friend and acquaintance of several racketeers.
- Owner of the Vegas and Carousel clubs in Dallas.
- Killed Lee Harvey Oswald on November 24, 1963.
- Sentenced to death on March 14, 1964.
- Died of cancer on January 3, 1967, while still in custody and one month before retrial.

MAX RUDBERG
- Bail bondsman.
- Saw Ruby morning of November 22, 1963, when he stopped in to say hello and gave him card.

RAY RUSHING
- Radio Evangelist from Plano, Texas.
- Claimed he rode up on elevator with Ruby on morning of November 24th.

HAROLD RUSSELL
- Witnessed Tippit's shooting.
- Beaten to death by a policeman wielding a service revolver in bar in Sulpher, Oklahoma, August 29, 1965.

RICHARD B. RUSSELL
- Democratic Senator from Georgia.
- Member of Warren Commission.
- Rejected single-bullet theory and dissented from other findings of Commission.

PETER RAYMOND RUSSO
- Identified "Leon Oswald" (FBI) as Lee Harvey Oswald and "Clay Bertrand" as Clay Shaw for Garrison.

DIAL RYDER
- Employee of Irving Sports Shop.
- Was interviewed along with owner Greener as to whether Oswald had rifle "sighted" in shop.

DR. KENNETH E. SALYER
- Doctor at Parkland Hospital.

"SAUL"
- Central character and supposed assassin in *Appointment in Dallas,* by H. McDonald, 1975.

J. HERBERT SAWYER
- Police inspector and man in charge of security at Dealey Plaza.

SCHLUMBERGER WELL CO.
- Munitions dump near New Orleans that was burglarized in 1961.

PAUL SCHRADE
- United Auto Workers official.
- Wounded during assassination of Robert Kennedy, June 5, 1968.

WILLIAM SCOGGINS
- Taxi driver who was eating lunch and saw police car pull up alongside man and policeman get out of car.
- Heard three or four shots.
- Identified Oswald in lineup as assailant of Tippit.

CARROLL HAMILTON SEELEY, JR.
- Attorney in U.S. Passport Office.
- Read CIA telegram informing Passport Office of Oswald's visit to Soviet Embassy in Mexico City and reviewed Oswald's file.

GEORGE SENATOR
- Jack Ruby's room-mate.

WILLIAM SEYMOUR
- According to Loran Eugene Hall, it was he who visited Sylvia Odio—an Oswald look-alike—and not Oswald.

LYNDAL L. SHANEYFELT
- Photography expert and FBI special agent who photographed rifle used in assassination.
- Identified that rifle as being rifle in photograph found in Paine house.

GORDON SHANKLIN
- Special FBI agent in charge of Dallas office.
- Reported to have stated that paraffin test of Oswald's face and hands was positive and "proved he had fired a rifle."

CLIFTON SHASTEEN
- Proprietor of barbershop in Irving, Texas.
- Remembers Oswald visiting Hutchinson's grocery store with a fourteen-year-old boy.

DR. ROBERT R. SHAW
- Surgeon at Parkland Hospital who operated on Governor Connally.

WILLIAM SHELLEY
- Foreman at Book Depository.
- Saw Oswald at "ten to twelve" on first floor.
- Seen by Victoria Adams with Billy Lovelady on first floor immediately after shooting.

DR. GEORGE T. SHIRES
- Doctor at Parkland Hospital.
- One of group of doctors who met with two Secret Service men to discuss autopsy findings.
- One of three doctors who attended Governor Connally.

BERT SHIPP
- Dallas TV personality.
- Received 30.6-caliber rifle shell after assassination.

JAMES W. SIBERT
- FBI agent.
- Wrote report with agent Francis O'Neill that showed the bullet hole to be lower—below shoulders—than final autopsy report.

RICHARD SIKES
- Prosecutor in Bolden case.

RONALD SIMMONS
- Army ballistics expert.
- Testified before Warren Commission on skill needed to gain "proficiency" with rifle.

RALPH SIMPSON
- Eyewitness to Dallas assassination.
- Canadian visitor who took movies of motorcade from southwest side of Dealey Plaza.

RICHARD SIMS
- Dallas police detective.
- Saw bag and shells on sixth floor of Book Depository.

SIRHAN BISHARA SIRHAN
- Assailant of Robert F. Kennedy on June 5, 1968, at Ambassador Hotel, Los Angeles.

MARILYN SITZMAN
- Abraham Zapruder's secretary.

W. DAVID SLAWSON
- Assistant counsel to Warren Commission.

TED SLACK
- Identified in "tramps" photo by Gary Patrick Hemming as "Frenchie."
- Naval intelligence instructor in Miami area.

J. M. SMITH
- Dallas police patrolman.
- After shooting, an hysterical woman told him "they were shooting the President from the bushes."
- Ran around to area behind concrete structure and checked cars in parking lot where he encountered an unidentified Secret Service man.

MERRIMAN SMITH
- UPI wire-service representative in press "pool" car.
- Wrestled for phone with Jack Bell of AP; called in story and won Pulitzer Prize.
- Committed suicide.

SERGIO ARACHA SMITH
- See: Aracha.

WILLIAM ARTHUR SMITH
- Witness to shooting of Tippit at Tenth and Patton streets.

RICHARD E. SNYDER
- Consul at U.S. Embassy in Moscow, October 1959.
- Visited by Oswald, who renounced his citizenship informally but never acted formally to expatriate himself.
- Again received Oswald in July of 1961 and heard Oswald claim he was a loyal American and seek visa to U.S.

FORREST V. SORRELS
- Head Secret Service agent in Dallas who served as liaison with police and was Washington contact.
- Walkie-talkie went out of control.

JOSEPH SPAGNOL
- Counterfeiter who testified against Bolden with Frank William Jones.

ARLEN SPECTER
- Warren Commission counsel.
- Gave name to "Specter Miracle Bullet" theory derided by critics of report.
- District attorney of Philadelphia.

C. I. SPEISEL
- Witness in Garrison case (*Louisiana* v. *Shaw*).
- Testified he saw Clay Shaw with Ferrie or Oswald in 1963.
- Recanted saying he was hypnotized by New York City police as part of Communist plot.

SPORTS DROME RIFLE RANGE
- Witnesses claimed Oswald used Dallas rifle range for target practice many times before November 22, 1963 (including several times when he was actually in Mexico City).

RICHARD SPRAGUE
- Computer technician and photographic analyst.
- Analyzed Zapruder film.

GERALD SPRINGER
- Dallas patrolman.
- Instructed to deliver mail to Tippit's widow on Sunday and then called back for no reason.

ROY STANDIFER
- Dallas police detective.
- Had known Ruby for thirteen years.
- Saw him on third floor of Police Building on Friday, November 22, 1963, between six and seven P.M.

SAMUEL STERN
- Warren Commission counsel.

ROBERT STEUART
- One of six Secret Service agents out of Dallas office.
- Assigned to Trade Mart on November 22, 1963.

ADLAI STEVENSON
- Democratic candidate for President in 1952 and 1956.
- United Nations Ambassador, assaulted in Dallas in October 1963, by right-wing mob.

PAUL M. STOMBAUGH
- Special agent of the Hair and Fiber Unit of the FBI laboratory.
- Found fiber on rifle matched Oswald's shirt.

RICHARD STOVAK
- Dallas police officer.
- Was with Officer Guy Rose when Oswald was brought into the station and asked him name before Captain Fritz excused them to commence formal interrogation.

MARTHA JO STROUD
- Assistant United States attorney for Dallas.

SANDRA STYLES
- Ran down back stairs from fourth floor of Book Depository Building to first floor with Victoria Adams after shots, where they saw Lovelady and Shelley.

H. W. SUMMERS
- Dallas police officer.
- Called in to dispatcher with "eyeball witness" account of "getaway man" sometime between one-thirty-three and one-forty P.M.

ROBERT SURREY
- Aide to Maj. Gen. Edwin A. Walker.

R. F. SWAIN
- Dallas police lieutenant.
- Preceded Oswald into basement on Sunday, November 24th.

ALLAN SWEATT
- Chief criminal deputy in Dallas sheriff's office.
- Reputedly source of information that Oswald was on FBI payroll.

JAMES THOMAS TAGUE
- Injured by piece of pavement struck by errant bullet while standing on Main Street at assassination site.

GEORGIA TARRANTS
- Cashier at A & P store in Irving, Texas.
- Told FBI that Oswald cashed a thirty-three-dollar unemployment check on the evening of October 31, 1963.

HARRY TASKER
- Dallas cabdriver.
- Was standing opposite Main Street ramp of Police Building on November 24th, waiting for a reporter who hired him and told FBI he saw no one resembling Ruby enter the basement while he was there.

ROBERT ADRIAN TAYLOR
- Mechanic in Irving service station.
- Believed man who gave him a U.S. Army rifle in lieu of paying a bill for repairs to car in March or April 1963, was Oswald.

GEORGE THOMAS
- President Kennedy's valet.

KERRY THORNLEY
- Marine comrade of Oswald.
- Told Garrison that Oswald conversed in Russian with John Rene Heindel every morning at Atsugi.

WILMA TICE
- Eyewitness who testified to Warren Commission that she had seen Ruby at Parkland Hospital while Kennedy was still in the Emergency Room.

J. D. TIPPIT
- Dallas police officer (badge number seventy-eight) shot between one-ten and one-thirty P.M. on November 22, 1963, in Oak Cliff section of Dallas after assassination of Kennedy.

MARIE TIPPIT
- Widow of Officer Tippit.

CONNIE TRAMMEL
- Young lady friend of Ruby's who went with him to the offices of Hunt Oil on November 21, 1963, in quest of a job.

GARRETT B. TRAPNELL
- Convicted skyjacker.
- Testified he met with three Cubans in May 1963, to plan killing of R.F.K.

ROY TRULY
- Supervisor of Book Depository whom Mrs. Paine called to get Oswald job.
- Noticed "missing" employee—Oswald on November 22, 1963.

F. M. TURNER
- Dallas police detective.
- Made inquiries at Irving Sports Shop concerning ammunition and reparation to Oswald's gun as the result of anonymous phone call.

JIMMY TURNER
- Television director.
- Testified he observed Ruby moving slowly down Main Street ramp seconds before shooting of Oswald.

KARL UEKER
- Assistant maître'd at Ambassador Hotel in Los Angeles.
- Witness to R.F.K. assassination.

JAMES UNDERWOOD
- Dallas newsman.
- Took pictures of mark on curb caused by bullet that struck James Tague.

IRA VAN CLEAVE
- Dallas police detective.
- Released data on April 10, 1963, stating the bullet that went through Maj. Gen. Walker's window was a 30.06.

ROY VAUGHN
- Dallas police officer.

- Stationed at top of Main Street ramp on Sunday, November 24th, and was thought to have let Ruby go by him into basement.

HENRY WADE
- Dallas district attorney who tried Ruby case.
- Assisted State Attorney General Waggoner Carr in Texas investigation.

THAYER WALDO
- Reporter for *The Fort Worth Star-Telegram*.
- Testified he was told by Lt. George Butler that Oswald would be removed by elevator into basement and then through ramps onto Commerce Street.

C. T. WALKER
- Dallas police officer.
- One of three officers who arrested Oswald.

MAJ. GEN. EDWIN A. WALKER
- Retired major general, U.S. Army.
- Resident of Dallas and right-wing spokesman.
- Attempt made on life April 10, 1963, allegedly by Lee Harvey Oswald.

IRA WALKER
- Television technician for WBAP (Fort Worth).
- Identified Ruby outside the Police Building on Sunday morning, November 24th, between eight and eleven A.M.

R. W. WALKER
- Dallas police officer.
- Officer who phoned in description of Tippit's killer.

MARILYN MOORE WALLE
- Dancer known as "Delilah" employed by Ruby at time of assassination.
- Shot to death by husband after one month of marriage, September 1, 1966.

MRS. CAROLYN WALTHER
- Eyewitness to J.F.K.'s assassination.
- Told FBI that after assassination she saw two men in the

window of an upper floor of Book Depository, one of whom was pointing a rifle at street below.

TRUETT WALTON
- Dallas police officer.
- Mentioned in testimony before Warren Commission as a frequenter of Carousel Club and a friend of Ruby's.

HUGH F. WARD
- Investigator for W. Guy Bannister.
- Member of Minutemen and Anti-Communism League.

ROGER WARNER
- One of six Secret Service agents in Dallas office.
- Assigned to Love Field on November 22, 1963.

EARL WARREN
- Chief Justice of United States Supreme Court.
- Chairman of the President's Commission on the Assassina-tion of President Kennedy, known familiarly as the War-ren Commission.

BERNICE WATERMAN
- Official in Passport Office in State Department.
- Based on Oswald's record, made up "refusal sheet" (or "lookout card") on Oswald, March 25, 1960.

DR. CYRIL H. WECHT
- Director, Institute of Forensic Sciences, Duquesne Univer-sity and chief forensic pathologist, Allegheny County, Pennsylvania.
- Analyzed J.F.K. autopsy report.

HAROLD WEISBERG
- Author of *Oswald in New Orleans*.
- Author of *Whitewash II*, 1966.

WILLIAM WEISEL
- ABC newsman.
- Wounded while standing near R. F. Kennedy when Sirhan started firing.

BERNARD WEISSMAN
- New York resident.
- Bought black-bordered ad in Dallas newspapers on November 22, 1963.

SEYMOUR WEITZMAN
- Dallas deputy constable.
- Scaled wall between railroad yard and Elm Street after assassination.
- In sporting-goods business prior to police duty, and identified rifle as a "Mauser."

TROY WEST
- Wrapping clerk for Book Depository.
- Testified Oswald had never borrowed nor used wrapping paper or tape.

W. R. WESTBROOK
- Dallas police captain.
- Originally credited with finding Oswald's jacket; later, this was disputed.

WESTERN CARTRIDGE COMPANY
- Division of Olin Mathieson.
- Manufactured the 6.5 M/M Mannlicher-Carcano ammunition used in the assassination.

W. R. WESTPHAL
- Dallas police detective.
- After assassination, instructed to search "605 Elsbeth," supposed residence of Oswald.

WILLIAM WHALEY
- Taxi driver.
- Took Oswald to Oak Cliff area.
- Had two notations on record—twelve-thirty–Greyhound and 500 No. Beckley.
- Killed in auto accident in 1967—first Dallas cabdriver in forty years to die in accident.

DR. MARTIN G. WHITE
- Doctor at Parkland Hospital.

B. EDWARD WHITTAKER, JR.
- Supervisor of Dade County Crime Lab in Miami.
- Examined "Second Gun" theory in R.F.K. assassination.

EDITH WHITWORTH
- Owner of furniture shop in Irving.
- Oswald, carrying package about fifteen inches long, asked if she repaired guns, and she directed him to nearby gun shop.

BONNIE RAY WILLIAMS
- Was watching motorcade from fifth-floor window of Book Depository Building on November 22, 1963.
- Had eaten lunch on sixth floor before motorcade went by.
- Debris fell on her head.

PHIL WILLIS
- Eyewitness to J.F.K.'s assassination.
- Took (at least) five pictures, with the fifth in reaction to first gunshot (less than a second after shot).

EUGENE WILSON
- Salesman at auto showroom where Albert Bogard was employee and where Oswald supposedly came in for demonstration on Saturday, November 9, 1963.

WINTERLAND SKATING RINK
- See: Chuck Rolland.

MARVIN WISE
- Dallas police officer.
- Took custody of three men with Officer Bass turned over to them by Sgt. Harkness.

WES WISE
- Newsman in 1963; later mayor of Dallas.
- Told TV cameraman Malcolm Couch he saw Ruby coming from grassy-knoll area around Book Depository Building minutes after assassination.

RONALD G. WITTMUS
- FBI fingerprint expert who confirmed Latona's findings.

DR. HOMER WOOD
- Witness who identified Oswald as being at Sports Drome Rifle Range.

RONALD WOOD
- Former inmate at San Quentin on Sirhan's cellblock.
- "Had information" on R.F.K. "slaying."
- Killed himself in Nevada State Prison.

WILLIAM WOOD
- Known as "Bill Boxley."
- Former CIA agent.
- Worked as chief aide for Garrison.

MARY WOODWARD
- Reporter for *The Dallas Morning News* and eyewitness to assassination of J.F.K.
- Wrote that bullets came from "behind her" as she stood on north side of Elm Street.

JAMES WORRELL, JR.
- Eyewitness to J.F.K. assassination.
- Told Warren Commission he heard four shots and saw man running from Book Depository Building.

RALPH YARBOROUGH
- U.S. Senator from Texas.
- In motorcade, November 22, 1963.

ELIZABETH EVANS YOUNG
- Wounded during R.F.K. assassination.

J. WALTER YOUNGBLOOD
- Alias "Jack Armstrong."
- Adventurer; CIA agent.

RUFUS YOUNGBLOOD
- Secret Service agent who threw himself atop L.B.J. after shots rang out on November 22, 1963.

JAMES A. ZAHM
- U.S. Marine Corps sergeant.

- Testified before Warren Commission on Oswald's marine marksmanship record.

ABRAHAM ZAPRUDER
- Took eight-mm. pictures that established timing and place of J.F.K. tragedy.

(17)   list of dead witnesses:

1. Hale Boggs (Warren Comm.) 107
2. Attorney Hunter (for Ruby) 113
3. Guy Bannister 136
4. Gary Underhill 146
5. Jerry Milton Brooks 169
6. David Ferrie 190
7. Bill Hunter 205
8. Jim Koethe 205
9. Tom Howard 206
10. Karen Bennett Carlin 206
11. Marilyn Magyar 206
12. Rose Cherami 207
13. Nancy Rich 207
14. Betty McDonald 207
15. Thomas Killam 207
16. Harold Russell 207
17. William Wahley 207
18.
19.
20.

dead witnesses after Wallace:

1. Dennis Salvatore Cossini 254
2. John McCleary 254
3. Herbert Spenner 254
4. Earl S. Nunnery 254 (disappeared)
5. Michael McHale   "   "
6. Michael Cullen   "   (deported)